Behind the Image

Behind the Image

The art of reading paintings

FEDERICO ZERI

Translated from the Italian by Nina Rootes

St. Martin's Press, New York

Translator's Acknowledgements

First and foremost, I should like to thank Professor Federico Zeri for taking the time and the trouble to resolve for me some of the queries that inevitably arise in the course of a translation. Meeting him was a very exciting and rewarding experience.

My thanks are also due in no small measure to Mr Peter Young and his colleagues in the Paintings Conservation Department of the Victoria and Albert Museum, and to Mr Carlo Dumontet of the National Art Library, housed in the same building. Their help has been invaluable and I am most grateful for it.

If any errors remain, the responsibility must be solely mine.

Nina Rootes

First published in Great Britain
by William Heinemann, Ltd., London.

ISBN 0–312–04724–X

First Edition
10 9 8 7 6 5 4 3 2 1

First Conversation

I should like to say that my lessons, here at the Università Cattolica, will not be in the conventional form this week; they will be more like conversations. These conversations will naturally have an overall theme – namely, the 'reading' of works of art – but this theme will be expounded in an informal and random fashion. You must not be surprised, therefore, if I tend to repeat myself, or if the same argument crops up again at a certain point, so that we can examine it in a different light.

In Italy, speaking of the evaluation or the reading of works of art is an arduous, if not a downright dangerous, task. We live in a country in which everyone believes he knows something about painting and therefore has a right to say his piece. I could tell you a good many anecdotes on this subject, but will confine myself to pointing out that, just as we have the legend of the musicality of the Italians, so we have, in parallel, the idea that we are a nation with a marked talent for the creation and, above all, the understanding of visual works of art. Yet, in this country, it is very often the case that people talk about works of art without adequate preparation, that is, without having educated their eyes to read the figurative data. What makes matters worse is that they often claim to interpret the work of art from a purely formal, stylistic point of view, totally ignoring the subject matter.

This unfortunate practice stems largely from the systematic, scholarly study of the artistic heritage of the past (begun in the nineteenth century, or rather, to be exact, at the very end of the eighteenth), a study that later found an extremely valid aid in that incomparable instrument, the camera. On this point, I would like to remind you that the first scholars, those who began a methodical study and organisation of Italian art, possessed nothing but their own eyes and their own acumen. The abbot Luigi Lanzi, for example, who wrote *La storia pittorica d'Italia*, a veritable miracle of balance and precision, had nothing to rely on but his own two eyes; the same may be said of Giovanni Battista Cavalcaselle, the greatest scholar of the second half of the nineteenth century, to whom we owe, in effect, the earliest foundations on which our current systematic study of the history of Italian painting is based. Cavalcaselle travelled around Italy by all sorts of unlikely means, quite often on foot, and made pen or pencil drawings on sheets of paper, most of which are now preserved in the Biblioteca Marciana in Venice and in the Victoria and Albert Museum in London. These records are marvels of erudition, of intuition, but above all they are illumined by that authentic passion which, all too often, has been lacking in later scholars.

Cavalcaselle's systematic classification (which shows, let me repeat, some remarkable intuitions) was then taken up, in a more markedly positivistic sense, by Giovanni Morelli. And Bernard Berenson, who can truly be considered as Morelli's greatest pupil, brought the method to perfection.

Working primarily from the bases laid down by Cavalcaselle, but also making use of his wide knowledge of Italian paintings housed in museums and collections abroad, Berenson went on to produce a systematic structure of the various schools, to recognise many hitherto unidentified painters, and, above all, to single out certain problems which up till then had remained obscure, due to the lack of that fundamental instrument of research, photography.

Berenson, as I can testify personally, maintained that the history of art is a great game of chance, in which the winner is the man who owns the largest collection of photographs. Rather a one-sided way of looking at things, however, since, with the aid of vast photographic documentation, one might quite easily identify the author of a work of art, and then fail utterly to comprehend what the artist is trying to say. On the other hand, what we are seeing today is the opposite phenomenon (which can lead to incredible excesses): a much greater interest in the subject matter than in the style and, most importantly, the quality of a painting. This reversal of tendencies is not confined to Italy alone, it is more or less universal.

But let us return for a moment to the bad habit of reading a painting without sufficient historico-cultural preparation, and to the stumbling-blocks that this can cause. Let us look at a very famous picture by Hans Holbein the Younger, in the National Gallery in London. This painting has always – and justly – been considered as one of the great Renaissance masterpieces of the German and northern European schools, but for at least two centuries, that is, from the time of its reappearance, people have been asking themselves what that weird blotch in the foreground represents. The picture shows two of the King of France's ambassadors, Jean de Dinteville and Georges de Selve, and is known, in fact, as *The Two Ambassadors*. But what is that strange piece of paper (that is how it was interpreted in an earlier age) which one sees in the foreground, at the bottom, and which has given rise to the most extravagant hypotheses? It is an anamorphosis, that is, an object inserted into the picture and drawn in an entirely different perspective from that which governs the principal subject. The constructional plan of the picture is three-dimensional. We have here a single focal point which, with the lines of perspective, determines an enclosed space. Within this space, polarised and precisely delimited by the external frame – that is, by the borders of the painting – the two figures are depicted according to precise laws of the relationship between depth and distance. The extraneous object, on the other hand, is constructed according to an entirely different system of perspective. What is it? It is a human skull, distorted by an altered perspective. It could have been recognised and examined only through a small peephole set, at an appropriate height, into the right-hand side of the picture-frame. From this, we can deduce that the picture originally had a projecting wooden frame with a peephole set into it, and that, by resting one's eye against this hole, the skull was perceived in its normal proportions, simply as a skull and not as a piece of paper or any of the other objects suggested in subsequent hypotheses.

The picture is, in effect, a *memento mori*. It shows us the images of two men at the very peak of their careers and their worldly success, their fame and their wealth, but, there in the foreground, is that warning object, a symbol to remind them that they, too, are mortal. This is a very common theme in paintings of the German and Flemish schools at the time of the Renaissance, especially from the sixteenth century on. How on earth did it come about that an element so vital to the reading of the picture was once lost? Because paintings, statues, miniatures, drawings – all figurative works, in fact – have, throughout the various ages, carried the same burden of expression, the same complexity of meanings, as words. What cannot be expressed by the written word was very often expressed visually, in accordance with the tastes and inclinations, the precise symbolical and iconographical codes of the different civilisations, but, with the passing of the generations, these keys to the understanding of such works were obliterated and forgotten. The purpose of art history is precisely this: to rediscover these meanings that have fallen into oblivion.

The identification of the skull in Holbein's picture has stimulated further analyses of Renaissance paintings from the point of view of the anamorphosis, and some very singular things have been discovered which, fifty or sixty years ago, would never even have been suspected. And yet, at that time, we already possessed in our libraries the texts which explained how to execute and read anamorphoses. But, let me repeat, there exist actual waves of oblivion that obscure the meaning of works of art. And this oblivion affects not only profane but also sacred works.

Let us examine another work with a profane subject, a painting on wood in the National Gallery, London, which has been submitted to various interpretations. It has always been recognised as the work of Agnolo Bronzino, an attribution that is fully confirmed whether one looks at its stylistic, compositional or qualitative aspects. The painting was commissioned by the Duke, later Grand Duke, Cosimo I de' Medici, and it was sent as a gift to Francois I, King of France. If it is true that each epoch possesses its own expressive structures, its mythologies, its predilections, it is also true that each work of art can be read, centuries later, at several levels. 2

In this painting by Bronzino, which is in a perfect state of preservation, we have the purely formal, stylistic level; then there is the historical level. Cosimo I, who ordered its execution, wanted to pay his respects to the French king for political reasons. Why did he send him such an elaborate and important work? Because as Duke, then Grand Duke of Florence, he found himself in a somewhat difficult position internationally, with the constant danger of seeing the dukedom of Tuscany annexed to Spain by Charles V, as had already happened with the dukedom of Milan. Therefore Cosimo sought to ingratiate himself with France by sending gifts. In the case of Spain, he did so by marrying Eleonora, daughter of the Viceroy Pedro of Toledo. To keep in good odour with the papal powers, Cosimo went so far as to hand over one of his most intimate friends, Pietro Carnesecchi, to Pius V when the former was accused of heresy – he ended up being burned at the stake. From the historical point of view, then, we could say that this painting was commissioned by Cosimo I for delicate political and diplomatic ends. This has happened very frequently throughout history; there are works of art that were created solely for the purpose of political manoeuvring or political propaganda.

1. Hans Holbein the Younger.
The Two Ambassadors.
National Gallery, London.

2. Agnolo Bronzino.
Venus, Love, Folly and Time.
National Gallery, London.

But we must read the painting at another level: we must try to ascertain what kind of society could have produced such a complex work, whose significance remains somewhat obscure even today, in spite of the infinite number of descriptions and interpretations that exist. Obviously, it is the product of an élite society, destined for an élite, since it is patently not a work that can be understood by everybody. What does the picture represent? It shows us a naked Venus (in the nineteenth century, she was partly clothed and, until a few years ago, the lower part of her belly was covered by a yellow drapery; this was then taken off during an excellent cleaning operation that revealed the underlying surface in perfect condition), a Venus, as I was saying, in a lascivious, almost obscene embrace with Love. Around them we see other figures, the most curious of whom is the woman in the near background on the right. Her hands are inverted, that is, her right hand is where her left hand should be, and in it she is holding a honeycomb. Moreover, this woman becomes a monster in her lower parts, half reptile and half lion. She symbolises Deceit. Obviously, this is an allegory. We understand, then, that the whole picture is an allegory of sensual love which, favoured by Deceit, is also accompanied by Joy, symbolised by the *puttino* who is advancing with little bells around his left ankle and with his hands full of roses which he is just about to scatter. However, on the left of the background, we see Desperation approaching, a woman who is clutching her head in an access of rage, and further back, high up in the right-hand corner, there is the winged figure of an old man who is about to cover the whole scene with a sombre curtain. He is Time who, in the end, extinguishes all passions.

The curious thing is that, in a picture of this genre, each time one studies it new details come to light. Up until a short time ago, notwithstanding the very rich literature concerning this painting, one detail had escaped everybody's notice: in the very act of embracing, Venus and Cupid are cheating one another. Cupid is stealing Venus's diadem of pearls and Venus, in her turn, is trying to extract the arrows from Cupid's quiver. The picture is an almost infinite series of superimpositions of symbolical and allegorical themes. A little while ago, I asked myself what kind of society could have produced a picture of this genre, and I came to the conclusion that it could only have been the extremely refined élite of a profoundly cultured and literate society. But it must be said that no painter, on his own, could have invented a subject of this order. Cosimo de' Medici would undoubtedly have consulted a man of letters and then furnished Bronzino with the subject matter for the picture.

Painters have often boasted of having themselves invented the subject matter of their works. One artist who, in my opinion, quite unjustifiably claimed the glory for having conceived a prodigious scheme, was Michelangelo. It is utterly impossible that the ceiling of the Sistine Chapel (a mine of complex meanings, drawn from the Old and the New Testaments and the Ten Commandments, and in which even the composition of the individual figures, especially those of the prophets, has a symbolical and allegorical significance) could have sprung full-born from the mind of Michelangelo himself – he simply could not have had such profound theological knowledge. It is impossible. Neither the ceiling of the Sistine Chapel, nor the first of the Raphael Stanzas, could have been conceived, in all their iconographical complexity, by the painters who executed them; they were certainly devised by theologians or erudite scholars from the court of Julius II. One may only make informed guesses as to who was the inspiration behind the iconological system of such sublime masterpieces, with their multiple meanings.

To return to Bronzino's Allegory, the fact that it is a work produced for and by an aristocratic élite is also indicated by the style. An idealistic style, cold and frustrated. Venus's body is made not of flesh, but of marble. Her hands make one think of ivory . . . In short, as Roberto Longhi said, it is a 'plastic idealism, superbly glacial'. There is something alien in this picture, something occult, which we are no longer able to perceive and interpret in its entirety.

Let us move on now to a painting with a sacred subject. It is the work of Francesco Bonsignori, an artist of secondary rank who was active in Verona during the latter half of the fifteenth century. The painting, which is signed and dated 1483, hangs in the Museo di Castelvecchio in Verona. It is a Madonna and Child. At first glance, it may seem to be just another Madonna, but, if we look at it a little more closely, we become aware of two or three very unusual features. The Child is sleeping on a slab of marble, which is totally improbable in the context of a naturalistic painting: no baby could sleep on a hard, cold stone. What is more, he is sleeping in a shift that leaves the lower part of his body and his sexual organs completely exposed. You will also see that the joined hands of the Madonna seem to be protecting the baby's genitals. What does this mean? Why on earth is the Child Jesus sleeping on a marble slab, and why are the Madonna's hands placed in that particular relationship to her son's body? In order to understand the picture, it is necessary to see the original or, at the least, a good reproduction in colour. Only then does one perceive that the marble on which the Child is sleeping is reddish, veined with white. It is the same marble slab which appears again in a picture in the Brera, the celebrated *Dead Christ* by Mantegna. What is the significance of this red marble speckled with white? Before we answer that question, note that the Child is lying down, he is sleeping in a rather rigid attitude, as if he were dead. The fact of the matter is this: the red stone veined with white is the so-called Stone of Unction, one of Christianity's most sacred relics which, up until the twelfth century, was kept in the basilica of the Holy Sepulchre in Jerusalem. In the twelfth century, this much-venerated relic was carried off to Constantinople and it is not known what became of it. However, it was evidently a well-known object to the Italian artists of the quattrocento. Perhaps it still exists, it may have been stolen during the sack of Constantinople in 1204, brought to Italy and then lost. Who knows whether it is still around today, lying unidentified in some sacred Italian building? In Jerusalem, the Stone of Unction has been replaced by a copy, and you will find it exactly half-way between Calvary and the Holy Sepulchre. According to tradition, it was the stone on which Christ's body was laid out and anointed after the deposition from the cross. Hence its name. According to the same legend, the stone was originally red, but the Madonna's indelible tears stained it with white.

3. Francesco Bonsignori.
Madonna and Child.
Museo di Castelvecchio, Verona.

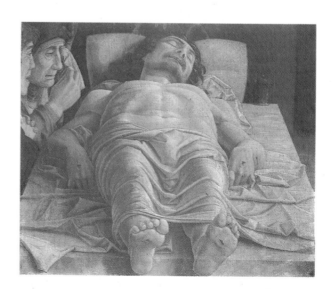

4. Andrea Mantegna. *Dead Christ*.
Pinacoteca di Brera, Milan.

These white veins, against the red background, can be seen in both Bonsignori's picture and in Mantegna's. In the latter, the Virgin is crying immediately over the stone and the reference to the legend is much more direct.

Having explained these specific points, the significance of Bonsignori's painting becomes clear. It is based on the rhetorical figure known as prolepsis, which is the depiction of an object or an episode in such a way as to foreshadow its final destiny. Here we have the Madonna with a still infant Jesus, but the baby is sleeping in the same position as the dead Christ after the Passion. So, the picture has a double meaning: it is a Madonna and Child, and, at the same time, it is Christ the Redeemer, for, lying stretched out on what will later be known as the Stone of Unction, the Child prefigures his own death. But why is the lower part of his body nude? This detail indicates that God is incarnated in Christ as a real man.

In the late fifteenth century, many of the theologians who compiled prayers for the Papal court, especially for Innocent VIII, Sixtus IV and Julius II, laid great stress on the second person of the Trinity, whom they held to be almost more important than the other two. In their view, while the creation of the world was to some extent imperfect, since man was created without the possibility of salvation, the Incarnation in Christ was more perfect, inasmuch as it gave to man the possibility of being saved. The Redeemer gave us something above and beyond the original creation. In stressing His sexual organs, Bonsignori's picture represents Christ as a true man. These concepts may seem impious to us today, accustomed as we are to the mentality of the Counter-Reformation and its sex-phobia. But, as you see, it is specifically by joining her hands in the attitude of prayer that the Madonna is protecting the most delicate parts of her son's body: His genitals.

We know that, in painting and also in philosophy, the human body is polarised. The upper part, above the umbilicus, is the noble part; the lower part, from the umbilicus down, is the ignoble, the carnal part, the seat of the stimuli we repress. Therefore, in Bonsignori's painting, it is precisely these lower parts that are exalted, as a sign of the Incarnation.

Let us take another look now at Mantegna's picture, in which the essential element is the red and white-veined Stone of Unction. Here, the painter has made it very apparent that the Virgin, seen as an old woman, is weeping onto the stone and veining it with white. Let me repeat: this outstanding relic must have been brought to Italy, possibly by Crusaders in 1204, and subsequently lost. I have suspected for some time now that, at a certain moment, it finished up in Mantua, or in some other locality between Lombardy and Veneto.

Do not forget that Italy is a country whose historical and cultural stratification has endured for more than two thousand years. Objects which, in their time, were extremely important, venerated, rich with religious significance, or, at any rate, highly valued and complex, can be mislaid or lost; they can be lying, unrecognised, in some church or convent, in the vaults of some museum, and this is precisely because of this country's continuing stratification and because, in Italy, works of art have always been an integral part of our religious, social, civic and cultural history, unlike the United States, where almost all the works of art to be found in its museums today were imported quite arbitrarily. It is no wonder, then, if we hear of great discoveries being made in Italy. If anything, the wonder is that certain objects – even some of outstanding importance – remained neglected for so long, in spite of the fact that they were right under somebody or other's nose. In this field, all things are possible. In Italy, any discovery, of any type whatever, may occur.

Another picture in which the theme of the Incarnation is treated in a completely different way is the small painting on wood by Carlo Crivelli which belongs to the Accademia Carrara in Bergamo. This is also a Madonna and Child. At this point, I would like to underline the fact that, when one comes upon a work of art, the first aspect to be considered is its state of preservation. The little picture in Bergamo is in good condition except in one area: the gold of the Madonna's mantle has been lost. Probably someone in the seventeenth, eighteenth or early nineteenth century cleaned it with unsuitable materials which removed the gold. For the rest, the surface is in excellent condition. How are we to read this picture? The Madonna, holding the Child, is set behind a parapet and against a hanging ornamented with branches, a large apple and a peach. In the background we see a landscape; in the foreground a carnation, a cucumber and a cherry. For a long time it was believed that these fruits and flowers were simply decorative, a caprice or predilection of Crivelli's, but, on the contrary, they have very specific meanings. Why is the Child holding such a large, heavy apple? Because the apple represents original sin and the forbidden fruit plucked by Eve. Therefore, Jesus the Redeemer, through His incarnation, takes upon Himself all the weight and burden of original sin. This same theme is taken up again in the background: the apple and the peach are further very precise allusions to original sin and salvation.

The cucumber in the foreground also has symbolic value. Assuming that a great deal of thinking in the Middle Ages was directed towards finding concordances between the Old Testament and the New, the cucumber can be seen as a symbol of the resurrection. According to the biblical legend, when Jonah was vomited out of the whale's mouth (after spending three days in its belly), he reawoke to the light of day under a pergola of gourds. The three days Jonah remained in darkness inside the marine monster are compared, in the concordance, to the three days Christ spent in Limbo after the crucifixion.

Moreover, in Renaissance times, gourds and cucumbers (both cucurbitaceae) were considered to be the same thing. Thus the cucumber symbolises the awakening of Christ after three days in the Beyond. I must add, however, that this interpretation of the figure of Jonah was not current during the first centuries of Christianity. While it is a fact that many sarcophagi from the era of paleo-Christian art are decorated with the figure of Jonah stretched out naked beneath a pergola of gourds or cucumbers, he simply represented Divine Providence at that time. The concordance between the episode in the Old Testament and that in the New was only made centuries later.

Returning to Crivelli's picture, we see that the cucumber in the foreground is placed between a cherry and a carnation. The latter is a nuptial symbol. In northern Italy and in Flanders, a great many pictures of the quattrocento portray a young man and woman holding carnations in their hands. These are wedding portraits, which were sent from the fiancé to his betrothed, or vice versa, especially in cases where – as was common in those days – the bride and groom had never actually met. So, they were shown with the carnation, symbol of marital love. Apart from the fact that the carnation (like the cherry which we see on the right) is also a symbol of sweetness, why in the world should there be a carnation – which, as we have seen, is a nuptial symbol – in this painting of Crivelli's? We must not forget that the Madonna was not only the Holy Virgin, crowned Queen of Heaven after the Assumption: a great many theologians also identified her with the Church, the 'Sponsa Christi' (the Church, Bride of Christ). Therefore here, too, albeit in a mystical sense, the carnation is a nuptial symbol. Amongst the numerous symbolic connotations in this picture, there is one in the landscape which, although in my view very evident, has never been commented upon.

The landscape presents entirely different aspects on the two sides. On the right, the trees are withered and sere; on the left, they are green. They represent, respectively, the aridity, the deadness, the drought of the world before the Incarnation, and the vigour and renewal of life in the world after the Incarnation. This detail can be seen in many of the paintings from Crivelli's own hand or from his studio. These works are not confined to a simple representation of the Madonna and Child, they are, rather, a sort of theological compendium; they are mines of information as to the beliefs, the theological preferences of the time. In this connection, however, we must note that the same image and the same theme can be rendered, over the various periods of art, in completely different ways.

The figure of Christ is a subject that has continued to develop uninterruptedly over two millennia, and it is among the richest and most varied themes in Christian art in the West (oriental Christianity, under the aegis of the Orthodox Church, poses radically different problems). The image of the Redeemer, therefore, changes drastically over the centuries, but often it changes over a period of only four or five years. Each generation portrays our Saviour in its own way, but none of these portrayals satisfies the succeeding generations. Very often, we would be baffled by the image of the Redeemer if there were not some written indication to guide us. Let us look, for instance, at a Roman glass panel from the third–fourth 6 centuries; it is now in the British Museum. Originally, it was set into the wall of a Christian sepulchre in a catacomb in Rome. Dating was obtained by comparative studies of style. The glass is of the kind known as *eglomisé*, that is, gilded and engraved on the reverse side. Similar glass panels were very common, and generally every arcosolium [the arched area above the niche serving as a tomb in a Roman catacomb] had one above the walled-up cell where the corpse lay. During the Middle Ages, they were stolen or carried off as relics (not to mention the depredations of scholars, collectors, and others). This panel depicts Christ as an adolescent; round his shoulders is something that looks like a stylised fur collar but is, in fact, a sheep. The four Evangelists are shown in the four corners of the composition. Notice how the image of Jesus, in these first days of Christianity, is always youthful and sweet. There is never anything awesome about him, never a

5. Carlo Crivelli.
Madonna and Child.
Accademia Carrara, Bergamo.

6. Roman glass.
The Good Shepherd and the Four
Evangelists. British Museum, London.

7. Ivory, fourth–fifth century AD.
The Crucifixion and the Suicide of Judas.
British Museum, London.

grim-faced Christ, but the Approachable One, the Kindly One. Later, when Christ became the protector of the Roman Empire, he was transmuted into the Supreme Judge and Chastiser. The glass, except for the upper part, is in a perfect state of preservation and, even better, it is untouched by restorations. I stress this point because very often works of this kind have been ruined by retouching and alterations.

From the same period and place – Italy between the fourth and fifth centuries – comes this fragment of some ivory object. Here, the image of Christ is in the process of mutation: he is more adult, and beginning to assume those attributes which were to become constant during the Middle Ages and endure until very late. But in this fragment, next to the scene of the Crucifixion, there is a very rare subject: the suicide of Judas. For many centuries, Judas was never portrayed, or, if he appeared at all, he was always standing apart, and in the shadows. In this ivory, on the other hand, he is shown hanging from the tree, and below him is the bag containing the thirty pieces of silver, which has fallen open. Note, moreover, the remarkable fusion of classical tradition and a new spirit. It was not until the Roman Empire was transmuted into a Christian Empire that there existed a true and proper Christian art. It is a curious fact that, while all the periods into which we subdivide the history of art are based on characteristics of style, or at least on a reading of the form, so-called Early Christian art is the only one that is defined solely according to the subject matter. In reality, the paintings and visual products of the early Christians show no formal difference whatever from those of the pagans; in some cases, we are even in doubt as to whether the theme is Christian or pagan, since the form itself offers no clues. Only when the Roman State adopts Christianity, that is, when the new religion is recognised and tolerated, to become, later on, the sole authorised creed (before Constantine, then under Theodosius I and Theodosius II), can we speak of a Christian art. Then, there is a real separation, the forms of the old pagan art fossilise, and it is as if a dehydrated art were born, which will find new life and new splendour only with the Renaissance. In the late Empire, when the State becomes totalitarian, we see a curious phenomenon: a kind of hibernation of the forms of classical art.

After the terrible crisis of the third century, the Roman Empire rises again, thanks to Diocletian and Constantine the Great, as a totalitarian structure. Within this structure, Christianity comes to play a role which is not dissimilar to that of Marxism in the Soviet Union: it becomes the only tolerated ideological form. The other religions, and most particularly paganism, had been eliminated earlier. In the meantime, figurative works that derived from the huge output of Greco-Roman art, crystallised and fossilised into those forms that, today, we define as Byzantine. Or perhaps I should say they became, not fossilised but dormant, for this art had only to reach the West and come into contact with more liberal societies to flower into, first, the Italian Renaissance and then the European Renaissance. And that is not all: Venice, which was considered during the Middle Ages as an appendage of the eastern Roman Empire, and as the most influential area of Byzantine civilis-ation, produced a figurative culture capable of the most perfect and the most prodigious classical revival in the entire Renaissance. In painting, there is nothing more classical than Titian, from about 1515–20, and, in my opinion, there is nothing more classical than the marriage between the sculpture of Vittoria, the architecture of Palladio and the painting of Paolo Veronese in Villa Maser, near Treviso. Venice was a city that, of herself, had such a lively hellenistic tradition that she was later able to create those miracles which are the purest expression of European classicism: the works of the Venetian cinquecento. In comparison, the neo-classical seems coldly pedantic and tiresomely academic.

In the late eighteenth century, neo-classical art had a moralizing function, but it was, above all, a political fact, which emerged as a reaction to the *ancien régime* and the social structure. Later on, neo-classicism degenerated, transforming itself into a propaganda instrument for the Napoleonic tyranny. Venetian classicism, in contrast to this, is innate, free and spontaneous; truly one of the highest achievements ever seen in Europe. It would be difficult to match anywhere some of the works produced in Venice and in Veneto province from the time of the late Giovanni Bellini up to 1580–90.

To return now to the figure of Christ, here is one that is completely different from those we have already looked at. It is the cover of an evangelistary in the Museum of Zurich; it belongs to about the middle of the twelfth century and is in a perfect state of preservation. The cover is worked in embossed gold and ornamented with precious stones cut in the form of cabochons (that is, not faceted but rounded and mounted in a setting). The gold lamina is decorated with *cloisonné*. Here I should explain that there are two techniques for working in enamel: *cloisonné* and *champlevé*. In *champlevé* work, suitable cavities are made in the block of metal and these are then filled with enamel. This is the oldest method, and it was soon abandoned because one had only to give the object a hard knock, or shake it violently, for the pieces of enamel to fall out of the holes. So then a more durable technique was devised – and, curiously enough, this happened simultaneously in both the West and the East. Thin strips of metal are bent to form the outline of the design and are soldered edge-on to the surface of the metal object. This creates a series of small partitions, almost like a network of fields enclosed by fences. The liquid enamel, at a very high temperature, is then poured into these 'fields', where it is protected and held in place by the metal partitions. The Zurich evangelistary is an example of *cloisonné*.

Observe the figure of Christ. We have already established that each historical and cultural period portrays Him in its own way and that no single style of representing Him is ever definitive or exhaustive. Here we have Christ the Judge, surrounded by the symbols of the four Evangelists and the mandorla, or stylised almond, which symbolises His ascent into heaven. This image was designed for the cover of the evangelistary and clearly demonstrates that even objects intended for everyday use can be works of art; it is a refutation of the totally absurd and irrational theoretical distinction between major and minor arts.

But to come back to the figure of Christ: look at this page from a Swiss psalter, dated 1312. A century and a half later, figurative art is responding to entirely

8. Cover of an Evangelistary,
mid-twelfth century.
Landesmuseum, Zurich.

9. Page from a Swiss psaltery, 1312.
Landesmuseum, Zurich.

different canons. At the top, this illuminated page shows Christ on the road to
Calvary and, at the bottom, the two donors of the psalter. Here, nothing whatever
remains of the majestic, or the awe-inspiring, especially in the figure of Christ
Himself; we are returning to something more human, more earthly, and gentler. In
this case, too, we have a work of art in a perfect state of preservation. I cannot stress
this point too strongly, since, if the work is in poor condition, it can very often lead
us into completely erroneous readings.

10   Here is an example. This painting on wood portrays a half-figure of Christ in the
act of benediction. But if you look at the hand in perspective, in the third
dimension, you will see that there is another hand underneath it. At first, the artist
had imagined the hand that is raised in blessing in a position of less dramatic
perspective. Then he had second thoughts and painted it over with his new idea,
that is, he carried out what we call technically a *'pentimento'*, or change of mind.
In the nineteenth century, presumably, this delicate painting was submitted to a
harsh cleaning which ruined the outer epidermis and revealed the original design.
The picture is the *Salvator Mundi* by Antonello da Messina. It is signed and
hangs in the National Gallery, London. As you can easily see for yourselves,
the picture has been spoiled by cleaning, not only in the hand but in other areas,
too.

It is a healthy principle that, if a picture is dirty, it is better not to touch it unless
it can be entrusted to really competent technicians. Time destroys, time ruins, but
not so much as bad restoration. Restoration has been one of the scourges of the last
200 years. A restorer can do far more damage than an air raid, for the splinters of a
bomb (provided they do not destroy it completely) mutilate a picture, but as long as
there is even a fragment left intact, we can still read the style. The restorer, on the
other hand, flays the painting, so that, for want of the final skin, it is impossible to
make analyses and formal interpretations. It has proved possible to interpret
certain pictures from a few minimal details that happened to survive in good
condition.

On the other hand, incautious cleaning has ruined more than one outstanding
masterpiece. For example, perhaps the most important public work of Beato
Angelico, the *Pala di San Marco*, the altar-piece in the eponymous church in
Florence, has been utterly devastated. A parish priest, perhaps, or some other
church official, entrusted it to someone who washed it with a caustic substance.
The picture is in a deplorable state, while the series of tablets painted with scenes
from the lives of Saints Cosima and Damian, which made up the *predella* of the
altar-piece and are today distributed amongst various museums, were saved
(probably because they were no longer *in situ*). These tablets are in perfect
condition, but, if they had stayed where they were, they would have met with the
same fate as the principal section of the marvellous altar-piece. Very often these
cleanings were carried out to remove the smoke of the candles, which had
blackened the surfaces. And in fact, by washing a picture with ashes or with caustic
soda, the surface seems, for the moment, to regain its pristine splendour. But then
the caustic continues to work, not just for decades but for centuries, and it is

impossible to halt the corrosive action. There are a great many ruined paintings in existence, and sometimes the museums that own them are not even aware of their ruinous state because old restorations, old and by-now-oxidised patinas, covered with dirt, conceal the disaster.

There are also a number of self-appointed restorers. I have seen a fine, highly important painting by Sebastiano del Piombo ruined by a restorer who started life as a dentist. This man did irreparable damage to the portrait of Christopher Columbus, a picture that once belonged to Talleyrand and is now in the Metropolitan Museum, New York. I repeatedly recommended leaving the painting untouched, but unfortunately there was nothing to be done – the dentist needed the work. This happened in the late 1950s. In the case of certain painters, notably the artists of the cinquecento, a breath will suffice to destroy them, for they covered their canvases not with a thick layer of paint, like the Venetians, but with a film a fraction of a millimetre thick. This is true of Pontormo, Rosso Fiorentino and especially of Fra Bartolomeo and Mariotto Albertinelli. Once their works are ruined, nothing can be done to repair them.

The same thing happens to statues. Many sculptures which had been stained by exposure to the open air, or were dug up from the earth, were then washed with muriatic acid, a substance which continues to corrode for centuries. These marbles have completely lost their original patina. If you lick a statue that was washed with muriatic acid even half a century ago, you will immediately taste the acid; this shows that the corrosive substance is still working and preventing the formation of a new patina.

There is another very deleterious habit from the past. Until the beginning of the nineteenth century, antique sculptures which were found in a corroded and mutilated state were not only completed (like the Apollo Belvedere, for instance, who was given new hands), but they were also polished. The epidermis was submitted to a washing process that completely altered the character of the statue, to such an extent that, nowadays, we do not know whether we are looking at original Greek statues or at Roman copies, since they have all ended up with the same epidermis. In most museums, such as the Vatican Museums and the Louvre, and in the antique collections made before the nineteenth century, there are antique sculptures which have been worked on and have acquired a new skin. In some cases, as I said, these statues were completed by artists – even by great ones. The marbles from the 'Aphaia' Temple in Egina, which are in the Museum of Sculpture in Munich, were restored by Thorvaldsen. Today, many of these restorations have been removed but, in my view, this is a mistake. Once the statue has been restored, and becomes known in its 'completed' aspect, it is folly to cut off the restored parts because, in order to do this, these fragments must once again be submitted to amputation and polishing. Now that Thorvaldsen's restorations have been removed, the sculptures from the temple in Egina look like painfully truncated stumps. The first man who refused to restore classical masterpieces was Canova, who was asked to complete the statues from the Parthenon, brought to London by Lord Elgin. Canova declared that he was incapable of executing this

10. Antonello da Messina.
Salvator Mundi.
National Gallery, London.

11-12. Antonello da Messina.
Christ and (on the back) St Jerome.
Private collection, New York.

work and advised leaving them alone. How fortunate! Otherwise, we should also have had the Elgin Marbles completed, restored and polished.

But, to return to the various interpretations of the figure of Christ, let us look at another work by Antonello da Messina in which Christ is making an extraordinary grimace, an expression that today we would define as *mafioso*! It is a work of the artist's youth, still ignored by the literature of art. It is a double-sided painting: on the back there is a very fine landscape (which confirms it as the work of the painter's early years) with the kneeling figure of St Jerome. But, while the landscape is in excellent condition, the face of the saint is obliterated. How can we explain this? The picture was certainly kept in a little leather wallet (of the type of leather known as *cuir bouilli* or *cuir cuit*, which was then hardened and stamped with decorative tooling); it was, therefore, a picture to be carried when travelling. The owner was a devotee of St Jerome and, by continually kissing it, year after year, he destroyed the face.

Another picture, which was in the Monastero degli Angeli in Rimini until the early nineteenth century, and is now in a museum in Miami, suffered a similar fate. In this picture, too, the surface is in very good condition but the head of the Virgin is completely missing. A source from the mid-eighteenth century, Cardinal Garampi, when describing this picture, underlines the fact that it was damaged by 'the filth of kisses': the nuns in the convent, by perpetually kissing the same detail, ruined it. A similar thing has happened to the famous bronze statue of St Peter, in the basilica of St Peter's in the Vatican. For over a thousand years this statue has been repeatedly touched and kissed in the same place (the right foot, which projects forward), with the result that the detail is virtually rubbed away. And, again, it is like the famous column in the Sanctuary of St James of Compostella, Spain, where for centuries and centuries pilgrims have touched the same part of the column, where their fingers have worn five grooves. But it was not sculpted like that, it is the erosion, the wearing away by millions and millions of devout hands that has made the stone, at that point, look like a root.

Coming back to Antonello da Messina's picture with two faces, the wood (about 3 or 4 millimetres in thickness) is so thin that it cannot be divided without ruining both surfaces. In many other cases, however, the thickness of the wood makes this division possible. The so-called '*deschi da parto*' (literally 'childbirth boards' but known in English as 'birthsalvers') have very often been treated in this way. These trays, painted on both sides, were in use in Florence in the fourth and fifth centuries. Their purpose was to carry the first bowl of broth to the newly delivered mother.

Reverting to the preservation of paintings, I would like now to speak about an enormous picture with a christological theme, executed by Sebastiano del Piombo between 1517 and 1519. It is the *Resurrection of Lazarus*, painted for the Cathedral of Narbonne and today in the National Gallery, London. The state of preservation is good, but not perfect because the picture was transferred from wood to canvas. This type of transfer becomes necessary when the wood of the backing is in such a rotten state (due to humidity, wood-worm, or because the wood was not properly prepared) as to prejudice the survival of the painting itself. It is not a difficult operation and today we have highly skilled technicians. Unfortunately, many of the paintings purloined from Italy after the French Revolution and carried off to Paris for the Musée Napoléon suffered because the transfer of the paint from wood to canvas was done clumsily and in haste. These include some of the great masterpieces stolen from the Papal States, such as the *Madonna di Foligno* and the *Transfiguration* by Raphael. These and many other pictures were damaged beyond repair, either during their transportation to France, on carts, or through incompetent transference from wood to canvas.

Looking again at Sebastiano del Piombo's painting, one can recognise various portraits in the middle of this evangelical scene, and these would certainly be of the people who commissioned the painting and of their friends. But does this picture represent nothing more than the resurrection of Lazarus? Is it simply an image that alludes to the resurrection of the dead, or has it other connotations? We can confidently state that it is a picture of great ideological complexity, as, indeed, is all the work of Sebastiano, in whom, the more one studies him, the more one discovers a connection with certain reformist tendencies of the Catholic Church, which were manifest in Rome during the first half of the sixteenth century and later suppressed by the Counter-Reformation. One always finds Sebastiano in contact with people who were in trouble later, when the Counter-Reformation came, and one meets him in places which were considered suspect at that time. For example, he was in touch with Vittoria Colonna; one of his masterpieces was painted in Viterbo, where the Spanish reformer, Juan de Valdés, also spent some time; it seems he was an intimate friend of Pietro Carnesecchi, who was later burned at the stake by the Inquisition. We know that certain cardinals, who commissioned work from Sebastiano, later suffered considerable difficulties during the Council of Trent. Probably the painter himself had reformist tendencies. After all, we must not imagine that, just because the Council of Trent later prevailed in Italy and Spain, these countries never felt strong urges to move in the same direction that Protestant reform was taking in the north. But while, in northern Europe, Protestantism led to a splitting into an infinite number of sects and innumerable variations of belief, in the south a substantially orthodox tradition dominated. But this does not preclude the fact that, in the early phase, there were strong thrusts towards reform. Indeed, there are those who maintain that the Council of Trent, addressing itself to this impetus, had no other purpose than to make reforms, but in the Catholic sense, in the southern, Roman sense.

What can the connotations be, then, in this picture by Sebastiano del Piombo? In the background, we see a city which reminds us of Rome, of her buildings and monuments. There is also a river, with a bridge across it, that looks like the Tiber. And everything appears debased, decadent. The group of washerwomen on the riverbank seem to signify that the nobility of the Imperial City has been ruined and sullied. From this we can read what is almost an invitation to revive the city, just as Christ is reviving Lazarus. In short, it is a protest, expressed in symbolic code. It is probable that there are religious themes in the work of Sebastiano del Piombo

13. Roman art, fifth century AD.
St Peter. Basilica of St Peter's, Rome.

14. Sebastiano del Piombo.
The *Resurrection of Lazarus*.
National Gallery, London.

which have not yet been recognised or deciphered; perhaps it is too early still for them to be recognised, studied and confronted in all their implications.

All themes, in fact, and all works of art, must await the propitious moment to be intuited, read and interpreted in an adequate manner. Moreover, we live in a continuous state of mutation. Our world changes unceasingly: for example, it changes even in the way in which we perceive colours. We do not see colour nowadays as the ancients saw it.

The Romans were extremely sensitive to black and white. Their vocabulary included two words to indicate white: *candidus* and *albus. Candidus* is sparkling white, the white of snow; *albus*, on the other hand, is a non-reflecting white, like the white of an egg. There was a Roman villa called '*Ad gallinas albas*' (at the place of the white hens). We, today, are content with saying simply that snow is white and eggs are white. The Romans also had two specific words for black: *niger*, which is the shining black of certain stones (such as the '*Lapis Niger*', the enormous black slab in the Roman Forum beneath which was the so-called Tomb of Romulus; or obsidian, which was known as *nigra*); and *ater* which is the inert, extinguished black of coal (the Romans always used the word *ater* in connection with the infernal regions because, in hell, there is no reflection of light).

The Romans, then, possessed a kind of sensibility that we today have lost. In the same way, when reading Greek texts, one often suspects that they did not perceive green as a separate colour from blue, but interpreted it merely as a shade of blue. It is only in a later period that blue and green begin to be distinguished from one another. And, in fact, in the language of some central Asian cultures, certain colours are absent altogether. We can deduce from this that certain colours may not be perceived, not for physiological reasons, but for purely cultural reasons.

But we really need not look so far afield: let us consider the colours used in fashion. When we look at the clothes we wore only 20 years ago, we are disconcerted: the incongruity of their colours surprises us because our chromatic sensibilities are no longer the same. There are, moreover, colours which only gradually make their appearance in art. I challenge anyone to find the mauve colour of wistaria in any painting earlier than 1875. You will not find wistaria shades in figurative works until the Impressionists – Monet or Renoir, for example. In Italy, we discover them again in the pictures of Armando Spadini. In fact, that particular shade of violet did not exist in art until the art nouveau period which, partly because of its intense interest in the vegetable world, discovered and revealed an extraordinary variety of colours, tones and shades.

As our chromatic sensibility changes, so does our palate. We experience tastes in a totally different way from – I am not even going to say the ancients, but, much closer to home, our grandparents. The gustatory appreciation of the ancients was so completely different that the dishes Apicius describes in *De re coquinaria* strike us as repellent and inedible. The entire cuisine was based on *dulcamara* (bittersweet): flavours were at once honeyed and salted, sickly sweet and sour, rather like *mostarda di Cremona* [a dish consisting of fruits, sometimes candied, in a hot, spiced sauce of honey, mustard and vinegar] which is, in fact, a gastronomic survival from antique and medieval times. In the Roman era, everything was seasoned with *garum*, a sauce made from the intestines of fish fermented in vinegar. The very idea of it is inconceivable to us, and so is the Roman way of treating meat. Since there were no refrigerators, and not enough ice and snow available all year round to preserve it, meat was smothered in layers of spices, which kept it from going off for many months. To us today, such tastes would be horrible, but in those days people thoroughly enjoyed them. Spices were of vital importance in the ancient world, during the Middle Ages and even up until fairly recent times. Alaric, the Visigoth king who sacked Rome in AD 410, is a case in point: when demanding the city's ransom, he specified not only precious metals but sacks of pepper. To sum up, the culinary arts which influenced the palate and taste-sensitivity of the ancients have today changed beyond recognition. Even the savours of the *haute cuisine* of the seventeenth, eighteenth and nineteenth centuries would seem exaggerated nowadays, not at all well balanced in relation to our modern palates. Just take a look at the interminable and highly complicated menus of the last century, and you will realise that there has been a profound change in tastes.

The same thing occurs with works of art. Every day we grow, we mature, we mutate, we are ever-changing. There are artistic periods which can only be intuited and understood when the moment is ripe, but, in any case, the past is dead for ever. Yesterday remains yesterday, it is impossible to resurrect it. No force, no belief will ever arise that will enable us to understand the past in all its implications. But, although dead and gone for ever, the events of the past have left us with a vast quantity of clues, connotations and meanings in works of art and in literature which we can re-read and interpret. We must remember, however, that it is always a matter of exhumation and not of total knowledge of the living thing. If we look back only 20 years, we find music, songs and newspapers containing allusions that are already totally obscure to us. Imagine, then, the abyss that divides us from complex works of art, full of messages, like the *Resurrection of Lazarus* by Sebastiano del Piombo, which belongs to the sixteenth century!

The more we know about literature and history, the more we can master the significance of a visual work. The greater our knowledge of a period, the easier it is to penetrate the spirit of its artistic texts. But we must have no illusions: many of its essential meanings escape us. A vast number of these meanings, with their cultural, social, allegorical and symbolical stratifications are lost once and for all. Because of this, we may be tempted to fall back on a false interpretation, a surrogate which consists of a reading based, not on the work of art itself, but on what we would like it to be. As happens, generally, in human relationships: the only way to get on with people is to seek in others what already exists within ourselves.

Here is an example of how the misreading of a work can hinder its correct identification for a long time – in this case, it was due to the *idée fixe* of the person who owned the panel I am showing you. From the stylistic point of view, we can immediately recognise here the hand of one of the greatest artists of the fifteenth century: Piero della Francesca. This picture was put up for sale on the Milanese

15. Piero della Francesca.
San Nicola of Tolentino.
Museo Poldi Pezzoli, Milan.

market in the second half of the nineteenth century and purchased by a great local collector, Gian Giacomo Poldi Pezzoli. He, and with him many critics and scholars, believed for a long time that the saint portrayed was Thomas Aquinas, who is described in the sources as a fat man. It was also thought that the habit was of the Dominican order, to which Thomas belonged. The parapet behind the figure looks as if it were part of a continuing succession of images. The solution to the problem was found when, nearly 25 years ago, the true subject of the picture was identified as, not Thomas, but Nicola of Tolentino. It is not an orthodox rendering of this saint, for, in the traditional iconography of St Nicola, the sun-image appears on his chest, whereas here it is in the sky, and the saint usually has a lily in his hand. It must be added that the face is, quite evidently, a portrait. The habit is not Dominican but Augustinian, of the order to which Nicola belonged.

Having established this, it became clear that the panel was part of a polyptych painted by Piero della Francesca for the church of St Augustine in Borgo San Sepolcro. The polyptych was composed of a central panel, now lost, which showed the Madonna enthroned with the Child, and four side-panels with saints. Of these four saints, only St Nicola of Tolentino remained in Italy. The position of his body indicates that he was on the right-hand side; there was a St John next to him which is now in the Frick Collection in New York. The St John had travelled from Milan to Vienna (before reaching New York) and belonged to a collector who acquired it in the same year in which Poldi Pezzoli discovered and bought his St Nicola. On the left-hand side of the Madonna there was a St Michael Archangel, now in the National Gallery, London, and a St Augustine. The latter, under an erroneous attribution, was discovered by chance some years ago in the Museu de Arte Antiga in Lisbon.

The identification of the polyptych, which is well documented, is certain because in the lower edges of the two inner panels (the St John and the Archangel Michael) we can see the outermost folds of the Madonna's cloak on the steps of the throne. As for the central panel, given up for lost, I do not in the least exclude the possibility that it is still in existence somewhere, unrecognised, in some Italian or foreign collection, perhaps in the Soviet Union. Unless, of course, it was destroyed in one of the great catastrophes of the last few hundred years.

When and how did the great destruction of works of art come about? Partly, in the fire in Madrid in 1734, when many masterpieces from the great royal collection went up in flames, including the series of the Twelve Caesars by Titian, painted for the ducal palace in Mantua. That was a real holocaust. Other great disasters were the French Revolution and the English Civil War, which destroyed mainly the works of art in churches, though not the most important pictures. During the Russian Revolution, nothing was destroyed. In 1917 everything officially belonged to the state, but it was left in the custody of the owners, except in cases where these people were considered a danger to the new régime.

Further wholesale destruction occurred during the Paris Commune: the fire in the Tuileries, for example. During the First World War, Belgium and northern France suffered, and in the Austro-Hungarian Empire there was huge devastation, especially in Galicia, where there were a great many private collections. In the Second World War, there were catastrophic bombings which destroyed, amongst other things, a large part of Bridgewater House, London, and with it the master-pieces of Annibale Caracci; the great fire that broke out in the heart of Berlin, in May 1945, after the fighting was over, and which destroyed the *Flak-Turm*, containing the masterpieces from the Kaiser Friedrich Museum; the horrific fire-bombing of Dresden; the enormous damage to the store-rooms in Munich, to the *Accademia Albertina* in Turin, and many other public collections. But, and I must stress this point, our artistic heritage has not generally suffered serious damage during the great revolutions, unless there were holocausts of works of art from religious motives, as happened in England at the time of the Reformation.

Second Conversation

In the First Conversation, we saw how certain works of art are of great cultural complexity, but these are not to be found in every period or in every society. Entire civilisations have existed, whole cultures which did not express themselves through the visual arts or, at most, only in a very limited way. Their artefacts and the figurative works that have come down to us are often surprisingly poor.

This is what happened in Europe during the era of the great migrations, from the third to the ninth–tenth centuries. During this period, some of the peoples living beyond the northern and eastern confines of the Roman Empire were driven to uproot themselves and cross the frontiers into the Empire itself. The force that drove them was located further out, deep in the heart of Asia, but we are still not very clear about who or what it was. At first, these invasions were only brief forays of the kind that had already taken place elsewhere (we know that there were similar pushes into Thrace and Asia Minor as early as the first, second and third centuries), but, later on, in the third, fourth and fifth centuries, whole populations transmigrated, only to be annihilated in the first clashes. Then, little by little, as the western Empire grew weaker, these peoples managed to establish themselves definitively on their new soil and even to set up associated kingdoms. This was the case with the Visigoths in Spain, the Ostrogoths in Italy and the Vandals in north Africa.

While it is true that, in certain areas, the Roman population lived separately from the invaders (as happened with the Ostrogoths, for example), there is no truth whatever in the idea that these associated kingdoms devastated or scorned the local culture; on the contrary, they maintained and sometimes even restored the ancient buildings. The last restorations to the monuments of ancient Rome were carried out by Theodoric, at the beginning of the sixth century, when he repaired a number of buildings that were in a dilapidated state.

We also know that, during the reign of the Vandals, the city of Carthage, one of the great metropoli of the ancient world, was in no way ravaged or transformed. In spite of this, the Roman Empire which had its seat in Constantinople, and was an empire with an absolutist and totalitarian mentality, never recognised these associated kingdoms. There was also a religious factor behind this intolerance, a kind of crusading spirit, since, in most of the associated kingdoms, it was the Arian version of Christianity that was practised. And so the Emperor Justinian, with a remarkable team of collaborators which included the Generals Belisarius and Narses, first set up diplomatic precedents and then resorted to force; in a series of wars of reconquest he destroyed the Vandal kingdoms in north Africa and the Ostrogoth kingdom in Italy; he also recovered part of the Iberian Peninsula. It is this campaign of reconquest that really signals the end of the ancient classical civilisation. I will not go into details about the tremendous damage it did, especially in Italy (the city of Rome, for instance, never recovered from the effects of the Gothic war: the population was decimated, aqueducts cut, cultures abandoned, and so on). In reality, Justinian's victory was catastrophically short-lived, it was a pyrrhic victory. Once the absolutist system, and in particular the Roman fiscal system were re-established, the provinces of north Africa and the eastern Mediterranean began to withdraw from the political and ideological centralism of the Empire. First, through the *fronde* of the Monophysites and then through Islam.

Islam came into being as a direct result of the reaffirmation of totalitarianism by the eastern Roman Empire, and it was a true, full-scale secession. In the early days, Islam did not repudiate the great patrimony of the Hellenistic-Roman culture, and in fact was at its greatest as long as it continued to live in the classical tradition. Then, gradually, what had originally been a liberating factor changed its aspect and became a restrictive and even suffocating structure.

This Islamic secession was crucial, because it deprived Greco-Roman culture of three out of four of the great metropoli of the ancient world (Rome had already been ruined and reduced to a village by the long Gothic war); Antioch, Alexandria and Carthage were forever divorced from Western civilisation.

As if that were not enough, Islam, at the height of its eruption, had such force that it not only spread into Sicily and southern Italy, but occupied the whole of the Iberian Peninsula, pushed right up into the heart of France and, from the Saracen base in Fraxinetum (modern Frainet) in Provence, even made incursions into Bavaria and parts of the Danube region. The advance of Islam was a phenomenon that created one of the greatest upheavals of the last two thousand years.

Then came a wave of reaction. The Arabs were chased out of Gaul. After a long series of wars ending only in 1492, they were expelled from the Iberian Peninsula. They had to abandon southern Italy, Sicily and Malta. But none of this alters the fact that the whole of the north coast of Africa was thus lost for ever to western European culture. Nor must we forget that this African coast was one of the great cultural areas of the ancient world, not only because it included Alexandria, one of the most important centres of artistic production (and yet not even the ruins of this culture remain standing today), but also because, during the first centuries of our era, Tunisia and eastern Algeria were extremely important to Christianity.

It was in this zone that many of the extraordinarily rich debates took place and a great number of the texts were written. Above all, it was here that one of the doctors of the church, St Augustine, lived and worked. (Once again, however, no living heritage remains of this Roman and Christian past.) Some cities were abandoned and left to the ravages of the sand, or rather, to neglect and oblivion: this is the case with Leptis Magna, Sabrata, Bulla Regia and Sufetula in Tunisia. Other cities were razed to the ground and the salvaged materials used to build new urban centres. Modern Tunis is largely built with the marble and stone saved from the ruins of ancient Carthage . . . not the Carthage that was destroyed by the Romans in the second century BC, of course, but the immense metropolis of Carthage that flourished during the Empire and was probably second only to Rome.

However, to go back to the artistic output of the peoples who lived in the era of

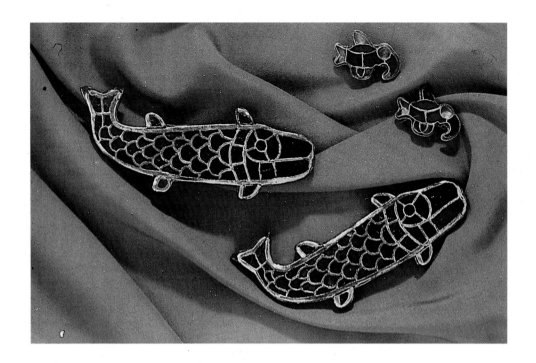

1. Fish in gold with red enamel,
fourth–sixth century AD. Found in the
necropolis of a Germanic tribe in
Switzerland. Landesmuseum, Zurich.

the great migrations, the first thing to note is that these objects are often very small
and almost always of the same type: little crosses, brooches for fastening cloaks
and dresses, or else objects that were sewn or applied to robes for special occasions.
There exists no appreciable body of plastic works, or paintings, from the first period
of the transmigrations. This applies to all the nations of Germanic stock. As an
example, let us take some articles that were found in Switzerland, in a cemetery
belonging to what was probably a German tribe that happened to arrive in that area
between the fourth and the sixth centuries. Here we have a few little gold fish,
filled with red enamel by the *cloisonné* technique. The use of this technique
which, as we saw in the first conversation, is the most advanced, indicates that the
tribe already had a certain tradition of craftsmanship. Moreover, the fish are
symbols of Christianity, because in Greek the word 'fish' (ιχθύς) is formed from the
initials of the expression 'Jesus Christ, Son of God, Saviour' (Ἰησοῦς Χριστός Θεοῦ
Υἱός Σωτήρ) and so was read and interpreted as an acrostic.

   This tribe was Christian, but not Catholic; they belonged to the Arian sect. Now
it would take a long time to explain exactly what Arianism was, but the important
point is that many Germanic tribes, including the Ostrogoths, had been converted
to Christianity of the Arian variety by the Alans, a nation generally thought to be
Germanic but who were, in reality, of Iranian origin. So, the penetration of Arian
Christians into the territories of what we may call Catholic Christians was a
further contributing cause to the friction between the native population, in this
case the Romans, and the invaders. For example, in the time of Theodoric there was
a clear-cut separation of invaders and the indigenous peoples which led to some
curious episodes in the figurative arts.

   Faced with these articles, one wonders how on earth these people could have
expressed themselves through such minute and secondary products. The easy
answer would be that they were inferior cultures – but that is *too* easy. The truth is,
they were very different from the Hellenistic-Roman civilisation with which they
came into contact, and apparently – indeed, we can say certainly – these cultures
expressed themselves in other ways.

   In all probability, they had an extremely rich heritage in textiles, but none of
these has survived to bear witness. Very likely they worked figurative compositions in felt, like the ones that have been found from other nomadic cultures in
tombs in Siberia. It is also possible that they possessed an immense repertoire of
music and songs, all ephemeral forms of expression which have not come down to
us. At all events, it is certain that these peoples expressed themselves through
means that were entirely different from the essentially figurative arts of the
Greco-Roman world.

   Nowadays, we can have only a very dim idea of what the cities of the Empire,
great and small, must have looked like in the fourth and fifth centuries, swarming
as they were with a multitude of statues in bronze and marble, a vast quantity of
sculpture of all kinds. Apart from the statues (we have evidence of many of these in
the form of inscribed bases with holes where the bolts went in to fix the statues in
place), we must reckon with the huge quantity of mosaics, frescoes and stuccoes

which also depicted the human form. Today, almost all the bronze statues have been lost, only a very few remain. But when you think that, in the city of Rome alone, the number of equestrian figures and single statues ran into thousands, and that in the great public buildings of Alexandria, Antioch, Carthage and all the minor cities, the statues were counted in tens and tens of thousands, then you begin to realise how profound the gulf between the nomadic invaders and the cultural context they found really was. They were truly two different worlds. And we can also understand why Islam prohibits the representation of the human figure. It was banned precisely because the human figure in effigy symbolised the Imperial authority that Islam opposed and, by banning it, her followers claimed autonomy in the face of that power.

We must not overlook the fact that this Islamic secession occurred in a region that, from a religious point of view, had been a thorn in the side of the Imperial power for centuries. We are talking about the region that stretches from Algeria to the confines of Turkey with Syria. The whole coast was teeming with Christian churches at a time when Christianity was forbidden. So, in this instance, Christianity was a form of opposition to the official paganism.

When Christianity was, first, tolerated and then given full recognition, the area that today constitutes Tunisia and eastern Algeria began to give birth to heresies and various sects: the Donatists, the Circumcellion (the latter perpetrated violent and unprecedented acts, like modern terrorists). When the Donatist heresy was suppressed, religious agitation spread, this time throughout a vast area which became the seat of another heresy, Monophysitism, which considered that Christ was of one nature only: the divine, and not the human. It was the source of infinite problems for the government in Constantinople.

The Monophysite heresy was sharply attacked by the emperors of Constantinople, but later found a sort of *modus vivendi* in the time of Justinian and Theodora. The latter, a woman gifted with a fine political mind, seems to have protected the Monophysites. No sooner was Theodora dead, however, than Justinian's advisers, and his successors, once more turned against the Monophysites. Note that the area of Monophysitism later succumbed to Islam. This change came about, admittedly, under pressure of attacks by Arab warriors, but it was really what we today would call a military take-over. Great cities like Damascus fell before a few hundred Islamic cavalrymen. The West, Byzantium, thus lost one of the most important territories for the Christian religion: the Holy Land. Bethlehem, where Christ was born, and Jerusalem, where he was crucified and where much of his activity was carried on, became Islamic cities.

However, we must not believe – and from the artistic point of view, this is most important – that the advent of Islam meant destruction, the burning of churches, and so on. Quite the opposite. In Damascus, for example, one of the most venerated sanctuaries of Christianity, the church where the relics of St John the Baptist were kept, was converted, with some modifications, into what is today the Mosque of the Omayyad. During the work of conversion, it was apparently the Emperor of Constantinople himself who sent craftsmen to execute very fine mosaics

2. Enamel clasp, found in the Sutton Hoo
sepulchre. British Museum, London.

depicting landscapes and buildings. (Obviously, no human figures were shown.)

The church in Bethlehem, built by Constantine and rebuilt by Justinian, was not destroyed either. The church we see today, marvellously preserved, is still Justinian's. It was only at a much later date that some slabs of particularly precious marble were taken away to decorate local mosques. This church in Bethlehem was often desecrated, however; camel-drivers would even go into it with their beasts, which is why the doorway was eventually made narrower to prevent such trespasses. But the Arabs never destroyed such venerated buildings.

We must also remember that the figurative Greco-Roman civilisation, even though Alexandria became one of its most brilliant, inventive and prolific centres, was still an alien civilisation, imported into north Africa and the Middle East for political reasons. And it is an infallible law that, sooner or later, the local civilisation will always rise up again to dominate the imported one, even if it takes centuries, or millennia. There is always a humus of the old culture which continues to ferment underground until it bursts into new and exuberant life. Alexandria was once the seat of the greatest library of the Greco-Roman world, and of the first museum, where Aristotle's manuscripts were kept; it was the home of schools of mosaicists whose work was exported throughout the whole of the Mediterranean (the famous Alexandrian *emblemata*); it was the source of illustrious architectural examples, imitated even in Rome in the time of Nero; yet Alexandria today is a city in which even the ruins are dead. Almost nothing remains. And remember that her lighthouse, the Pharos, was one of the Seven Wonders of the ancient world. But the indigenous culture prevailed and finally suppressed everything that had been imported. The same thing happened in the great cities on the Libyan coast, Sabrata and Leptis Magna, homeland of the Emperor Septimus Severus; in our century, they have been rediscovered, not destroyed but abandoned, buried in sand, because once the representatives of Imperial Rome had gone the civilisation of the Libyan nomads flourished once more.

So much for the nomadic peoples who came from north and south to invade the Empire. Now we must consider a truly vast European region which also, before the Roman occupation, possessed a very limited, and in some places practically non-existent figurative civilisation. I am talking about the cultural region of Celtic origin which extended from the Appenines as far as our modern Bohemia and Moravia, including almost all of Gaul and a large part of Belgium. Its purest expression, however, was found in the British Isles.

It should be remembered that, while the main island was occupied by the Romans as far north as Hadrian's Wall along the southern borders of Scotland and became the province of Britannia, the other large island, Ireland, was never occupied, in spite of an initial project described by Tacitus. And so, in Ireland, the Celtic culture remained in a pure state until well into the Middle Ages. It then made a direct leap, without intermediate stages, from the purest Celtic culture to what later became Irish Medieval art. However, as I have already said, the original features of the autochthonic culture always remain lively and functional.

The figurative products of Celtic Ireland must have been very limited. We know, on the other hand, that it was a culture that gave tremendous importance to music, song and verbal expression. Even today, if you go into any of the large pubs in Dublin or other Irish cities in the evening, you become aware that, beneath the anglicised, Western skin, there lies a culture that still has a striking partiality for the word. And let us not forget that, in modern times, Dublin has been the home of three of the greatest artificers of words: Oscar Wilde, James Joyce and William Butler Yeats.

England herself was under Roman domination for centuries and saw the growth of great cities within her own confines: Londinium, now London, which was probably built to designs made by the Emperor Claudius's military engineers; Eboracum, now York, and other large cities, not a few of whose ruins have been discovered; great thermal centres, like Bath, where the Roman baths are still in use today. And even now it is still possible, in England, to observe the difference that existed between what was, and was not, Roman.

As soon as you cross the border that separates England from Scotland, you feel you are in a different world, a different civilisation, a different culture. This is because, south of the border, the local culture is still active, still functioning, in spite of the fact that, after detaching herself from the Roman Empire, England suffered, first, the great invasions of the Picts and the Scots, those indigenous tribes who had not been subjugated by the Romans, and then, during the Middle Ages, the great Anglo-Saxon and Norman invasions which completely changed the social canvas.

What figurative arts did this culture possess? It was in the fifth century that the Roman province of Britannia detached itself from the Empire. We do not know much about the details of this secession, but it is very probable that the guiding minds of the Empire, in both Rome and Constantinople, realised the impossibility of defending such a distant province without the aid of a great fleet, and this was either non-existent or unavailable due to commitments elsewhere.

As soon as Britain divorced herself from the Empire, she split up into a multitude of little kingdoms, with minor monarchs, all impregnated with the local culture.

These kings were buried under enormous tumuli of stone together with their private treasures and very often – like the Vikings at a later date – with their ships. During the course of the centuries, many of these tumuli were sacked and looted. We have accounts from the seventeenth century which speak of the ruthless search for these mounds, where people went treasure-hunting. Some tumuli escaped these ravages until recent times, and so it has been possible to excavate and study them scientifically. A very important tumulus, probably a king's, was investigated at Sutton Hoo, in eastern England, in the 1930s. Together with the wooden ship, which was in a poor state, the king's personal treasure was discovered. It consisted of objects of two types: looted articles, especially of silver, which were the booty from raids along the southern coasts of Europe, or had been taken from villas in cities or other inhabited centres of Roman Britain, and gifts sent by Roman governors to British notables.

3. Reliefs on the base of Theodosius's
obelisk, in the Hippodrome in
Constantinople.

The silver was usually found in pieces. Since it was booty, it had been divided up amongst the various members of the raiding party, who, rather than exchange whole articles amongst themselves, preferred to break them up into equal shares. And so, very often we find finely wrought rectangles of silver, or even of gold and silver, which are in fact the remains of large serving dishes, splendid dinner services or other luxurious wares. This practice was common amongst the populations of the British Isles as well as with the nomadic peoples of continental Europe.

In the National Museum in Dublin there is a quantity of this classical silverware, in particular Roman silver of the fourth and fifth centuries, all cut up into little squares.

There are traces of the same phenomenon in Italy, too. For example, the great bronzes that were found at Carroceto, not far from Ancona, in the 1930s, are cut into pieces; they are the remains of a series of sculptural groups in gilded bronze portraying male and female figures and a triumphal car. Apparently, some invading nation had carried them off from a public Roman building. It has even been suspected that they came from Trajan's Arch in Ancona, but more probably they were taken from some commemorative monument in a city in central Italy.

These statues, enormous and weighty, although not of sublime workmanship, were literally smashed to pieces. A few have been recovered almost complete, others are missing parts that evidently, in the division of the spoils, fell to the share of men who carried them off elsewhere.

Besides these objects of classical, that is of Mediterranean or Roman, origin, the sepulchre at Sutton Hoo and other tumuli have revealed objects of local manufacture. In general, these consist of small pieces worked in metal and enamel, small decorations for utensils, sometimes very elaborate but rather solid and lacking in delicacy. But, as well as these mediocre objects, there are some of very great aesthetic value.

2 For example, this clasp in vividly coloured enamel, which shows a remarkable balance and harmony in the stylisation of its forms, and in which we can already see, in embryo, what will later become the primary characteristics of medieval Irish miniatures. But this does not necessarily mean that these articles were made locally, because we know that in the late Middle Ages and, even earlier, in classical times, a very dense commercial network already existed in central and southern Europe, although we have only the vaguest notions as to how it operated.

Let us take an example: in Oslo, in the relatively more recent Viking tombs, a small decorated wooden bucket has been found, with a metal handle and with enamel-work certainly executed in Ireland. There was, therefore, trading in enamel between Ireland and what is now Norway.

Another example. We know from Roman literary sources and from archaeological finds that many Roman merchants settled along the Baltic coast (in the part around Stettin and Danzig, today eastern Prussia and Pomerania), where there was amber to be found. Amber, highly sought after by the Romans, who also worked it, was sent to the Mediterranean along a road that ended at Aquileia. So we can see that there was a vast amount of trading.

4. Celtic mirror, found at Desborough,
Northamptonshire. British Museum,
London.

We have, also, both written and archaeological proofs that Mediterranean merchants ventured, by the crude means then available, into territories of the Nordic world about which they had only the scantiest knowledge, places we would never imagine they could have frequented. Throughout the entire Middle Ages there was this continuous commercial interchange. Another thing that gives one pause: for centuries the personal bodyguard of the Roman Emperor at Constantinople was made up of soldiers who came from Iceland. Periodically, a contingent would set out from Iceland, cross the North Sea, disembark in the country we now call Norway, cross the Scandinavian peninsula, re-embark, cross the Baltic Sea and come down to Constantinople by crossing what is today Byelo-Russia. An almost inconceivable journey when you consider the means of transport they had to use and the dangers these men inevitably incurred. But the fact that, in the fourth and early fifth centuries, the Emperor's bodyguard was formed of soldiers who came from the north is confirmed by the reliefs on the base
3   of Theodosius's obelisk in the Hippodrome in Constantinople, where we can see that the Imperial box is guarded by soldiers with long hair that somehow gives the impression of being blond, who are unequivocally men of Nordic origin.

In this connection, I would like to mention some extraordinary mosaics, datable to the third or fourth century, which were found in Tunisia, in what was one of the great metropolises of late antiquity and then almost completely disappeared. Today, it is the little city of Susa. Amongst the sparse ruins of Adrumetum some large mosaic pavements were found, some depicting the custodians of wild beasts from the circus, or bestiaries, as the men who were destined to fight against wild animals in the circus were called. The physical type to which they belong is unquestionably Germanic, or indeed, even more Nordic.

This huge commercial traffic never diminished. According to some historians, it was perhaps only the rupture with Islam that broke up the commercial network of the Mediterranean basin, but the relations between the Roman Empire and northern Europe continued throughout the Middle Ages. For example, the city of Constantinople, and its government, earned a great deal of money from a trade in sacred relics which, once central and northern Europe were converted, were sold to the uncultured nations.

Coming back now to the Sutton Hoo and analogous treasures, I have already mentioned that, along with minor articles, others of a very different aesthetic level
4   were discovered. Here is an outstanding one: it is a mirror with a smooth, reflecting face (of metal, naturally), in which one could see oneself, and a decorated back, like Etruscan mirrors. The latter were decorated with *graffiti*, with figures of Hellenistic derivation. This one, on the other hand, belongs to the Celtic culture. It is covered with an exceptionally sustained and austere abstract motif of superb quality. There is no need for me to describe the perfect stylistic coherence of each minute detail; the whole thing is constructed with the same imaginative unity, and the same formal rigour. At first, the motif may appear to be an arabesque and nothing more, but in reality it is upheld by very complex cultural precedents. The end result is this apparent or false simplicity, typical of great masterpieces.

When a work of art stands out above the norm and approaches the absolute, it can happen that it gives the effect of something simplified, even crude. This is what a lot of incompetent people fail to understand in, for example, Raphael's drawings which, at first glance, may seem to be simply sketches dashed down on paper without adequate forethought and preparation. In point of fact, this is the feigned simplicity, the feigned poverty of something extremely elaborate. The same thing occurs in some of Verdi's music which, if you have not been educated to listen to it, can sound like a popular song. Even some of Dante's verses can have this effect.

We are talking, of course, about the way people who are not educated react, but a lot of professional intellectuals and critics, who prefer things to be obscure, react in the same way. In our day, there is in fact a sort of sub-culture which prefers anything that is involuted and obscure, anything which requires professional exegesis, to simplicity. These intellectuals live directly off the ignorance of the public and the obscurity of texts, so anything the masses can understand annoys them, since, in the long run, it can put them out of work.

With this mirror, then, I must again stress the extraordinary harmony and integration of the form. It was probably made around the years AD 40–50, and it is not impossible that it was of Irish workmanship and happened to land up in England for reasons we shall never know. This object is one of the most significant, and the most perfect, survivals of Celtic culture which, as I have already said, was not confined solely to the British Isles, but occupied almost the whole of the region which is our modern France, a large part of Belgium and extended so far as to touch the borders of Czechoslovakia, in what is now Bohemia. It also included Slovenia and, in Italy, the whole of the Po Valley between the Alps and the Appenines.

It would be interesting to know how these Celtic peoples expressed themselves, what their language and their music were like, but unfortunately we know absolutely nothing about them. It was certainly not a written culture. We have no Celtic inscriptions and no Celtic books. We have songs which come from Ireland, but these are from a much later period and cannot be taken as typical. Almost all of what little information we have about Celtic society comes from Roman sources, from Julius Caesar, who was a very biased and tendentious observer and must therefore be taken with a pinch of salt.

Once again, let me repeat that there existed cultures to whom figurative expression was quite alien, but who expressed themselves in other ways. The culinary arts, amongst others, can play a primary role. Sometimes, just one recipe for a certain kind of dish can be significant. In baroque Italy, the preparation of desserts actually became an important artistic event.

We know from written sources, and from certain engravings, that great artists like Gian Lorenzo Bernini devoted their talents to the manufacture of monumental sweets for the Roman aristocracy. These were made of gelatine, whipped cream and custards of various colours and consistencies. Such creations must have been very free and inventive, because it is much easier to model in gelatine than it is in clay, or, more particularly, marble. Working with culinary materials, there is none of the resistance, none of the refractory element which the sculptor experiences

5. Coptic textile. The Louvre, Paris.

6. Coptic textile. The Louvre, Paris.

with marble, and which hinders the imagination from expressing itself in as free and unbridled a fashion as it can in ephemeral works.

Here, I do not want to be too paradoxical, I do not want to praise what is, after all, only a marginal product, to the detriment of the principal works. Nor would I want to fall into the absurd posture of people who cite ephemeral works as if they were on the same plane as monumental works. I am thinking, for example, of one of the contributors to the *Enciclopedia Italiana Treccani*: in the entry for 'Michelangelo' he cited, amongst the lost works of this sublime artist, a statue he made out of snow when he was a boy, just for fun.

There are also many other cultural areas which have not produced any figurative works of art. Sardinia is a typical case. If we examine the plastic and pictorial works of Sardinia from 1200 down to the present day, we soon realise that the earliest sculptures were imported from Pisa. In the fourteenth century, we have a few pictures that come from the Naples area. In the fifteenth century, we have works which came from central Italy to the eastern side of the island, while those on the western side are strongly influenced by Spain and Catalonia. Then, in the sixteenth century, we have a great painter: Michele Cávaro, but unfortunately, due to the ravages of time, or the neglect of the people who owned his works, very few have survived. Cávaro belongs mainly to the Romano-Neapolitan culture of Polidoro da Caravaggio. In the seventeenth and eighteenth centuries, there are many pictorial works, including some important ones (not yet recognised or published) which were mostly imported from the area around Rome.

So, can Cávaro, linked as he was to the Romano-Neapolitan culture, truly be considered Sardinian? Culturally, I would say no. For a painter to be considered as belonging to a specific culture, he must be a descendant of it, he must have antecedents in that culture and, in his turn, produce his own descendants, which is not the case with Cávaro. I consider him to be a painter of the Romano-Neapolitan school. In fact, essentially, Neapolitan. In the same way, I refuse to consider the much more famous Modigliani as belonging to the Italian School. Modigliani has his antecedents and his descendants in Paris. He therefore belongs, without question, to the school of Paris.

But does this mean we can discard Sardinia from the list of regions which produced a figurative culture? No. Sardinia had an extraordinary output of bread, in a thousand different shapes, full of a thousand inventions, some of them quite brilliant and ingenious. These forms are now beginning to become collectors' items, and are deemed worthy of study. There is another field in which Sardinia expressed itself artistically and that is the popular song.

There are, therefore, various forms of artistic expression and not all can be evaluated according to the criteria appropriate to great art: great architecture, great painting and great sculpture.

Coming back to our discussion of Celtic art, it is important to note that, when the Roman Empire came to an end and the Hellenistic-Roman culture began to break down, many other parts of the Empire started to produce expressive forms that reverted to earlier, more abstract models and so pointed the way to the dissolution of Hellenistic-Roman naturalism. One of these areas is the Coptic, noted primarily for its textiles.

First and foremost, the Coptic area is a populous region of Upper Egypt, far from the Mediterranean coast. It has a humid climate along the banks of the Nile, but is very dry in the interior, near the desert; a great many sepulchres have therefore been preserved, in which the corpses were wrapped in sheets with embroidered borders, or with embroidery all over them. Enormous numbers of these fabrics have been recovered in the last hundred years and are now distributed amongst various museums.

The Louvre possesses one which is worked with the Jonah motif (the same one we have already seen in a different context): Jonah waking up beneath a pergola of gourds or cucumbers – we have seen that the two are interchangeable – after spending three days in the belly of the Leviathan. It is obvious that anyone who has himself buried in a shroud decorated with this theme must have been a Christian, although we must remember that, in the early days, the story of Jonah referred to Divine Providence rather than the Resurrection. The outstanding point about this is that all the models, through which this motif must certainly have been handed on as far as Egypt, tend towards abstraction, towards a non-realistic, non-naturalistic interpretation.

Another Coptic textile, also in the Louvre and datable, I believe, to the fifth century, depicts a female figure, apparently a dancer but, as she has a halo, she may have some sacred significance, too. Once again we notice that the original motif is Hellenistic, but the end-product is diametrically opposed to the style of Hellenistic-Roman art. This Coptic art represents, really, the petrification as well as the tendency towards abstraction of one offshoot of Greco-Roman art.

Even after the conversion of Egypt to Islam, Coptic art survived and was still the art form of those parts of the population which had remained Christian. In fact, it is alive today: Abyssinian art is the last offshoot of what was once the Coptic art of ancient Egypt.

There are innumerable stages between Coptic art and Abyssinian art, but a vast number of iconographic and stylistic themes still to be seen today in Abyssinia, especially at a popular level, derive directly from motifs that were already in use in the fifth and sixth centuries. Moreover, while this tendency towards abstraction manifested itself in more or less all the peripheral zones of the Empire at the twilight of the ancient world, it later manifested itself even at the centre of the Empire, for what we call Byzantine art is none other than the hardening, the mummification of the classical heritage.

Byzantine art, which continues up until the fall of the eastern Empire in 1453, is based on classical motifs fossilised into a certain number of stylistic and icono-graphic schemes and, in the fifteenth century, it was these same schemes that, once they came into contact with the West (especially in Italy, in Florence and Venice) took wing again, like the Phoenix rising from his ashes.

It is very probable that, when the ancient world was dying, a phenomenon we might call 'generalisation' took place, and that the mutation in the figurative arts was due not only to the influx of art amongst the migratory peoples, or to the resurgence of local cultures,but also to the fact that there was something already present in the Greco-Roman culture itself which favoured this tendency. Personally, I am convinced that the great Greek figurative tradition was already becoming barren during the Hellenistic period, and that, although it was then perpetuated through the Roman Empire, it lacked by that time the creative urge which had characterised it earlier, especially in the fifth century BC.

The same trend towards abstraction also appears in Italy. I would like to show you now a detail from the large mosaic pavement in the Basilica at Aquileia. You will notice at once how in this figurative detail everything tends towards a succinct description of the forms, everything is moving towards the abstract.

Let me show you another detail: it is Victory with the palm. The figure of Victory undoubtedly derives from pagan sources. The palm, however, once an element in profane victories (we see Victory carrying it in her hand on the triumphal arches in Rome), has now become the martyr's palm. The same applies to the bread. This is no longer the bread that was given to the poor citizens of the Roman Empire (an empire of grants and distributions, especially in the great cities like Rome, and also Constantinople, where there was an immense stratum of the population who lived like parasites, receiving their food gratis and producing nothing). The bread, now, becomes symbolic: it is holy bread, the bread of the Eucharist.

So we have these two trends, one towards abstraction, and the other towards symbolism. Very gradually, these two tendencies become dominant, and when we reach the Dark Ages, the seventh and eighth centuries (a period in which little was produced), we have a figurative language which verges on total abstraction. Throughout the whole of Europe we find plastic examples of a very curious international figurative language: the language of intricate knots. These elaborate patterns are seen on reliefs that were mostly designed for the ambos in early Christian churches and for the plutei and capitals which can be discovered throughout a vast zone that stretches from northern Gaul right down to Sicily, from Jugoslavia to Spain. This motif is derived from the intricate knots found in the pictorial works of the nomadic populations, but it flourished all over Italy.

The Istituto dell'Alto Medioevo in Spoleto is publishing a corpus of these reliefs, and it is astonishing to see how, everywhere, they are practically identical. Once removed from their context, it is impossible to establish what area they come from, except, perhaps, by analysing the marble.

During these centuries, we have then, on the one hand, a purely abstract and symbolic figurative language, and on the other, populations who no longer knew what the things they saw around them represented, for, although the cities were still standing, the end of the Empire was accompanied by an almost total eclipse of literacy. Nobody knew how to read any more, nobody knew what the inscriptions meant or what the innumerable figurative works of art represented, works that were to be seen virtually everywhere, in the form of reliefs, paintings, statues or goldsmiths' work. It is hardly surprising, therefore, if a human mass, already reduced in number, and illiterate and completely ignorant to boot, proved a

7. Modern copy of a detail of mosaic
pavement, early fourth century.
Basilica of Aquileia.

breeding ground for legends about the ancient monuments, nor that these same monuments came to be abandoned and, as they started to deteriorate, were simply destroyed. This phenomenon is common to the whole of the western Empire.

Notice, however, that in both the Coptic textiles and the mosaics of Aquileia, every detail is pervaded by a perfect consistency of style. Note, also, that there is a total discrepancy of idiom between these and figurative Hellenistic-Roman art.

Now I want to show you a fragment from a fresco discovered in Pompeii or Herculaneum, which today belongs to a small American museum. There could not be a greater disparity, a more immeasurable gulf between the Coptic works, or the Aquileia mosaic, and this descriptive form executed with liquid brush. As you can see, there is also an attempt here to render spatial depth, something which is completely lacking in the works we have seen so far.

9   While on the subject of this Pompeian fresco, let me remind you that we know almost nothing of ancient painting, because all the great pictorial works, which were celebrated in their day, have been lost. We no longer possess a single picture, in colour, large or small, which was considered to be the work of a great artist. And yet we can definitely assert that painting was the foremost art in the Greco-Roman world.

Every epoch has one leading art which all the others follow. It is not true, as is generally believed, that sculpture was the leading art in the classical world. On the contrary, it was painting and, in fact, in the ancient sources, sculpture is always interpreted in painterly terms. When Pliny talks about the Venus of Cnidus by Praxiteles, he does not expatiate on the plastic qualities of the sculpture, but speaks of its violet eyes. Antique statues were covered with coloured wax, called ganosis, which was sometimes in naturalistic colours and sometimes positively gaudy; it was frequently renewed. The fact that Pliny cites the violet eyes of the Cnidian Venus makes one think that the goddess's eyelids must have been lightly painted with purple, and that this made a great impression. Not only all the sculptures but all the buildings, too, were coloured. The Parthenon itself still retains faint traces of the original polychrome. Polychrome! That seems almost impossible, even absurd, to us, because we look at antique art through the filter of neo-classicism and this has conditioned us to a totally false and misleading idea: we see statues as white and classical buildings as white marble.

One of the great merits of contemporary Pop art is precisely that of having brought sculpture back into the heart of everyday life, and painting it in lively colours like Greek sculpture. Even works in terracotta were painted; they did not have that monotonous colour we see in museums today. Sometimes during excavations, particularly in Rome, sculptures turn up which still have their polychrome on them, or at least the bole which is the ground for this polychrome.

In the second and third centuries, this colouring on marble becomes abstract, parallel to the abstraction which we have seen in mosaics and textiles. Few colours are used in this era, mostly gold. On the front of many sarcophagi, for example, only a few details are gilded. Sometimes the gold is still intact, much more often it has fallen off, leaving only the ground underneath, that is, the bole.

We have seen that, during the whole of the Hellenistic-Roman era, the leading art in the antique world was painting. You might well ask me: what is the leading art of our day?

I will answer you: the cinema, because it is the form of expression that draws all others in its wake. Much of the best music of our time has been composed as the incidental music to a film. Superb costumes, for both men and women, have often been created for the screen. Set designers flock to the cinema. But, above all, the cinema has conditioned us to judge figurative works of art, including paintings, according to a different framework of values.

Other epochs have had different leading arts. In Italy in the mid-nineteenth century the leading art was certainly music. Operatic music, in particular, which influenced both painting and architecture. Think of the enormous effect the operas produced at the Scala, Milan had on Lombardian painting between 1830 and 1860. Think of the architecture of that period, and of the ornamentation on the buildings. If you compare them with the set designs for opera during these years, you will see that the operas of Verdi, Donizetti and Bellini influenced all other visual forms.

In the Renaissance, on the other hand, the leading art was architecture. Apart from the fact that the great genius of the Florentine Renaissance, Brunelleschi, is primarily an architect, many of the most important paintings and sculptures, from Donatello to Fra Angelico and Piero della Francesca, are conceived purely in architectonic terms.

Antique painting, especially Greek painting, must also have contained a wealth of hints and tendencies, as well as technical problems and solutions. The literary sources give us only the faintest echo of these things. As for the actual pictorial works, nothing remains. Not one masterpiece of ancient painting has come down to us.

A lot of people claim to read and interpret ancient painting from the painting on Greek vases. Now, it is obvious that these vases derive from what must have been the great masterpieces of Polygnotus and Apelles and, in some cases, this has been established beyond all possible doubt. But what exactly does this derivation consist of? A few hints, some forms, the postures of certain figures, but it is absolutely impossible for us to understand, from these vases, what the authentic, monumental painting was like. Imagine for the moment that the great paintings of Raphael or Michelangelo were lost, and we tried to visualise and interpret them through vases from Casteldurante or Deruta. In this majolica from central Italy, we have direct reflections of the great pictorial cycles (mediated especially through prints); but from this to attempting to reconstruct Raphael from a piece of majolica is a very long step indeed. In the same way, it is absurd to assert that the ancient world knew nothing of reasoned perspective. How much could we understand about Raphael's reasoned perspective simply by looking at the majolica products of Deruta and Casteldurante? Absolutely nothing.

The same goes for Pompeian painting. It is utterly impossible to interpret the great themes, the great riddle of monumental Greek painting through the decorative works of two provincial cities, which is what Pompeii and Herculaneum

8. Victory with the Palm, detail from
mosaic pavement, early fourth century.

9. Fragment from a Pompeian fresco.
J. Paul Getty Museum, Malibu, California.

were. Very often, the decorators copied the compositional themes of great master-pieces in a clumsy and distorted fashion. Some of the themes – Perseus and Andromeda, for instance – appear, with variations, in more than one example. This means there must have been a prototype from which these works derived. The Pompeian decorators must have been very much like those wall-and-ceiling painters who, up until about fifty years ago, were to be found in quite large numbers in the workshops of central and northern Italy, and also in the south of France. For a very modest fee, these itinerant painters would embellish ceilings with frescoes whose motifs often included reflections of the great painting of the nineteenth century. There still exists a series of these ceilings in Abruzzo and in Puglia (a very beautiful book about the latter has been published), and there are others in France. Amongst the elaborate decorations are medallions containing landscapes that sometimes (especially in France) faintly reflect the compositional motifs of the Impressionist landscape. But, from the products of these workshops, could we ever grasp the greatness of a Monet? Can we look at certain nineteenth-century Spanish ceilings and comprehend Goya? At the most, we can understand some of the themes, pick up some clues from the composition, especially the attitudes of some of the figures, but it is utterly impossible to understand a great picture which has perished.

How did these great ancient paintings disappear? In the first place, many masterpieces of the Greek world were looted by the Romans and taken to Rome; the journey alone must have done them a lot of damage. Then there was the long, agonised dying of the city of Rome, and in the consequent neglect, the abandon-ment of these works, which must, in any case, have been very fragile.

During the fourth and fifth centuries, the emperors in Constantinople collected a great number of masterpieces from all over the world, especially from Greece, with the express purpose of preserving them from ruin, and from invaders. But there were two appalling disasters. The first was the Nika riot in 532, during which the entire centre of the city of Constantinople was put to the torch. The greater part of the Imperial palace was destroyed, as well as the so-called Baths of Zeuxippus and the Church of Santa Sofia itself (later rebuilt by Justinian). A great many Greek masterpieces were certainly lost in this colossal fire. Mostly paintings, but some sculptures, too. Probably Phidias's Athene Parthenos herself, a figure in gold and ivory which had been brought to Constantinople, perished or disappeared in the flames.

Much of what was saved from the Nika riot was later lost in the terrible catastrophe of 1204, when the Crusaders, instead of devoting their attention to the Holy Land, sacked the capital of the eastern Empire, destroying an extraordinary number of works of art. Some very famous statues, such as the Athene Promarchos, taken from the Acropolis in Athens and up until now safely preserved, disappeared at this time.

In spite of the fact that the great Greco-Roman output of painting is irremediably lost to us and we have no hope of finding anything much (except, perhaps, for a few painted steles of second- or third-rate importance), we have a very precise echo of the technique of these great works in the portraits from el-Faiyûm. During the Roman period in Egypt, these were customarily inserted into the bandages of mummies. They were head-and-neck likenesses of the people who had been mummified and wrapped in bandages. Why are they called el-Faiyûm? Because, although at least two examples were already known (both were destroyed in the bombing of Dresden in 1945), the majority of these portraits came to light, from around 1880 on, in an oasis in the Egyptian desert which is called el-Faiyûm. However, a great many other examples have been found in various localities, including Antinoöpolis, which was the provenance of many of the portraits now in the Musée Guimet in Paris. They are nearly all painted with encaustic on wooden boards and have been preserved in admirable condition because the mummies were buried in extremely dry soil.

It is not certain whether these portraits were painted when the person was still alive – as I personally believe – or were carried out *post mortem*. In all probability, they were painted in life and then the frames were removed and the pictures inserted into the mummies. In the British Museum there are mummies that are still complete with the portraits in the wrappings.

These portraits date from the end of the first century to the fifth, and they, too, follow that evolution from naturalism to abstraction and simplification that we have noted in other expressions of the antique world. Some of them have an extraordinary expressive power.

Observe the truth-to-life, the profound naturalism of this portrait. Bear in mind, 10 also, that these are products of a small provincial city and certainly had nothing to do with the artistic output of the great cities of the Empire: Rome, Carthage, Alexandria and Antioch. And yet, in spite of this, the portrait is a clear pointer to what the paintings from the major centres must have been like – you have only to look at the *impasto*, the brushwork, the chromatic richness of these examples.

And so, as I have repeatedly reminded you, nothing remains of the huge output of paintings in the Greco-Roman era, and very little indeed of the great sculptures. (The recently discovered bronzes of Riace are an almost unique example of what the great Greek bronzes of the fifth century BC must have been like.) On the other hand, we do have some outstanding objects of minor art which have been saved by their very nature. Here we see one of them: the so-called *Gemma Augustea*. It is a 11 large cameo in several layers that was once part of the Imperial treasure of the Hapsburgs; today it is in the Kunsthistorisches Museum in Vienna. It is, as we shall see, one of those works which were never buried and cannot be considered as archaeological finds. The subject of the design is very complicated: it is an allegory relating to an expedition against the Germans which took place in the first half of the first century AD during the Julio-Claudian dynasty. It would take a long time to explain here the meaning of the scenes. The interesting thing to note is that this cameo must have formed part of the Imperial treasure of Rome. Carried off to Constantinople by Constantine or one of his successors, it must have remained in the Imperial palace until it was stolen by Crusaders, in 1204. Whoever stole it must have taken it to an area that eventually fell to the Hapsburgs, who then kept it

10. Portrait of a Woman, of the type known
as 'el-Faiyûm'. National Gallery, London.

11. The *Gemma Augustea*.
Kunsthistorisches Museum, Vienna.

amongst their treasures. It is, therefore, one of those objects that was known throughout the Middle Ages and cannot, in any way, be classed as archaeological finds.

Now, the *Gemma Augustea* was certainly seen and known in Constantinople, as were the innumerable works of Greek and Roman art kept there, including some of the supreme masterpieces of the sculptors of the golden age of Greek art. And yet works of this kind had not the slightest influence on local artistic production.

The same can be said of many works which remained in the West and were never lost to sight, or buried. There was an extremely famous and important one in Lombardy: the *Reggisole* in Pavia. This was an equestrian statue of a Roman *condottiere* with his arm raised in a gesture of salute. Legend claimed that it was the sun he was saluting. The statue remained intact, or very nearly so, until 1797, when it was smashed to pieces by local radicals who saw it as an allegory of absolute power. It is not really known whether, as some maintain, it was a portrayal of the Emperor Severus Alexander, circa AD 230, or a work from the first half of the fourth century (and therefore extremely rare) which portrayed Theodoric, King of the Ostrogoths.

The *Reggisole* was very well known during the Middle Ages, yet it failed to make even a minimal impact on the work of local artists. The same is true of many works which, being preserved in Rome, were constantly visible. The most celebrated is the statue of Marcus Aurelius which today stands in the Piazza del Campidoglio (the Capitol). Nowadays, it seems certain that, during the Empire, this sculptural group (some years ago, what appears to be its original base was discovered) was kept inside the house near the Lateran where the Emperor Marcus Aurelius was born. At any rate, during the whole of the medieval period, it stood in front of the Papal palace in the Lateran, and it was saved only because it was erroneously believed to be a figure of Constantine, the Emperor who sanctioned Christianity. For the same reason, the Arch of Constantine is the best-preserved of all the thirty-six Imperial arches in Rome. So, the statue of Marcus Aurelius was preserved through a case of mistaken identity, but, throughout the entire Middle Ages, there exists not a single hint, not the palest reflection of it in the plastic products of the epoch.

The same applies to many of the works that, nowadays, are mainly kept in the Capitoline Museums. The Capitoline She-Wolf, for example, or the Boy Extracting a Thorn from his Foot, or the so-called Camillo (a young priest), or the colossal head, once identified as Constans II but now believed to be Constantine the Great. In all probability, this head came out of the Sessorium, the Imperial palace near the Lateran which was the residence of Constantine's mother, St Helena; in medieval times, it was kept in the Church of St John Lateran.

Another example? Let us consider the objects transported to the West after the sack of Constantinople in 1204: the Colossus of Barletta, for example, which is a portrait of the fifth century emperor, Marcian, and can very probably be identified with a statue described in the old guides to Constantinople. This statue was loaded on to a ship that sank in the Adriatic near Barletta; during this misadventure, it lost its arms and legs (which are now being restored). It was later erected in front of the

Cathedral of Barletta where, of course, it was highly visible. Yet it did not have even a minimal influence on local creative endeavour. These works were looked upon as curiosities, nothing more. It was as if the artists simply did not see them.

And remember the most famous of these plundered objects: the four horses of St Mark's in Venice. In all likelihood, they came from a Roman monument, were taken to Constantinople to adorn the Hippodrome there, then brought back to Italy, to Venice, by the Doge Enrico Dandolo. These horses were well known throughout the thirteenth and fourteenth centuries, but even they did not have any effect on stylistic conceptions or on the local artistic output. However, they were to become extremely important during the Renaissance.

And we have not yet mentioned the two groups of porphyry figures of the tetrarchs: Diocletian and Maximian, Constantius Chlorus and Galerius, which today are to be found set into the walls near the Porta della Carta of the Doge's Palace in Venice. These, too, were looted from Constantinople, wrenched from the column which supported them. Their provenance is certain because, not many years ago, during excavations in the Forum (the piazza built by Theodosius the Great in the capital of the eastern Empire), a foot was found, made of porphyry, which had been missing from one of the two groups of tetrarchs.

But let us come back to the horses on St Mark's. Their tremendous reverberations began in the fifteenth century. Why precisely then? Because every work, if it is to have a rapport, a nexus with posterity, must be seen at just the right moment. Only then is it possible to perceive it in the entirety of its meaning and significance. We can have plastic, pictorial and literary works of supreme importance right under our noses; we can see them, read them, we may even find them interesting, and curious, but they remain separate from us and do not solicit that profound re-evaluation that happens only at the right moment. This is true of every epoch, every civilisation (even the greatest), and for every work of art.

Years ago, there was a travelling exhibition of the four restored bronzes, and it was most impressive to realise how many artists had been influenced, and in how many different ways, by the four prototypes of St Mark's, which, after all, are not even outstanding masterpieces. And yet, deriving from these four models, there is an entire, precisely traceable geneaology. Let me repeat: in order for a model to work effectively, the person exploiting it must have reached a degree of maturity that will give him a very clear insight into the model to be re-elaborated.

One last example, to show how this phenomenon of the delayed comprehension of works of art is not confined to the West, but can be seen in the capital of the eastern Empire itself. I am thinking of a wonderful marble bust of a woman 12 (probably a poetess, or a gifted and illustrious lady), datable to the end of the fourth or the beginning of the fifth century. It was found in Constantinople and is now kept in the Metropolitan Museum in New York.

A work of this type must have been well known in Constantinople, but its influence on local artists was nil. It is important to note, however, that the models, the prototypes created in the great centres are always of very high quality. I do not believe in 'instant' art, nor do I believe in naif art. The true naif is always a great

12. Female bust in marble, end of the fourth or beginning of the fifth century, found in Constantinople. Metropolitan Museum, New York.

13. Cover of an Evangelistary, with figure of
Christ. Musée des Thermes et de l'Hotel de
Cluny, France.

artist who returns to the naif through a stylistic evolution. I consider the Douanier Rousseau to be a born painter and a true artist. But when somebody starts drawing and painting all of a sudden, and then somebody else starts shouting about 'masterpieces', to me it is nothing but an imposture, a stunt got up for commercial or literary ends. I do not believe in improvisers, in people who, never having done a drawing in their lives, take a sheet of copper and produce an etching that other people then declare to be an outstanding work of art. To me, they are all frauds.

In reality, all great art is the product of extraordinary technical ability. And this technical ability must be legible even in the most minute details. Look, for instance, at this cover of an evangelistary and notice the remarkable consistency of style that informs every last detail. It is the expression of a kind of stylistic will that refuses to slacken or be deflected. Observe the way the folds of Christ's robes and his cloak are delineated. This is a work of consummate technical skill. The same exceptional skill is always at the basis of every great work of art. You find it in Michelangelo, both as sculptor and painter; you find it in Leonardo in all his various manifestations; you find it in Dürer; you also find it in Picasso, in spite of certain acrobatic tricks that, at first sight, can be disconcerting. These artists were, above all, great technicians. The more profoundly they had mastered their technique, the greater the works they produced.

A great artist, even if he is a craftsman, or a supposed craftsman, always maintains this congruity. In fact, in this respect, one must carefully avoid dividing the arts into major and minor, or considering one type of art as pure and another applied. Art is only art. It was idealism that made the distinctions between more or less noble types of art according to the canons of the old aesthetics, and maintained that applied art was a sub-species. Nowadays, we see things in an entirely different way. The old aesthetics, for example, considered still life to be secondary. Today, we have realised that a still life can often be of great artistic value, its powers of aesthetic communication can be equal or even superior to those of paintings depicting human figures or historical events. Often, it speaks the truth in a much more intimate fashion. Just as we have realised that a piece of furniture, in its lines and in its structure, can be a far more significant example of its period than are certain florid or conventional decorations.

Even a plate can be a great work of art, and one of the great merits of modern design is that it has often produced utensils, objects of everyday life, of a very high artistic quality.

The old aesthetics divided art into a kind of hierarchy (beginning with the noblest type of art and finishing with the least noble) because the society in which these critieria held sway was itself hierarchical.

I do not want to sound like a Marxist missionary, but, in fact, there is an intimate connection between the way art is conceived and the structure of the society which expresses that conception.

A society based on a hierarchy conceived of art as a succession of genres: from the noblest (religious, historical or allegorical subjects) down to the least noble (scenes representing everyday life). This, of course, is the reason why some outstanding or even great artists were despised in their own day and enjoyed little respect up until very recent times. This was the case with the Dutch painter, Peter van Laer (known as *Il Bamboccio*), who was active in Rome in the first half of the seventeenth century and painted small pictures portraying poor people, social outcasts, artisans, and street scenes. Van Laer and his followers were always disparaged and held in contempt. The other side of the coin is that we often find that painters who no longer have anything to say to us today were exalted as sublime artists by their contemporaries. A case in point is the Dutchman, Adriaen van der Werff, who is interesting nowadays only as an academic phenomenon. He was active between the end of the seventeenth and the beginning of the eighteenth centuries. If we glance through the written appraisals of van der Werff, we become aware that his contemporaries regarded him more highly than they did either Titian or Tintoretto. These *critiques* amaze us because, although he was a very fine, a very meticulous painter, and sometimes interesting in his choice of subjects, to exalt him above Rembrandt or Aert de Gelder is simply inconceivable today.

I would like to show you some other examples of genres, or kinds, of figurative production which were once considered minor: miniatures, for instance. There are miniatures which have the quality, the intensity, of sublime works of art; and there have been periods in which the miniature was the most important means of expression, more so than painting, more than the great wall paintings. Lombardy in the fourteenth century, for example, produced frescoes but not paintings on wood, and there were outstanding personalities in the field of miniatures, artists who later influenced Burgundian art and were very important to the development of northern art.

Here is a page from one of the most important northern European texts of the 14 quattrocento that exist: *Les très riches heures du Duc de Berry*. It is a Book of Hours created by the brothers Jean and Paul de Limbourg for the Duc de Berry. Today, it is kept in the Musée Condé in Chantilly. Amongst other things, this Book of Hours contains twelve marvellous illustrations of the months of the year. Here you see the month of February: observe the miraculous balance between naturalism and stylisation which is typical of northern art, especially French art at this period. Note, also, that the illuminated page depicts snow, a subject which generally defeats artists as it is extremely difficult to render satisfactorily. A lot of paintings with snow are pure fraud, nothing but gimmickry. There are, however, a few very beautiful examples, including this one which, for me, is the crowning achievement. There is also a fifteenth-century Neapolitan predella in a private collection in Munich. You can also find some very successful, absolutely spot-on paintings of snow amongst the work of the Impressionists.

Recently, I saw a picture of Monet's where, again, there was snow, and it exuded that extraordinary sense of silence which you can also read from this miniature by the Limbourg brothers.

When it comes to painting snow, northern European art reached its zenith in the work of Pieter Brueghel the Elder, the finest northern painter of the sixteenth century. His picture, *Hunters in the Snow*, in Vienna, is an absolute masterpiece.

14. The Limbourg Brothers, page from
the Book of Hours of the Duc de Berry.
The Month of February. Musée Condé,
Chantilly.

15. The Master of Flémalle.
Portrait of a Woman.
National Gallery, London.

The miniature by the Limbourg brothers is interesting, furthermore, for a curious detail. In the first conversation, I said that we have lost the art of reading sex correctly in works of art. I showed you the picture by Bonsignori in which the Christ Child is sleeping with his genitals exposed, and made the comment that, in our eyes, this seems profoundly indecent (or did until very recently). Then we saw how, on the contrary, the baby's sexual organs were symbolically relevant to the Incarnation of Christ, as true God and true Man.

Observe, in this miniature, the posture of the woman in the foreground: she is warming herself in an attitude which, according to the canons of respectability, might be considered indecent. And in fact, when this miniature was first reproduced in colour, in the magazine *Verve* in the 1930s, the woman's skirts were retouched so as to make them reach her ankles. Nowadays, following the struggles for sexual and social liberation, this does not happen any more, and perhaps we have come to understand a little better that in life, everything is connected, everything has a meaning which, in turn, is linked to other, parallel meanings.

Be that as it may, in this miniature from *Les très riches heures du Duc de Berry*, we note a contradiction typical of international Gothic: a very austere and ritualistic type of gesture and pose united with an uncommon capacity for the obervation of nature. We find this same surprising contradiction in the works of one of the greatest representatives of international Gothic, Gentile da Fabriano; the interiors of his paintings are extremely stylised, as are the gestures of his figures, but, in the frames, the decoration is often of plants and flowers painted with an objectivity and a precision that would grace a botanical treatise. And remember that this was also the period of the great *sanitatis* albums – that is, the kind of book which describes plants and flowers according to their medical uses – which means that the descriptions had to be extremely precise and true to nature.

But – let me say it once more – the most important thing is always the evaluation of the quality of a work of art. We must never let ourselves be tempted by other considerations, because the qualitative standard is always the most valid and the most exact. And quality can be found in works commissioned by far less prestigious men than the Duc de Berry; sometimes, it can even be found in works commissioned anonymously.

Now I want you to look at a portrait of exceptional artistic quality which belongs to the National Gallery in London. It is the work of one of those painters who are nowadays identified by the provisional name 'Master of . . .', because, with many recognisable artistic personalities, we possess a group of works so similar in style that we know them to be the work of one artist, but we do not know his historical name. (It also happens vice versa, we know the names of many artists for whom we have no definitely attributable works.)

15   The portrait in question belongs to a group which a number of scholars have put together under the name of the 'Master of Flémalle' [in the National Gallery, London, this painting is labelled 'Ascribed to Robert Campin']. In each of these provisional collections, there is one work, called the name-piece, which gives its name to the whole group. Generally, it is the most important work, or the work

whose provenance is certain. In this particular case, the name-piece is the remnant of a great altar-piece, a triptych, executed by this artist for the Abbey of Flémalle, in Belgium, which was later partly destroyed and partly dispersed. Around the remains of this work, critics and scholars of Flemish art have grouped a number of works with sacred subjects and some extremely beautiful portraits, including the one you see here. We have some antique copies of the triptych from the Abbey of Flémalle as it appeared before it was partly destroyed and scattered.

Who this wonderfully integrated painter was remains an enigma. One hypothesis is that he could be Robert Campin, concerning whom we have some documentation but no positively identified works. Others have gone so far as to suggest that the group of paintings attributed to the Master of Flémalle is none other than the early work of a great painter, one of the fathers of Flemish art whom we know in his mature phase: Rogier van der Weyden. If this were so, we would have a case where, as new works became known, an anonymous group assembled by experts under the name 'Master of . . .' would eventually be absorbed into the opus of an already-known artist.

At the end of the last century Bernard Berenson grouped together a number of works which showed a notable similarity of style and devised the name 'Friend of Sandro' for them because they were strongly influenced by Sandro Botticelli. (It was not difficult, however, to distinguish them from the technique and the individual idiom of the great master; there were also certain sensibilities of colour and design that differed.) As time went by, it was discovered – and this is generally accepted nowadays – that Berenson's group was none other than the artistic début of the young Filippino Lippi, which took place in Sandro Botticelli's studio. And so the riddle as to who the 'Friend of Sandro' was resolved itself in the historical name of Filippino Lippi.

A similar case, again picked up by Berenson, was confirmed when he realised that, in an altar-piece by Domenico Ghirlandaio (now in the Museum of the *Spedale degli Innocenti* [Foundling Hospital] in Florence), the principal figures in the foreground were indeed by Ghirlandaio, but the figures in the background were by a different hand. The same hand that you can recognise in a conspicuous number of paintings of the Madonna, on altar-pieces, and on the fronts of coffers with mythological or historical scenes. Berenson had provisionally named this collaborator (whose work was easily identifiable and very distinct from that of his master, Ghirlandaio), 'Pupil of Domenico'.

As research into the archives progressed, Berenson was seen to be perfectly correct: it became clear from the documents that, together with Ghirlandaio, another artist, called Bartolomeo di Giovanni, had worked on the painting for the *Spedale degli Innocenti*.

And so, in this case, the work grouped under the provisional name of 'Pupil of Domenico' was later definitely ascribed to Bartolomeo di Giovanni. But sometimes the philology is not so simple because, during the Renaissance, there are cases where artists deliberately camouflaged their work. I mention this because, at one moment in his career, Bartolomeo di Giovanni did precisely this.

16. Lucas van Leyden. Portrait of a Man.
National Gallery, London.

17. Rogier van der Weyden.
Portrait of a Man (St Ivo?).
National Gallery, London.

The most important case of 'camouflaging' by artists happened in the Sistine Chapel. When Sixtus IV decided to decorate the papal chapel he had had rebuilt in the Vatican palaces, he entrusted the work to Pietro Perugino. Not only did this artist carry out the altar-piece, a fresco depicting the Assumption of the Virgin in the presence of the Apostles, but, on the right wall, he also began the christological cycle with a *Nativity*, and, on the left, he initiated the Moses cycle with the *Finding of Moses in the bulrushes*. All these works have vanished because Michelangelo destroyed them to make room for his Last Judgement. Perugino called in artists from his own province of Umbria to work beside him: Pinturicchio, Andrea d'Assisi, a certain Rocco Zoppo, and Piermatteo da Amelia. In the first works executed by these painters, that is, up until a certain point in both the christological and the Mosaic cycles, it is extremely difficult to pick out the individual painters, because they all strove to adapt themselves to a common denominator of form and composition. They all tried, in fact, to paint in the same manner. Later on, however, this group from Umbria was replaced by a group of Florentines: Ghirlandaio, Botticelli, Cosimo Rosselli and Biagio di Antonio. We do not know why, but it is not impossible – though this is only a hypothesis – that political pressure was brought to bear. Probably Lorenzo the Magnificent realised the importance of these decorations to the Sistine Chapel and therefore wanted Florentine artists to participate in the project. Lorenzo actually used Florentine artists to establish a kind of Florentine cultural hegemony. This explains why Verrocchio was sent to Venice and Leonardo to Milan. Faenza itself, under the Manfredi dynasty, suffered considerable cultural deprivation when Lorenzo the Magnificent sent Biagio di Antonio to work on the Sistine Chapel. In Naples, *Il Magnifico* found it impossible to assert this hegemony; he sent gifts but did not manage to send artists because the political situation was too tense. It was very probably through his intervention, however, that the Umbrian predominance in the Sistine Chapel was brought to an end.

The Borgia apartments, those splendid apartments in the Vatican which became the seat of the Borgia Pope, Alexander VI, present another typical, yet quite extraordinary case. The Pope decided to have the vaulted ceilings and some of the walls of his residence decorated with a series of highly complex frescoes portraying profane, sacred and astrological subjects. Many artists were summoned, mainly from Umbria, but also from the Abruzzi, from Latium and Florence. They all worked, however, under the guiding intelligence of Pinturicchio and they all tried to paint in his manner. And so it is extremely difficult to distinguish the work of the various artists. Amongst those who were called in to decorate the Borgia apartments was Bartolomeo di Giovanni, but we would never have discovered him except that, by pure chance, there came to light a drawing that was unmistakably from his hand. It was a preparatory drawing for a large lunette depicting the Nativity of Christ. Once the drawing was discovered – and only then – it was easy to pick out certain traits characteristic of Bartolomeo in the fresco, but suppressed, almost muted. Without the drawing, I defy anyone to have intuited a thing of this kind, it was practically impossible.

There are several cases like this, in spite of the fact that art history claims to set up very clear distinctions between one artist and another, as if the artist was privileged never to imitate the art of an earlier time.

In reality, 'retakes' of this kind, and very specific ones, are commoner than is generally thought. A case in point (and one which has led some art historians to indulge in very rough and ill-mannered polemics amongst themselves) is the fresco entitled *Guidoriccio da Fogliano* which hangs in the main hall of the Palazzo Pubblico in Siena and is presumed to be by Simone Martini. In my opinion, this is definitely a 'retake' of later date, or a reworking that imitates an older theme. But historiography ignores the fact that very often imitations are actually requested by the person commissioning the work, and this may happen with the most unexpected people, and in the most unlikely periods. I live near Monte Rotondo, where, in the Town Hall, there is a remarkable case of this kind. In the courtyard of the building, which was originally a palace belonging to the Orsini family, there is a fifteenth-century colonnade whose travertine capitals are sculpted with the coat-of-arms of the House of Orsini. So far, everything is perfectly plausible. But the colonnade continues with the same type of columns, the same type of fifteenth-century capitals, but, instead of the Orsini arms sculpted on the capitals, there is the bee of the Barberini family. And in fact, in the third decade of the seventeenth century, the palace passed from the Orsini to the Barberini. At first, it was thought that the Barberini had had the Orsini coat-of-arms removed and substituted with inserts of stone decorated with their own heraldic bee. The mystery remained, however, as to why this change had not been completed, why, on the first arches, the Orsini bearings had been left in place. And then, some years ago, following the discovery of some archives, it came to light that the Barberini, after buying the palace, considerably enlarged it. However, they wanted the original form of the courtyard to be retained, with the sole difference that the new capitals should be sculpted with their own heraldic emblem. And so, here we have a case where the Barberini themselves – great patrons of Bernini and Borromini, considered, in fact, to be the *non plus ultra* of Baroque patrons – actually commissioned a building in the fifteenth-century style, in perfect imitation, that is, of the style of a hundred and fifty years earlier.

The idea that there exist precise breaks, datelines when a certain style ceases to be (the idea, in fact, that the historiographic scheme has a historical reality), is typical of the mentality of certain scholars, who cannot conceive that men could have continued to paint in the Gothic style well into the Renaissance. It was not by chance that, in Arezzo in 1452, Piero della Francesca carried on work on the frescoes that had been interrupted by the death of Bicci di Lorenzo. There are scholars who actually consider the terminology of art history as facts which possess an autonomous life, for whom it is inconceivable that certain artists could have continued to work in a style that, according to the rules of art history, belongs to an earlier period. This mentality has given rise to a great many mistakes.

It happens that concepts which are purely empirical and historiographical (such as Medieval, Romanesque, Gothic, Renaissance, Baroque) end up by taking on a life

18. Piero di Cosimo. Portrait of a Man.
Dulwich College, London.

19. Juan de Flandes. The Beheading of John
the Baptist. Musée d'art et d'histoire,
Geneva.

of their own, and so impede our understanding of the reality of things. We have just cited the case of Piero della Francesca who, two years after the middle of the fifteenth century, worked on a cycle of paintings begun by a Gothic artist. Very often, this same confusion occurs in the case of what is called mannerism, which in the minds of some art historians has taken on autonomous life, so that they continue to talk of mannerism and anti-mannerism. But things are not that simple. The most sensational case, actually in this field, concerns Bartholomeus Spranger, the most celebrated painter of the last wave of international mannerism. Spranger worked for Rudolph II in Prague and had a very large following in central Europe. At a certain point in his career, under orders from Pius V, he copied a triptych by Fra Angelico; he even went so far as to imitate a work of 1480, the *Massacre of the Innocents* in the Church of St Augustine in Siena. Today, this copy is in the vaults of the Art Gallery in Munich.

Whenever an artist tries to imitate a past era, his own hand can still be recognised through certain idiosyncrasies of style, because, however much goodwill the artist brings to his work, he still belongs to his own time, and therefore his own personality will insinuate itself into the imitation of the work from the past; it will condition it, and alter it, in small details, perhaps, and that is exactly where the eye of the expert is put to the test. We shall examine this point in greater depth when we come to talk of fakes and their unmasking.

There is also the fact that, no matter how hard one strives to understand an ancient work of art, or how hard one strives to imitate it, one will never succeed in grasping it in all its complexity. This is especially true of the supreme works of art, like the Raphael Stanzas, Leonardo's *Last Supper*, the ceiling of the Sistine Chapel and many of the great Venetian paintings, which contain elements that are incomprehensible to us nowadays. As I have already said, every work of art can be read at various levels, and beyond the formal and iconographic levels there are allusions and connotations which are lost forever. The past is dead for ever.

In the Raphael Stanzas or in Leonardo's *Last Supper*, there may be allusions to actual personages, to their style of dressing, or moving. There may be allusions to theatrical performances, or references to prayers or literary texts, which we shall never be able to identify, or, at best, only very partially. There exist, in fact, connotations which escape us, which can never be recovered; only occasionally it happens that, by pure chance, or after lengthy research, some of these come to light.

16   You see here, for example, a portrait from the National Gallery in London; it is the work of a great Dutch artist of the first half of the cinquecento, Lucas van Leyden. You will see that the picture can be clearly read insofar as its extraordinarily austere technical and formal qualities are concerned. Notice the chromatic scale, which is extremely limited and yet powerfully expressive. And then you can see that, beneath this wonderfully integrated formal and stylistic level, there is something which is lacking in the portraits of the quattrocento, and that is a kind of morality. You feel at once that this portrait was painted in that specifically Dutch ambience of the sixteenth century, when the struggles between

Catholics and Protestants were beginning. You sense that the man in the picture is either a relentless defender of Catholicism or a fanatic of some extremist persuasion. This portrait has its roots in the period and in the society that spawned it, and you can certainly feel this. Unfortunately, we do not know the name of the sitter; this very important element, for the moment, eludes us.

Another thing I wanted to point out to you is that, generally, a further test of quality is how well a painting stands up to enlargement, as now, for instance, when the images projected on slides during the course of these conversations are mostly blown up larger than the original dimensions of the work. This painting is small, and yet it can stand up perfectly well to being shown on any scale. Enlargement shows up a painting of poor quality, making it look like a deflated balloon. Its compositional defects become very apparent. On the other hand, some works of splendid quality, Rembrandt's etchings, for instance, can be enlarged to as much as 40 metres by 60 without even minimally losing their expressive power.

Here is another portrait, also in the National Gallery in London. It used to belong   17
to a private collector in England who did not recognise it for what it was. Eventually, it was identified by an English scholar, the late David Carritt. It is a typical work by Rogier van der Weyden, a painter we have already talked about. The main reason I am showing you this picture is to prove that enlargement does not in any way impair the compositional density of the work. The same cannot be said of, for example, the works of a great many nineteenth-century painters which, at first viewing, may also seem to be very fine, meticulously done, and composed with intelligence, but which, blown up, are seen to be vacuous, inconsistent and lacking a rigorous formal texture.

Another reason for showing you this picture is that recently, in a really crazy book, the writer condemned it as a fake. He maintained that a group of works – which were, incidentally, entirely different from one another – are all from the same hand, the hand of a forger working in our century, a decade or so ago.

Apart from the inconsistency of the argument, I must stress the point that no faker could possibly attain such a high technical and qualitative level, and still less could he succeed in penetrating the mentality of an artist of five hundred years ago to the extent of creating a work for which no model and no precedents exist. There is no effective model from which this portrait, identified as St Ivo, could have been taken, nor are there any analogous works with a similar composition.

The argument invoked to invalidate the picture is that the writing on the page the Saint is holding is meaningless, since the forger did not know what to write, and could not guess what the calligraphy of the time would have looked like. But this is a specious and irrelevant argument. What counts is the marvellous expressive quality of the painting and its equally marvellous technical intensity.

Let us look again at the first problem that confronts anyone who wants to examine a work of art: the state of preservation in which the work has survived. The painting illustrated here belongs to Dulwich College, London, and the eye of   18
the expert will immediately recognise a quantity of data which will enable him to

20. Arcimboldo. Allegory of Water.
Kunsthistorisches Museum, Vienna.

21-22. Claude Gelée (Claude Lorraine). Landscapes (drawings). British Museum, London.

attribute it to Piero di Cosimo, a Florentine of the late quattrocento and early cinquecento. In what condition has this painting come down to us?

First of all, the dimensions of the picture have been reduced, probably due to a habit that was very widespread in the past, right up to the nineteenth century: pictures were considered as part of the interior decoration, and when it was necessary to have a pendant, or companion picture, nobody thought twice about mutilating the larger one and cutting it down to match the smaller.

May I remind you that this happened to Leonardo's *Gioconda*, which originally had two columns, one on either side of the figure. These were cut off. The *Mona Lisa* was put at risk because it was required as a pendant to another, slightly smaller picture that hung in one of the rooms belonging to the King of France. As we see it now, therefore, it has been altered, but we have an idea of its original appearance from antique copies and, above all, from the imitations and derivations of Leonardo's painting carried out in the early cinquecento in Florence, even by great artists such as Raphael.

Piero di Cosimo's picture has also been spoiled in the red-coloured area. Many artists of the late fifteenth and early sixteenth century carried out technical experiments (you have only to think of Leonardo). We do not know much about these experiments, or what ingredients they used, so paintings of this type are extremely vulnerable, under their varnish, and in cases where they have fallen into the hands of over-zealous cleaners, they have been ruined beyond repair. Piero di Cosimo is one of these artists. The red colours he used can be removed even by substances which, normally, should not cause any damage. When the picture was cut down, the landscapes on both sides were also mutilated, as they must once have been larger. And it is landscapes of this kind (usually spring landscapes, with blue skies) that make Piero di Cosimo one of the greatest lyric poets of nature. Notice, however, that in a picture like this, the hand of Piero di Cosimo can also be recognised by the psychological overtones, by that freshness and immediacy which are characteristic of the way this great painter captures the personality of his sitter.

Let us move on now to a picture which has not been wrecked by too-drastic cleaning and still has its epidermis intact in spite of being painted in an extremely delicate manner. This is a small painting on wood from the Musée d'Art et d'Histoire in Geneva, and it shows the beheading of John the Baptist. It is the work of a Flemish painter, Juan de Flandes,who was active in Spain (his work is rarely found elsewhere, and I would say he is little known outside Spain). The scene is set in the courtyard of a fortress, and you notice at once the quite extraordinary delicacy with which the stones of the walls and the moss that clings to them are painted. Another remarkable feature is the outline of the wall against the sky, from whose limpid transparency we realise that the event is taking place in the early hours of the dawn. Here, then, is a very rare painter, scarcely known outside Spain, but whose work always displays this same intensity of form and composition.

Now let us look at another painter: Arcimboldo. This picture we are going to examine is also in good condition, down to the last detail. It is an allegory of water. Arcimboldo, of Lombardian origin, was one of the strangest personalities in the history of art; he devoted himself to all kinds of research, attempting, amongst other things, to build a musical instrument in which each note would correspond to a particular colour. It is a curious fact that this theme turns up again and again in the history of European culture and, early in our own century, there were certain members of the avant-garde who were interested in it.

Arcimboldo's curious personality and his extraordinary activities led to his being summoned to the court of the Emperor Rudolph II, one of the most important patrons of the second half of the sixteenth century, who was anxious to have the artist with him in his castle in Prague.

It is my belief that, for Arcimboldo, who was also a great costume designer for ballets, painting was not his principal occupation. If it was not actually a spare-time activity, it was one to which he devoted only a limited amount of time. And I am convinced that there are not many pictures by Arcimboldo in existence, he cannot have painted more than fifteen or twenty.

This panel belongs to a series dedicated to the four elements: earth, air, fire and water. It was painted for Rudolph II and is exceptionally well preserved. The subtlety of the pictorial description is worthy of Jan 'Velvet' Brueghel. Arcimboldo was immensely successful, and a host of imitations, made throughout the whole of the seventeenth century, still exist. The formula he invented proved to be highly attractive and museums are full of pictures derived from Arcimboldo, none of which, however, is executed with the finesse of the originals.

How can we distinguish Arcimboldo's paintings from those of his followers? In the works by his imitators, what we miss is, precisely, that delicacy of execution, the finesse of the maestro; the approach is always vulgar, the subject matter crude. And they lack that brilliantly witty inventiveness through which, in Arcimboldo's compositions, every allegorical detail excites our curiosity while being, at the same time, integrated into a satisfyingly homogenous texture. And so, there is no possibility of confusing the works from Arcimboldo's own hand with those of his followers and imitators.

This same extraordinary quality of execution, this same marvellously sustained harmony of form and composition, can also be found in many drawings. Here we see two examples by a painter who is also one of the greatest draughtsmen of all time: Claude Gellée, known as Claude Lorraine, or Le Lorrain, as he came originally from Lorraine, although he settled in Rome before 1630 and remained there for the rest of his life. Claude Lorraine painted a great many landscapes with mythological themes. They were large oil paintings on canvas and most of them are still preserved today. His pictures were immediately imitated and, being anxious to distinguish his own authentic work from the spurious, he created a *Liber veritatis*, a volume in which, from a certain period on, he reproduced in drawing all his finished pictures, noted down the dates and who had bought them.

Apart from those in the *Liber veritatis* (which is now in the British Museum), Claude Lorraine made a large number of drawings which are amongst the finest specimens of European landscape and, at the same time, works of genius, amongst the highest achievements of all time in the art of drawing.

23. Georges de la Tour. The Fortune Teller.
Metropolitan Museum, New York.

Take this view, for example. Observe the dexterity, I would like to say the magic, with which the colour has been spread over the surface, and note also how the consummate skill of the artist has succeeded in incorporating the white of the paper itself into the picture – an absolutely unique feat. This other drawing by Claude Lorraine is, for me, one of the greatest masterpieces of all time. It shows a view of the Tiber, probably from the direction of Orte. Here, you can see how the slow flowing of the river during the summer season has been rendered by using the paper itself, that is, the grain of the white paper has been woven into the pictorial texture with a gradation of shading so subtle that we are tempted to consider the paper itself as the painter's creation, and, after all, it is, since it is he who has conferred a formal dignity and function on the amorphous material.

It is strange that a draughtsman of such power was not an equally brilliant painter. The pictures signed by Claude Lorraine contain heavy, often rather dull subject matter and are sometimes executed in such a perfunctory fashion that one is induced to suspect that collaborators had a hand in the work. Their only value, I would say, is in their overall effect. I believe this to be a rather rare case of a dichotomy between the draughtsman and the painter.

In conclusion, here is another picture, one which has recently been the subject of an absurd debate. It is a canvas from the Metropolitan Museum in New York and depicts a subject that was very widespread in Rome in the early years of the seicento: a fortune teller who is reading the hand of a naif young man to distract his attention while her accomplices rob him.

In the same book that accused the Rogier van der Weyden of being a fake, this picture was also declared to be a forgery from the same hand. How absurd! It was claimed to be a fake on the pretext that, according to the author, the costumes are not of the period to which the painting is generally dated.

The reality is that the painting is not only a genuine antique, but it is also in an exceptionally good state of preservation, so good, in fact, that one suspects it was precisely this happy state that suggested the hypothesis of a fake.

Amongst other things, the canvas is signed by Georges de la Tour, another artist from Lorraine. This region, on the borders between Germany and France, has known two outstanding moments of importance: one in the early Middle Ages, the other in the seventeenth century. In short, the culture of Lorraine is one of those European cultures which, despite being a kind of buffer state between two major cultures, retains its individuality and re-emerges periodically.

The most extraordinary aspect of this picture is actually the signature, admirably executed, with characters that are of the same formal integrity as the whole canvas. Note the similarity, or perhaps I should say the affinity, between the profile of the woman on the left and the letters of the signature. They are unmistakably by the same hand. But this is not a unique phenomenon. Anyone who knows the signatures of Raphael will know that they, too, have the same intensity, almost the same figurative quality that we find in his paintings and drawings.

Third Conversation

In this Third Conversation, I am going to show you works of art that illustrate some of the problems the expert comes across in the course of his studies. Not all these pictures are of great artistic, aesthetic or historical value, but they are very interesting as examples.

Often, the scholar or connoisseur is faced with pictures whose surfaces have become severely blackened due to neglect; for long periods, sometimes for centuries, they have lain abandoned in the vaults of museums, in private houses, monasteries or convents, without ever being cleaned or varnished.

In the galleries in Florence, for example, there is a spectacular collection of still lifes, amassed by the Medici grand dukes; there are dozens and dozens of these paintings – some of them cited in the archives because of their unusual subjects – but many are without frames, dirty and disfigured, and some are actually at death's door because none of them has been cleaned or relined since time immemorial. If canvas is left for long periods without being varnished or refreshed, and without being relined, it dries out completely and becomes very brittle. In this state, the slightest knock, even a little friction, will perforate it or reduce it to shreds.

A great many paintings on wood, from the early era of Italian painting (from the thirteenth century to the beginning of the sixteenth) also met with this fate; for hundreds of years, they were left hanging above altars, or in sacristies, and nobody took care of them or varnished them. Often the sunlight beat monotonously, day after day, on the same part of the picture, so that the paint skin and the gesso underneath (that is, the priming between the board and the paint itself) dried out and the work finally became powdery. Such paintings have come down to us in very poor condition.

However, as I have said elsewhere and will never tire of repeating, the damage caused by wear and tear is infinitely less than that caused by restorers, particularly by incompetent people who clean and restore works of art with harmful materials.

Fortunately, even when a picture is reduced to a flaking and dilapidated condition, we can still judge of its quality as long as there remains one small detail with its outer skin intact. And very often that little detail will be enough for us to establish the period (even dating it to within a few years) and, if it is the work of a known painter, to make the attribution. But very often paintings are totally blackened. What do you do in such cases? First, you have to approach a really good restorer, someone in whom you have confidence; if the picture is on canvas, he will make a new lining, taking great care neither to crush the paint surface by using excessive weights nor to overheat the canvas during the relining process. In the second phase of the operation, he will go on to the actual cleaning. It is sometimes possible to take a picture in a practically illegible state and bring it back to the light in perfect condition.

Here is an example. When I first saw this picture, it was black, totally illegible. Relined, cleaned and varnished by expert hands, it was revealed in pristine condition and its author was immediately apparent. It is a work by Pompeo Batoni, a celebrated portraitist of the Roman school of the first half of the eighteenth century; he was also very well known in England. Sometimes, as in this case, an engraving of the picture exists and this makes the attribution much easier, it gives us the name of the sitter (Cardinal Prospero Colonna di Sciarra) and, of course, the name of the painter.

Why was a print made from this picture? In general, no sooner had the artist finished the portrait for whoever commissioned it (in this case, it may have been the Cardinal himself, or a member of his family), than a skilled and reputable engraver would make prints of it to be distributed amongst the acquaintances or the protégés of the family, especially if it was the portrait of a famous person. Then, it often happened that copyists made copies from these prints. That is why there are an infinite number of copies of certain pictures, and they can be found in the most far-flung places. It was the printing process that diffused the models, and for many centuries (say, from the end of the fifteenth up to the nineteenth century), the print was tremendously important for European art. There are periods – such as the late cinquecento – which simply cannot be studied, cannot be examined in depth without a thorough examination of the graphic works, and of engraving.

And, as a further example, if you are not familiar with the engravings of the time, you cannot possibly comprehend the chapter of European painting which we call international Mannerism, which blossomed, to some extent, all over Europe. This movement reached its peak in Bavaria and at the court of Rudolph II in Prague, but there were also very important and very varied manifestations elsewhere: in Utrecht, in Fontainebleau and in Milan. The school known as the Lombard Mannerists represents one Italian contribution to international Mannerism. Others existed in Venice, in Florence and in other less important areas of central southern Italy.

How did this diffusion of painting through graphic art come about? In some cases, there was already a finished painting which the engraver took as his model. In others, the painter gave the engraver a drawing without ever having painted the picture. There are some outstanding compositions which were never actually painted, and which are known only through engravings. There are also artists who produced more graphic works than paintings, precisely because the black and white image had such tremendous importance.

There are even artists whom we know solely through their graphic work and not through their paintings. A borderline case is Jacques Bellange, one of Europe's greatest artists, who came from Lorraine; we have an abundance of marvellous drawings, almost always in sanguine, and of prints taken from his graphic works, but only one painting (now in the Hermitage in Leningrad), which is very different, both in style and quality, from his graphic art.

There are also minor artists who are extremely important to us because their graphic works influenced other artists. Hans Speeckaert, for instance, who is

1. Pompeo Batoni. Portrait of Cardinal
Prospero Colonna di Sciarra. Walters Art
Gallery, Baltimore, Maryland.

2. Cosimo Tura. Madonna and Child.
Accademia Carrara, Bergamo.

virtually non-existent as a painter, but very important as a draughtsman and for the engravings that have been made from his drawings.

These prints were avidly sought after from one end of Europe to the other and had an enormous influence on artists of the most diverse origins. Today, we can have only a faint notion – through the reflections we see in art – of this vast market which reached the most unlikely places. Take, as an example, the Flemish artist, Marten de Vos, whose drawings were a fount of ideas for the engravers who collaborated with him. In one case, it can be demonstrated that his engravings reached the dukedom of Muscovy. In fact, there exist icons executed and signed by Moscow artists, from the end of the cinquecento and the beginning of the seicento, which derive from engravings taken from drawings by Marten de Vos, and it has even been proved that some engravings travelled as far as India – the evidence is clear, since there exist Indian works dating from the seicento that definitely spring from easily identifiable European graphic models.

In Europe, engraving fulfilled the same function that photography fulfils today, but the most curious thing about it is that, while some artists' work was published in vast quantities through graphic art, there are others, even great names, for whom we have not a single engraving. This is the case with El Greco: no contemporary engravings of his pictures exist. This could be because El Greco lived in a small centre like Toledo, where, probably, there were no engravers, but it is still a mystery why his compositions were never published in the form of prints.

There are artists whose pictures were distributed from Russia to Portugal, from Sweden to Sicily, while others (whom we consider to be very great indeed) remained virtually a dead letter, known only in the place where they worked. But the history of art is a series of historiographic schemes that extract from the past whatever is considered great according to the taste and fashion of that particular moment. It is by no means certain that what we admire as great works today were so highly esteemed at the time of their creation. Apart from a few well-established giants like Michelangelo, Raphael or Giotto, who have never faltered or lost prestige, there is an immense body of work which is continually being re-evaluated historiographically.

The graphic arts, then, were of fundamental importance to the sixteenth century, and also to the seventeenth, when the trade in prints became absolutely vast.

In some centres, particularly Rome, there were studios of engravers (such as the De Rossi) who immediately made prints from the paintings of the great artists. These were then sold throughout Europe and had a profound influence on local creative production, both in terms of composition and, still more, of subject matter.

Some artists, Maratta for instance, became extremely famous thanks to this trade in prints. His pictures in Casa Colonna were immediately engraved and widely published, and it was through this transposition on to paper that his work became highly appreciated throughout Europe.

Returning now to the painting by Pompeo Batoni, the print by Johann Georg

Wille confirms the attribution and the subject. But what really counts, in the final analysis, is the quality of the picture, because we can have the same portrait repeated *ad infinitum* and only a qualitative judgement can tell us which is the original and which are copies. There are innumerable versions of certain portraits, not one of which is the original, or, at least, where its identification remains very doubtful. Perhaps the most famous case is a half-bust portrait of the Duke (later Grand Duke) Cosimo I de' Medici by Agnolo Bronzino. All the many versions of this painting are on wood, and all of rather good quality, but none of them is quite good enough to be adjudged the prototype. Every now and then, someone declares he has found the original, painted from life, but, up until the present moment, I do not think any of them can be accepted without question. Bronzino's original, in my opinion, has yet to be discovered, or perhaps it no longer exists.

Why is it that there are so many versions of this portrait of Cosimo I in existence? Because it was the custom to send one's own portrait to both friends and potentates. This was simultaneously a sign of respect and a friendly gift. Therefore, while the original remained in the Medici collection, Bronzino himself would have had orders to produce copies in his own studio, copies which were possibly finished by the master's own hand. Sometimes, these copies were hung on the walls of important offices, in law courts and state departments, as happens nowadays. This explains why there are so many versions of certain portraits. The name, and the importance of the artist who had painted the original, also had a considerable bearing on the number of versions made.

In other cases, the art historian finds himself faced with pictures that have been seriously affected by alterations and manipulations over the last 150–200 years. A painting belonging to the Accademia Carrara in Bergamo is a case in point: it is a Madonna and Child by Cosimo Tura, a fifteenth-century artist from Ferrara. You do not need to be an expert to see that there is a great difference between the part that is actually painted on gesso and the background. The foreground is in good condition, quite readable, but the background looks flat and is crudely done; it is a metallic gold ground, which cannot possibly belong to the same period as the tempera. In fact, the original gold background was destroyed, and it was replaced with modern gold in the nineteenth century. Looking at the figure of the Virgin, you also become aware that the lower part has been mutilated. Almost certainly, the figure was originally full length and included the legs and feet of the Madonna seated on a throne. Very often, altar pictures of the thirteenth, fourteenth and fifteenth centuries were removed at a certain moment because they no longer conformed to current tastes. They were taken down from the altars and hung in the Sacristy, as we know from a mass of documentary evidence about pictures that were removed from their place of honour in the church and put in less prominent positions. It even happened that they were taken out of the important churches and banished to the provinces. This happened to Sassetta's large *Madonna of the Snows*, which was taken from the Cathedral in Siena and sent to Chiusdino, a little town in the environs of the city. In other cases paintings were removed, not because they were not admired any more, but because they had been damaged by

3. Attributed to Raphael. *Madonna del Popolo*. Musée Condé, Chantilly.

4. Raphael (?). *Madonna del Popolo.*
J. Paul Getty Museum, Malibu, California.

candles falling against the painted surfaces. When this happened, rather than restore them, they simply sawed off the damaged part of the picture, gave it a new frame and hung it somewhere else. Not infrequently, the gold is missing, as with Cosimo Tura's picture. When these gold backgrounds went out of fashion in the early cinquecento, they were considered, primarily, as valuable material to be salvaged: the gold was scraped off with a razor blade, a knife or a scraper so that it could be used again.

And we know that, between the end of the eighteenth and the beginning of the nineteenth centuries, there were merchants who bought up these paintings that nobody valued any more from the local priests. They then piled them up in a great bonfire and set light to them; the gold that melted out of the paintings and the frames was collected in stone or metal containers.

The majority of the gold backgrounds on paintings in the Orvieto area met with this fate. At Bagnoregio, where there must have been a wonderfully rich production of polyptychs in the fourteenth and fifteenth centuries, there are today no more than four paintings with gold backgrounds. Moreover, when the so-called Primitives came to be re-valued, a lot of dealers and collectors started renewing or touching up the missing gold, with very harmful results for the reading of the works themselves, because, until then, the gold, even when it had been scraped, retained traces of the original embossing. This was destroyed by scraping the gesso down still further and applying a series of fine gold leaves. This has made it very difficult for the modern scholar to identify the individual artist and establish what complex the painting belonged to.

In Cosimo Tura's Madonna, the embossing, the original halo and all the decorative detail incised in the gold have been lost. It is almost certain that this work was the central component of a polyptych destined for the altar of a church in Ferrara. But in cases like this one can only formulate hypotheses, because the data which would enable us to reach a definitive solution to the philological problem are missing.

There are also cases of paintings – even famous ones – where we do not know whether it is the original or a copy that has come down to us. The most illustrious example of this type of problem is the *Madonna del Popolo*, Raphael's painting for the church of Santa Maria del Popolo in Rome. Let me just remind you what the church of Santa Maria del Popolo was at that time. It was situated near Porta Flaminia (then known as the Porta di San Valentino), and had been reconstructed by Pope Sixtus IV, who intended to transform it into a church-mausoleum for his family, the Della Rovere. The same plan was taken up again and amplified by Sixtus IV's nephew, Julius II, who had the apse demolished and rebuilt on a larger scale to designs by Donato Bramante. He even planned to build his own tomb there, presumably in the most important position, in the middle of the apse behind the high altar. But when Julius II was persuaded by some of his advisers to demolish the ancient basilica of St Peter's, he conceived a new and completely different scheme for his tomb; he wanted a gigantic marble mausoleum to be erected in the centre of the new basilica, and it was to be designed by Michelangelo Buonarroti. The church of Santa Maria del Popolo was therefore abandoned as the site of this monument.

I need hardly remind you here that the tomb of Julius II was the great tragedy of Michelangelo's life. This elaborate and grandiose project included a mausoleum that was actually to consist of two storeys: on the ground floor there were to be gigantic figures of the prophets (but, in the event, only the Moses was executed, and this is now in the church of San Pietro in Vincoli); there were also to be allegorical statues and the so-called Prisoners, two of which are now in the Louvre and the others, barely rough-hewn, in the Accademia in Florence. On the upper floor, there was to be the figure of the Pope on his bier and a great high relief, or a large sculpture of the Madonna and Child behind him. Gradually, the project was cut down, reduced, ever more mutilated until it reached the compromise solution which can be seen in the actual tomb of Julius II in the church of San Pietro in Vincoli [St Peter in Chains] in Rome, where the only work by Michelangelo is, in fact, the statue of Moses.

In 1508, before he had changed his mind, Julius II ordered Raphael (newly arrived in Rome) to paint two pictures for the church of Santa Maria del Popolo. These were, respectively, a seated portrait of the Pontiff, and a Madonna uncovering the sleeping Child with St Joseph in the background, a composition that was called the *Madonna del Popolo* [the Madonna of the People]. The original plan was for the picture of the Pope to hang on the left side of the high altar and that of the Madonna on the right. I have personally verified that the nails on which they were hung are still there in the church today. These paintings were not visible every day, however, they were hidden behind silk curtains and revealed only once a year, on the occasion of the most solemn ceremonies. The two pictures must have had a symbolic significance for the Pope that totally eludes us. The strangest thing, however – and this is another of the problems of art history – is that, while we do not have a single copy of some world-famous masterpieces of Raphael's (or at most one or two) there are at least ninety known copies of the rarely visible *Madonna del Popolo*, and these have made the most astounding journeys and ended up in the most outlandish places. There is even one beyond the Urals, in an ancient Russian monastery. Others can be found, with variations, or adapted into compositions with more figures, in Flanders, France and Spain. But of Raphael's other master-pieces, the *Madonna della Seggiola* [the Madonna of the Chair], for example, I know of only one copy, which is in Jugoslavia. It is of extremely fine quality and I suspect was produced in Raphael's own studio with the personal intervention of the artist. Well then, why was the *Madonna del Popolo* copied so many times? Evidently, for both painters and the general public, it had some profound meaning we cannot even guess at. The two pictures remained in Santa Maria del Popolo for most of the sixteenth century. Towards the end of the century, they were taken (one might almost say raped) by a collector, Cardinal Paolo Emilio Sfondrati, who was the nephew of Pope Gregory XIV. Sfondrati had superb taste and was one of the greatest collectors in Rome during the cinquecento. Patently, he was a man with a profound understanding of painting, and in Palazzo Spada (nowadays the seat of the Italian Council of State) he had assembled what I can only call a sensational collection. It was gigantic, and famed throughout Europe. We possess documents which tell us that another outstanding collector, Rudolph II of the Hapsburgs, greatly admired this collection and sent emissaries to look at the pictures. They included some exceptional pieces: Titian's *Sacred and Profane Love* and Veronese's *St John the Baptist Preaching in the Wilderness*, to name just two. At a time when the collection was at the height of its splendour, Sfondrati suffered a religious crisis. He had become the friend of Cardinal Cesare Baronio, a man dedicated to the study and research of primitive Christianity, the Christianity of the Catacombs, and of the martyrs. Sfondrati decided therefore to get rid of this vast collection which, to him, now appeared sinful, or, at least, ill-suited to his new interests. In the early years of the seventeenth century, part of the collection was sold to Cardinal Scipione Borghese Caffarelli and today it can still be seen in the Galleria Borghese in Rome.

Raphael's two paintings, the portrait of *Julius II* and the *Madonna del Popolo*, were also sold to Cardinal Borghese and are continually cited in the inventories of the Borghese household. Then there came a time when the family began to sell off works of art to raise cash. Both *Julius II* and the *Madonna del Popolo* disappeared.

Thanks to recent research, the *Julius II* has, in all probability, been rediscovered in the depository of the National Gallery in London. I believe it to be the original. Apart from the quality, which is Raphael's own, there is another factor: the bottom left-hand corner is marked with a number which not only corresponds to the Borghese inventories but is applied with the same brush and in the same whitish colour that can be seen on other pictures which are still in the Galleria Borghese. It therefore seems to me that, in this case, the search is over.

3   There is also a *Madonna del Popolo* in the Musée Condé in Chantilly, near Paris, which some believe to be the original. This picture, too, has the same inventory number on the lower left-hand corner. The quality and the style are, however, suspect, so we cannot exclude the possibility that Raphael's picture, sold off separately, was substituted by a good copy on which the same inventory number was painted.

Moreover, there exists another version of the *Madonna del Popolo*, which is in
4   the Getty Museum in Malibu, California, and this one is worth examining. Even at first sight, it is obvious that the surface of this version is a total ruin. In the late eighteenth or early nineteenth century, the picture was subjected to a drastic cleaning operation with unsuitable materials (probably caustic soda) which completely wrecked the paint skin. The only part the cleaner did not dare to touch is that curtain in the background, which is painted in a masterly fashion worthy of Raphael. What you see, then, is not a painting but the corpse of a painting, impossible to judge. So why do I think it might be the original? Nowadays, we have means of research and investigation which have only recently become available to us. One of these is infra-red rays. The photographs of this painting taken by infra-red rays show that, beneath the ruins of the picture, there is a drawing of extraordinary quality and unity. Besides, the drawing shows a considerable number of *pentimenti*, of alterations, as if, during the course of the work, the painter

revised his ideas. One very notable *pentimento* is in the raised hand of the Madonna, another, equally important, in the leg of the Child Jesus. These *pentimenti* would not only be unlikely in a copy, but virtually inexplicable. The drawing of certain parts of the picture, particularly the face of the Virgin, shows traits which are characteristic of a very early Raphaelesque style, indicating that it was painted soon after his arrival in Rome. This style is not to be found in the version in Chantilly, and I have very grave doubts about that one. In my opinion, the uncertainties about the *Madonna del Popolo* will never be resolved. Unless a *Madonna del Popolo* appears which bears the absolutely certain and indisputable hallmarks of a Raphael, we shall go on arguing as to which (if any) is the original version of the painting.

The question of the *Madonna del Popolo* has recently been complicated by some collateral data. During the eighteenth century, it was believed that the original of the painting had found its way to the sanctuary of Loreto, and in fact the picture became known as the *Madonna di Loreto*, totally identified with the one visitors and pilgrims admired amongst the treasures of the sanctuary there.

The original of this *Madonna di Loreto* (the one that had been in the sanctuary) was acquired and brought to Rome by a man called Braschi, a nephew of Pope Pius VI; it is listed in catalogues of the collection in Palazzo Braschi in Rome. During the French invasion, the palace was plundered by Jacobins and the pictures were sent to France. However, when the crates were opened in Paris, it was discovered that some of the paintings had been substituted, including the *Madonna di Loreto*. So, we are left with an almighty mix-up which will probably never be sorted out, unless, as I said, a picture that is beyond question from the hand of Raphael turns up – if it still exists. An even greater mystery is that, apart from the pictures sold to Cardinal Borghese, all the rest of the splendid Sfondrati collection has also vanished.

When Sfondrati died, what was left of his collection was transferred to Sesto San Giovanni, in Lombardy, where the family had a palace, and we can more or less trace these survivors of the collection up until about 1890. After that, everything disappeared and no trace of it has ever been recovered. My own hypothesis is that the last works from this collection (and there were some extremely important paintings amongst them) are lying neglected, or forgotten, in some villa in Brianza.

Let us take a look now at some of the terrible vicissitudes that, for the most varied reasons, other paintings have suffered. Here is a picture from the Walters Art Gallery in Baltimore, Maryland. The greater part of the works in this gallery came from a collection formed in Rome in the second half of the nineteenth century by Don Marcello Masserenti, a prelate from the Vatican. The collection was bought *en masse* by the American millionaire, Henry Walters.

Some years ago, one of the paintings in this collection was brought out of storage and the decision was to have it cleaned. It was a most disconcerting picture because, while the face of the sitter was superbly painted and immediately showed characteristics of the style of Lorenzo Lotto, all the rest was exceedingly rough and of a quality altogether unworthy of such an artist. X-rays were taken and then the

5-6

5. Lorenzo Lotto. Fra Lorenzo of Bergamo dressed as St Thomas Aquinas. Walters Art Gallery, Baltimore, Maryland.

6. The same painting before restoration, with the religious connotations obliterated.

cleaning process began. Before this operation, nobody even knew what it was meant to represent: it was obviously a monk, but one could not tell what order he belonged to – some said it was the Augustinian, others (and they were proved right) the Dominican. After the cleaning, it was seen to be a portrait of a particular individual dressed in the habit of St Thomas Aquinas.

In the last century, the religious connotations of the painting had been obliterated. A restorer was instructed to efface the lily, which is the attribute of the saint, and to transform his habit. Alas, not content with painting over the parts he was ordered to change, the restorer first scraped them down with a razor blade, or a scraper. Not only did he ruin the lily in this way, and flatten out the whole of the saint's clothing, but he also spoiled the hands. What the modern restorer has recovered for us is definitely a Lorenzo Lotto, for, in the painter's diary, he speaks of a portrait of Fra Lorenzo of Bergamo dressed as St Thomas, painted in 1542. There is no doubt that the portrait cited is the one in the Walters Art Gallery, but we have it in a deplorable condition, three quarters of it virtually beyond recovery. I could quote you an infinite number of similar cases. My own feeling is that it is better not to restore pictures, it is better to leave the corpse in peace, without cosmetics, and to read whatever is still legible rather than attempt a reconstruction. This is not everybody's view, however, and all too often we find ourselves looking at paintings, even some of outstanding importance, which have been completely travestied by the restorer.

Let us look now at another picture from the Walters Art Gallery which presents a rather unusual problem. When studies on this picture began, all it showed was the half-length figure of a woman crying out in great distress. Once cleaned and restored to a perfect state of preservation, the picture disclosed an architectural frame that had been completely concealed by a black background painted over it at a later date. The most interesting point is that it shows, at least in the painting of the woman's head, the unmistakable characteristics of Ercole de' Roberti, a fifteenth-century painter from Ferrara.

This figure is similar to the figure of the Magdalen weeping at the foot of the cross, part of a cycle of frescoes (now destroyed) which de' Roberti painted in the chapel of the Garganelli family in St Peter's, the Cathedral of Bologna. Before the disastrous renovations to this church in the eighteenth century, there was a very famous cycle of frescoes with the Crucifixion on one wall and the Death of the Virgin on the other, both painted by de' Roberti. (Other parts of the fresco were from the hand of another great Ferrarese artist, Francesco del Cossa.) Before these frescoes were demolished, someone had copies made and one of these (part of the Crucifixion) can be seen today in the Sacristy of the Cathedral in Bologna. Two other copies, taken from the Death of the Virgin, are to be found, one in the Ringling Museum in Sarasota, Florida, and one in the Louvre. In the copy taken from the Crucifixion, we can see that the weeping figure of the Magdalen is identical to the one in the Walters Art Gallery. How can we explain this odd fact?

I rule out absolutely any suggestion that the head in the Walters Art Gallery picture is a copy; the quality is too good, and copyists are always on a considerably

7. Ercole de' Roberti. The Weeping
Magdalen. Walters Art Gallery, Baltimore,
Maryland.

8. Anonymous, end of fifteenth century.
The Redeemer. Walters Art Gallery,
Baltimore, Maryland.

less-exalted level. I believe this to be a typical case of one of those 'samples' which painters had to produce before being commissioned to paint a fresco. The patron would ask for a sample in which the artist had to show exactly what kind of appearance and finish he intended to give his fresco. In this case, de' Roberti must have painted just the head of the Magdalen to demonstrate how the fresco would eventually look. At a later date, somebody else completed the sample. Let us take a closer look: the quality of the head is infinitely superior to the lower part of the figure and the frame. Someone, desiring to transform the artist's sample into a complete picture, added the rest of the figure and the architectural frame. Why was this done? Because, in its original state, this sample of de' Roberti's would have looked too much like a fragment, and such things were not considered to be of any aesthetic value in the sixteenth and seventeenth centuries; it was therefore necessary to complete it. At a still later date, the architectural frame was obliterated by over-painting. There exist similar, unfinished pieces, carried out on terracotta or on wood, and some are the work of distinguished Florentine artists. It is my belief that they are certainly samples which the patron required of the painter before giving him the go-ahead for the fresco.

8   Here is another picture from the Walters Art Gallery, and this again is a case where cleaning brought about some very sad and, at the same time, rather problematic results. When the restoration began, this picture was as black as night, virtually illegible. After cleaning, it emerged in rather good condition except for one important detail: the head of the figure had been completely destroyed. The reason must be the usual one – the facial features did not please the owners and therefore it was decided to scrape off all the original paint and change them. The characteristics of this picture are hard to read, making an interpretation from both the iconological and the attributive viewpoints difficult. It appears to be a portrait of the Redeemer, but some of the iconological details here are inexplicable, they do not seem plausible. Why, for example, is this Christ figure holding a sort of crystal crozier with a cross at the top? What does it mean? And why is He wearing that belt strapped tightly around His body? What sort of belt is it, and what does it signify? I made long researches into this picture but they led me nowhere. These details must have a specific meaning, they must relate to a particular order or confraternity whose existence has not yet been discovered; probably, it was limited to a small neighbourhood, wherever this picture was painted. As for the attribution, it clearly belongs to the Venetian area, but it is difficult to establish who the painter was. I know of only one other painting from the same hand, it is a small tablet with a standing figure of St Benedict. It belongs to a private collection in Rome and is in good condition. It is undoubtedly by the same artist, as certain details can be seen in both: the type of landscape, the clouds and, above all, that parapet of ornamental marble in the background. Can one make an attribution in this case? No. We must leave the author in his anonymity. There are some scholars whose expertise is dedicated, first and foremost, to the marketplace, and for them there is no such thing as 'anonymity'. Everything must have a name, it must be christened at all costs. But you should be very sceptical of this method because, while we have a

great many anonymous pictures, we also have a great many names of painters – in written or printed documents – for whom we have not a single work. So, in certain areas, the systematic scholarly study is only in the early stages. And besides, you must remember that we possess only a small percentage of what was produced. Take a great artist like Piero della Francesca: we have no more than eight to ten per cent of his output. Piero's great pictorial cycles, in Ferrara and in Rome, have been demolished. Of the work of other sublime artists, like Domenico Veneziano, only two to three per cent has survived. The great series of St Egidio in Florence, executed by Neri di Bicci, Domenico Veneziano and Piero della Francesca, has been destroyed. The same thing happened to Pontormo's masterpiece, the choir in the basilica of San Lorenzo in Florence, which was demolished in the seventeenth century because nobody liked it any more.

Some of the most valuable works survived into later epochs. For example, the chapel Andrea Mantegna decorated for Pope Innocent VIII, in the Belvedere at the Vatican, was still to be seen in the late eighteenth century, when it was ruthlessly knocked down to make room for the museums of antique sculpture. Probably, all that remains is the altarpiece, the *Christ seated on a Sarcophagus and supported by two Angels*, now in the Staten Museum for Kunst in Copenhagen.

You must, therefore, be extremely wary of experts who have an answer to every question, and never take their declarations at face value.

In the majority of cases, figurative works of art are destroyed because, at a given moment, they are perceived as neither modern nor yet antique, but simply old-fashioned and, therefore, in bad taste. It seems, then, perfectly natural to get rid of them. This happens to objects, too. We have all had things from the 'art nouveau' and 'art deco' periods in our own homes and thrown them out with great satisfaction because we thought of them as old rubbish, things we did not want to look at any more. We have got rid of furniture, vases, dinner services, all considered as nothing more than the refuse of a past era.

Now that art nouveau has been re-evaluated, and judged artistically valid, many of us regret the beautiful things we sold to the junk man, or even put into the dustbin, without the slightest qualm or hesitation. This has happened even to distinguished works of art: pictures have been discarded without scruple only a few decades after they were painted. The most notorious case occurred in one of Christendom's holiest places, the Sistine Chapel in the Vatican. When it was decided that Michelangelo's *Last Judgement* should be painted on the end wall, Pietro Perugino's great fresco, the altar-piece of the *Assumption of the Virgin, with Sixtus IV kneeling*, was chiselled off and destroyed. The same happened to the two other frescoes painted by Perugino and his pupils, the *Finding of Moses*, which initiated the Mosaic cycle, and the *Nativity of Christ*, which initiated the christological cycle.

This desire for the new, and rejection of the antique, has had an even more drastic effect on profane works of art. Entire series with non-religious subjects, both in the form of frescoes and easel paintings, have been thrown out because they were no longer considered worthy of survival. You have only to think what happened to the

9. Pietro Longhi. Scene of Venetian Life, oil
on copper. Walters Art Gallery, Baltimore,
Maryland.

10. Raffaellino del Colle. Madonna and
Child with the Infant St John. Walters Art
Gallery, Baltimore, Maryland.

decorative works of art in the Visconti houses in Lombardy. In the eyes of Ludovico il Moro and Beatrice d'Este, the series of paintings by Gothic artists must have looked old-fashioned, even ridiculous, and they discarded them without a second thought.

So, we no longer have these great cycles, although we often have documentation concerning the commissioning of the work, and descriptions written by people who saw them. Apart from what we have already mentioned, you must remember all the decorative work on furniture, or on doors, that was sacrificed with as little compunction as if it were simply a matter of redecorating a room for practical reasons.

There are also cases in which a building was saved, not out of consideration for its aesthetic value, but because, in the meantime, it had become a place of secondary importance. The reason we still have the ducal palace in Urbino, with its very beautiful fireplaces, its inlaid doors and the small study of Federico da Montefeltro, is not because anybody appreciated their intrinsic value, but because, at a certain moment, the court of Urbino was transferred to Pesaro. In 1631, when the Dukedom of Urbino devolved to the Papal States, the palace built by Federico da Montefeltro became the seat of the local governor. Nobody, thereafter, dreamed of spending any money on renovating this building, and that is why it was saved.

We have other, tragic examples of works of art being destroyed just before it had become possible to document them, that is, just a few decades before the advent of photography. I have already mentioned Mantegna's chapel in the little palace of the Belvedere in the Vatican, built by Innocent VIII. This chapel was considered to be a supreme masterpiece, yet nobody made any drawings of it before it was torn down, so we do not even know what the subjects or the compositions of these celebrated frescoes by Mantegna were. In another chapel in the Vatican that was destroyed without the slightest compunction, there were frescoes by Fra Angelico. And so on and so on. The Borgia apartments, on the other hand, have remained practically intact, because they were no longer used. The Borgia Pope, Alexander VI, who had lived there, was so execrated and despised by the pontifical authorities that his apartments were virtually closed, and used only as store rooms. Nobody dreamed of renovating them, which is just as well or they would have been lost to us.

We possess an infinite number of documents regarding the continual destruction of profane series, pictures and decorations that has gone on over the centuries. The most glaring example is the ancient basilica of St Peter's in the Vatican. In the early decades of the cinquecento, when Julius II decided to demolish the ancient edifice and rebuild, the original structure, dating from the time of Constantine the Great, was still intact, although it had been enlarged. When the roof-structure of the nave was dismantled and the walls knocked down, it was found that many of the beams still bore the marks of Constantine the Great's branding-iron. They had become nests for rats and bats, but the wood was still the original from the great cedars of Lebanon brought to Rome on Constantine's orders. The church was sacrificed without qualm or scruple, and frescoes and mosaics were lost by the square kilometre, as well as numerous sculptures which testified to and illustrated the history of the Catholic church from about the year 330 up until the beginning of the sixteenth century. Perugino's decorations to the apse were knocked down; Pietro Cavallini's frescoes, innumerable sepulchres, including the Imperial and Papal ones, and the whole of the chapel of John VII, decorated with mosaics, were destroyed. A few things were saved, because some of the *monsignori*, horrified at the sight of this devastation, managed to rescue some fragments of mosaic and bits of fresco from the pick-axes and the chisels of the demolition men. We have, for example, two of Giotto's angels: one has been rediscovered at Bovile Ernica, in Latium, the other is still in the Vatican. A few fragments from the cycle of mosaics in the chapel of John VII were also saved; one is in St Mark's church in Florence, another in the church of Santa Maria in Cosmedin in Rome, and a third in the Duomo at Orte. Several sculptures were rescued but, apart from a very few pieces which were salvaged and put into the new church (including the large disc of porphyry on which, according to tradition, Charlemagne was crowned), all the rest of the building was ruthlessly torn down.

But let us come back now to paintings and the problems they raise. Here is another picture from the Walters Art Gallery in Baltimore, which is as it was when I first saw it, before it was cleaned. At that time, it was covered in layers of varnish, yellowed by age, and this made it rather difficult to read. Moreover, it had been very oddly baptised as: *French School of the seventeenth century, Voltaire visiting his mistress.* As soon as they started to clean the picture, and remove the layers of varnish that had made it almost illegible, an extremely fine work came to light: a typical piece by the Venetian painter, Pietro Longhi. Naturally, the picture has nothing on earth to do with Voltaire, nor with the French school. It is simply one of those scenes of Venetian life, interpreted with humorous *brio*, which shows an old gentleman visiting a young woman seated near a spinet.

The picture is painted on copper, and that makes it a rarity among the works of Pietro Longhi. Oil-painting on copper does not suffer chromatic changes, so it lasts very well and, in fact, other than some minute areas of peeling, this picture is in a perfect state of preservation. In this case, the attribution to Longhi, indicated by the stylistic data, was confirmed by a contributing detail. High up, there is a little cage with a parrot in it. Now, in a sketchbook belonging to Pietro Longhi, preserved in the Museo Correr in Venice, there are studies from the life of this parrot in his cage. This, then, is not an invented detail, it is something the artist had observed directly from nature. But how in the world did the picture come to be attributed to the French school? For a long time, it was considered much grander, much more *chic*, to own a French painting rather than a Venetian one. It was quite a common phenomenon for pictures attributed to Boucher, Fragonard and other French artists of the period to reveal themselves, after cleaning, as the work of Francesco Fontebasso, Gaspare Diziani or other Venetian artists of the eighteenth century. One should not be too surprised, therefore, at this confusion.

The Longhi painting in Baltimore is one of the most felicitous restorations I have ever come across. The fact that it is painted on copper might give rise to suspicion, as this is rather unusual in the case of Pietro Longhi, who generally used canvas, but there are a few other pictures, especially small portraits, on copper, so this is not a unique piece.

10   Here is another picture, again in the Baltimore Museum, which poses a most singular problem. It is a panel depicting the Madonna and Child with the infant John the Baptist. In the background, you see a classical building in the form of an apse. This is a work by Raffaellino del Colle, a painter of the school of Raphael.

Raffaellino began his career in Rome, where he carried out some very noteworthy commissions for private patrons, and then went to work in Umbria and the Marches, mostly in the Dukedom of Urbino. It must be said that his work is very uneven; side by side with some rather refined paintings of excellent quality, we find others, signed by the artist, which are so slovenly and incompetent as to make one doubt their authenticity. Evidently, he was a painter who 'gave what he got', and carried out his work according to the amount of money he was paid. I believe that, with certain artists, it is possible to see a direct connection between the quality of their work and the remuneration they received.

We know of at least four versions of this picture in Baltimore. The latter is, unequivocally, the prototype from the artist's own hand, and at least one of the others may also be his, but painted later and with less care.

There is a very strange mystery attached to this painting. There exists another,
11-12   practically identical version of it in the Galleria Borghese in Rome. And, in the same gallery, there is a second composition which also depicts the Madonna, the Child and the infant St John. When the Baltimore picture was taken to the laboratory for restoration, it was submitted to X-rays, and these revealed that, originally, the artist had painted the *second* composition in the Galleria Borghese, and in fact had taken it to a very advanced stage; then, later, he cancelled it out by painting the composition we now see over it. What possible reason can there be for the existence of both the twin version of the Baltimore prototype and a version of the painting which X-rays showed beneath the visible surface of this same prototype? What motivated Raffaellino to obliterate the composition that he himself, or one of his pupils, had copied in the second of the paintings in the Galleria Borghese? This is the strangest case I have ever come across in my career, and it is an insoluble mystery.

Often, the art historian is faced with incomplete pictures, mere fragments. This happens most frequently with pictures from the fourteenth and fifteenth centuries, triptychs or polyptychs or altar-pieces which have been dismembered; the predella is particularly vulnerable to separation. During these centuries, polyptychs were composed of a series of panels (three, five or seven) with a principal scene in the middle, generally a Madonna and Child, or a Crucifixion, and standing figures of saints at the sides. Underneath was the predella, a sort of stepped base, divided into compartments containing scenes relevant to the figures in the main panels above. Usually, under the Madonna and Child, we find either a Crucifixion or a Nativity, while, under the saints, we almost always find scenes from their legends. Sometimes, it is very difficult to identify these hagiographic episodes, and only after systematic scholarly reconstruction can we make out what they mean.

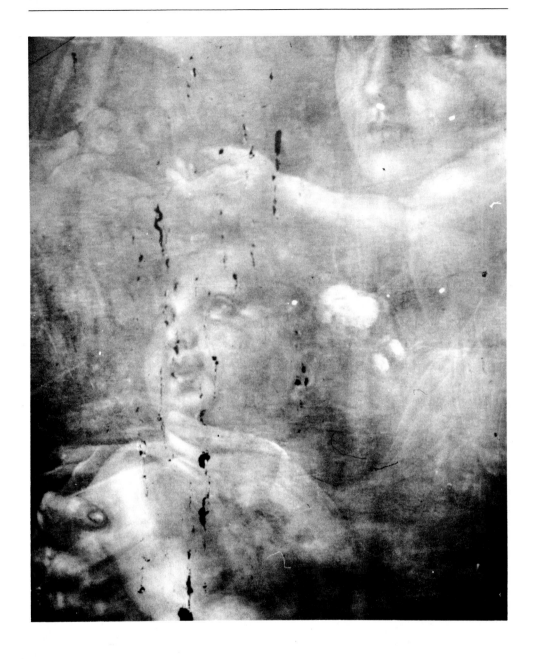

11. Under X-rays, the picture by Raffaellino del Colle in the Baltimore Museum reveals traces of the composition in the Galleria Borghese (see facing page). On the right, the extended arm of the Child is clearly visible.

12. Raffaellino del Colle. Madonna and
Child with the Infant St John. Galleria
Borghese, Rome.

13 and 14. Benvenuto di Giovanni. The
Beheading of St Fabian, and the Massacre of
the Innocents. Gigli Campana collection in
the Musée du Petit Palais, Avignon.

Why did these dismemberings and dispersals take place? For a variety of reasons. Sometimes, the polyptych was removed from the high altar and hung above a smaller one in a niche that was not big enough to contain the predella as well; sometimes, the latter was stolen; at other times, a collector coveted it, bribed the priest and bought it. These predelle are very common and in most cases it is with these pieces, in museums or private collections, that the expert has to prove his mettle.

We now come to an example in the great collection formed in Rome, around the middle of the nineteenth century, by the Marchese Gigli Campana who, at that time, was director of the Monte di Pietà. After the Marchese's financial, political and moral collapse, his collection was acquired by Napoleon III, and then, during the Third Republic, dispersed throughout a number of museums. A few years ago, most of this collection was happily reunited in the Musée du Petit Palais in Avignon.

13-14   This tablet illustrates the beheading of a bishop-saint. In the same collection there is a companion panel with the Massacre of the Innocents. Observing these two panels, we can be certain of one thing only: the panel with the Massacre of the Innocents, since its composition is perfectly symmetrical, must have occupied the central part of the predella. The identity of the saint in the other panel remains obscure, because, in hagiographic literature, a lot of bishop-saints were decapitated. We must therefore concentrate on the attribution of these paintings which, to the expert eye, is not very difficult. They are by Benvenuto di Giovanni, a Sienese artist of the second half of the quattrocento. We can tell that they are his work, and date them to around 1480, by studying the Morellian characteristics, namely, those traits of style, those forms that an artist repeats almost mechanically in the secondary details of his work. These characteristics are named after Giovanni Morelli, who was the first to identify them by a rigorous application of the positivist method, and they are still at the basis of the art of attribution. However, we have not progressed very far simply by stating that the Massacre of the Innocents occupied the central part of the series and that both pictures are by Benvenuto di Giovanni. The only other thing we can say is that, above the Massacre of the Innocents, there must have been a Madonna and Child, because the massacre, rather a rare subject, is almost always linked to the group of the Madonna and Child.

The riddle would have remained unsolved if a third element of the series had not
15   appeared, a few years ago, out of an English collection. This depicts a miracle performed by St James of Compostella, the miracle of the hanged man, with the saint supporting the victim in front of two pilgrims. The panel is of the same dimensions as the other two, the style is identical, the attribution to Benvenuto di Giovanni (at the same point in his career) is absolutely certain. All the facts lead one to suppose that the altar-piece to which this predella belonged included St James, a bishop-saint and, in the centre, above the Massacre of the Innocents, a Madonna and Child.

16   Now, this picture exists. It is a well-known altar-piece by Benvenuto di Giovanni

15. Benvenuto di Giovanni. Miracle of St James
of Compostella. Private collection, England.
16. Benvenuto di Giovanni. Altar-piece, the
Church of San Domenico, Siena.

and can be found in the church of San Domenico in Siena; it dates from 1483. In the middle of the altar-piece we see the Madonna and Child and, on the left, a bishop-saint, or rather, a Pope, St Fabian. Corresponding with him, on the opposite side, there is a St Sebastian who, in the late quattrocento, was always coupled iconographically with St Fabian. On the left, we also see St James. Therefore, as far as the predella is concerned, we know the compartments relating to St James and St Fabian, as well as the central part. Still missing are the scenes relevant to those two saints on the right, St John the Evangelist and St Sebastian. Probably the two panels still to be traced depicted the martyrdom of St Sebastian and the martyrdom of St John the Evangelist.

One thing that helped us to arrive at a definite solution to the problem in this case was the fact that quite a lot is known about the modifications carried out to the church of San Domenico over the centuries. Siena is one of the best-documented cities insofar as the appearance of her churches is concerned; there are numerous guides and a lot of informative manuscripts, one of which is actually from the hand of Pope Alexander VII, before he became Pontiff. These manuscripts frequently cite the pictures and which particular altar they belonged to, as well as their subjects, the artists's signatures (when present) and the writings that appear in the various panels. And so, in many cases where Siena is concerned, we can proceed with absolute certainty.

At other times, the systematic, scholarly reconstruction of a work is aided by 17-18 accessory data which act as beacons to the original provenance. These two panels, which I saw in the deposits of the Pushkin Museum in Moscow, are in an extremely individual style and, to the expert eye, immediately betray the hand of a Sienese painter of the quattrocento, Stefano di Giovanni, known as Sassetta. The style also indicates a date, not far off 1440. Having said this, we still do not know a great deal about the two panels, which portray two deacon-saints. The one with a grid-iron is St Lawrence, the other, most probably, is St Stephen. But we would never have been able to say where they came from but for the fact that they were still in their original frames. The very beautiful frames you see at the top, worked in gilded and embossed relief, are not nineteenth century, as might at first appear, but form part of the panels themselves and are the originals. Now, these same frames reappear in other components of what was Sassetta's masterpiece, and one of the masterpieces of Italian art: a gigantic polyptych with two faces, painted in about 1440 for the high altar of the church of San Francesco in Borgo San Sepolcro. This was sold, disastrously, around 1810 and is now scattered.

The structure of the polyptych was very unusual. It had two faces, the main one contained the panel with the Madonna and Child and four panels with four saints, or, to be exact, three saints and a *beato*, the Blessed Raniero Rasini, a Franciscan from Borgo San Sepolcro, who was buried nearby. The reverse side, which faced the choir, showed the standing figure of St Francis of Assisi in the middle and, at the sides, eight compartments, placed on two registers, with scenes from his life, four on the left and four on the right.

The polyptych was remarkably thick and the sides, or ends, were filled with

17-18. Stefano di Giovanni (known as
Sassetta). St Stephen and St Laurence.
Pushkin Museum, Moscow.

panels of the saints. Two of these are actually the ones in the Pushkin Museum in Moscow. Naturally, the polyptych was furnished with a double predella, one in front and one behind, and completed by cusps and pinnacles. Some pieces have been discovered, many others are still hidden and awaiting exhumation.

Unfortunately, this polyptych suffered rather a sad fate. Once it was sold, it was dismembered and today it is dispersed amongst various museums and private collections. The front face, with the Madonna and Child and two of the four saints, is in the Louvre in Paris. The centre panel of the back part, with the standing St Francis, and the other two saints from the front face, are to be found in the Berenson collection in Settignano. Of the eight panels relating the story of St Francis, seven are in the National Gallery, London, and one has ended up in the Musée Condé in Chantilly. All the known elements of the predella are distributed between the Detroit Museum, the Berlin Museum and the Louvre. But, as I said, a lot of other parts still have to be discovered. The same frames, in gilded *pastiglia*, the same ornamental motif, worked in the identical technique which we have noticed in the two panels from the Pushkin Museum, can be seen again in the eight panels narrating the life of St Francis, and so confirm the fact that the two Moscow panels were part of this gigantic complex.

Apart from the pieces already mentioned, we know that, in an exhibition in St Petersburg in the years 1880–90, two other parts of the polyptych appeared, but they are now considered as lost. Probably they are in some provincial museum in the Soviet Union or in some private Russian collection.

You see, therefore, how many fragments of a single work have been scattered, how an ensemble has been mutilated, so that now we can only reconstruct it mentally. Most of these dispersals took place during the nineteenth century, when it was the fashion to collect Italian Primitives, and there was an immense amount of trading. Italy was plundered for these works, which were then poured into France, England and Germany. The earliest collector of Italian Primitives on a large scale, however, was the Marchese Alfonso Tacoli Canacci of Parma, who went to Florence in about 1780 and acquired a considerable number of paintings on gold backgrounds – panels, triptychs, polyptychs, and predelle which came out of the suppressed churches and monasteries. He took them to Parma where, during the French invasion, the Tacoli Canacci collection was looted by Jacobins. One part was transferred to France, but one part is still in Parma, divided between the Pinacoteca and the little Pinacoteca Stuart.

During the nineteenth century, travelling collectors came to Italy to buy up works of art, and some immense collections were formed, especially in England and France. The French were the first with, for example, the Artaud de Montor collection, for which we have a catalogue of lithographs, and the Cacault di Rennes collection.

Then came the great English collectors, a truly impressive list. Not content with assembling a few dozen pictures, they often bought up hundreds, each more important than the last. Walter Davenport Bromley and Charles Butler were two particularly outstanding collectors. Then there were travellers enamoured of an individual artist; they, too, came to Italy and bought up every available work by their favourite painter. One of these was Alexander Barker, who loved the works of Crivelli and his school. Travelling in the Marches, he succeeded in buying some extremely important pictures and, in fact, many of the great Crivellis that are now found all over the world came from the Barker collection.

From the end of the eighteenth century on, when the religious orders were suppressed, great collections were also formed in Italy. You may well ask: but were there no laws to protect our artistic heritage? Certainly there were, but they were full of loopholes. Moreover, there were powerful political leaders who chose to run with the hare and hunt with the hounds: Napoleon's uncle, Cardinal Joseph Fesch, for instance, who amassed a huge collection in his palace on the Via Giulia in Rome. And there were political upheavals that made it easier to get masterpieces out of the country. Perhaps the most blatant case was the Lombardi Baldi collection in Florence, which was exported from Italy in 1859 just after the agitation that led to the suppression of the Grand Duchy of Tuscany and its annexation by the Kingdom of Italy. Many of the great pictures in the National Gallery in London, including the splendid *Rout of San Romano* by Paolo Uccello, come from the exquisitely chosen Lombardi Baldi collection. During the days of the Grand Duchy, it would never have been allowed to pass beyond the confines of Tuscany.

But the most extraordinary collection made at the end of the eighteenth century as a result of the suppression of the religious orders was the one formed, in the environs of Bergamo, by a priest who travelled round northern and central Italy buying up an unbelievable number of altar-pieces, especially from the quattrocento and early cinquecento. After amassing this vast collection, comprising hundreds of pieces, the priest sold the whole lot to a certain Solly, a London timber-merchant. Solly stored the works in his house in London and tried, in vain, to persuade the British government to buy his collection and found a national gallery. Having failed, he looked for other outlets. Finally, in 1821, he managed to sell the lot to the King of Prussia. The Solly collection constituted the main nucleus of what then became the Kaiser Friedrich Museum in Berlin, which is now split between East and West Berlin. The number of large altar-pieces Solly sold to the King of Prussia is nothing short of fantastic.

For those who deplore the departure of these masterpieces from Italy, it is only fair to say that, in many cases, this was really a rescue operation, a road to survival, since a great many of these works were found abandoned, uncared for, in dilapidated buildings with leaky roofs. If they had remained *in situ*, we should no longer be able to enjoy them today. Sometimes, it was the local people themselves who, out of concern for the safety of the pictures, begged the visiting collectors to take them away. And, after all, the Brera, Milan's splendid art gallery, was founded by the Viceroy Beauharnais, who literally sequestered a great many pictures that were already starting to deteriorate, 'kidnapping' them from Veneto, Lombardy, Romagna, Emilia and the Marches. But, as soon as the pictures reached Milan, they were dealt with in what seems rather a bizarre fashion. A committee divided them into three categories: Category A, to be exhibited; Category B, to be kept in storage; Category C, to be sold. So, some stayed in the Brera, where they are still on show. Others were sent to be stored in local churches, monasteries, convents and various institutions in Lombardy; many of the works in this category have been lost through lack of care and supervision. As for Category C, masterpieces were sold off along with very minor works, or, in some cases, parts of masterpieces which had been kept in the Brera. For example, the cusps, the pinnacles and the predelle of Crivelli's pictures were sold because they had been taken out of their original frames which, in line with the practice at that time, were then destroyed. The frame was not considered to be important, it was simply replaced with a contemporary, or even a nondescript one. These colossal concentrations of works of art were, therefore, a kind of ulterior incentive to dispersal.

Do not imagine, however, that only the huge complexes, taken out of churches and monasteries, suffered dispersal, mutilation and fragmentation. The same fate also befell small pictures, privately commissioned and destined for domestic use.

A very complex example concerns two tiny paintings (a little under 30 cen-
19-20 timetres high) now in the Kress collection at the National Gallery in Washington; they are by Sassetta and the subjects are Saints Margaret and Apollonia. For a long time it was believed that these two little paintings were part of the lateral pilasters of a polyptych, that is, that they had been inserted into the frames. However, a closer examination of the wooden backing, which was rather thin, showed that this was not the result of any recent planing down, but was actually the original thickness. This ruled out the existence of a polyptych, since pilasters would not have been painted on such thin wood. It became evident then that these were the wings of a little triptych for domestic use. Now a triptych of this type, with the wings portraying two female saints, belongs to the quattrocento, and the decoration embossed on gold, which forms the two arches, is typical of the Sienese school. We know this because each school and each period has a particular type of structure and a particular way of setting and framing the paintings. This applies not only to the general structure but also to certain subsidiary details. For example, the angulation of the cusps in fourteenth-century Florentine panels follows certain norms and evolves in its own individual way. Often it is possible to date pictures that are in a sorry state, virtually illegible as far as the painting itself goes, solely on the basis of the angulation of the cusps. When you know the data, and have the means to make the appropriate comparisons, you can date it very accurately, to within five or six years. The same applies to portable triptychs, whose wings, like these two panels by Sassetta, must finish with two cusps at the top and not with a horizontal line. The two cusps in this case have been identified, they are in the
21-22 Frick Museum in Pittsburgh, Pennsylvania. One depicts the Angel of the Annunciation and the other the annunciated Virgin. By opening the wings of the triptych, the two figures of the saints were seen to match.

These pictures are in a museum founded by an American citizen, Miss Helen Frick, daughter of the steel magnate Henry Clay Frick.

It is always interesting to learn the history of individual pictures, which can

19-20. Stefano di Giovanni (known as
Sassetta). St Margaret and St Apollonia.
Kress collection, National Gallery,
Washington.

21-22. Stefano di Giovanni (known as
Sassetta). The Angel of the Annunciation,
and the Virgin. Frick Museum, Pittsburgh,
Pennsylvania.

serve as an introduction to the complex world of the history of art. Miss Frick bought these two paintings from an incredibly bizarre and eccentric personality who lived in the first half of our century, Captain Robert Langton Douglas. A Protestant priest, five-times married, father of innumerable children, a great antiquarian, a great discoverer of Primitives, a great scholar, this man was a kind of cat-with-nine-lives, frenetically active as antiquarian, priest, seducer . . . And also writer, because he found time to write some essays that are by no means to be despised, and some unforgettable books. A history of Siena, for instance, that is very important in some respects. It was also Langton Douglas who brought to light a number of extremely interesting pictures whose discovery helped considerably to stimulate the study of Italian painting of the quattrocento, although the man himself hated art historians with a passion and never wanted to have anything to do with them. His great enemy was Bernard Berenson.

I think this antipathy arose from the fact that it was actually Langton Douglas and not – as is generally believed – Berenson who discovered Sassetta. Langton Douglas brought certain paintings to Berenson's attention and the latter based his essays on them. At any rate, amongst Langton Douglas's discoveries were these two *puntine*, as they were then called, illustrating the Annunciation, and Miss Helen Frick, who was a client of his, bought them from him.

When these two small panels were taken out of their modern frames, it was seen that, in thickness and type of wood, they were perfect matches for the two little female saints in Washington. Moreover, their shape (once you discounted the rectilinear lines of the new frames) made it possible to make an educated guess at what the centre of the little triptych must be like: a vertical rectangle ending at the top with a central cusp joined to the rest by two curves. It was then possible to identify the centre panel. It is the *Madonna of Humility* by Sassetta, which is in the 23 West Berlin Museum and is one of the pictures from the Solly collection which I have already mentioned. In fact, it is one of the very few small pictures from this collection, and must have been bought in Italy at the end of the eighteenth century.

And so the triptych can be recomposed, but we must still ask ourselves why the subject of the middle panel should be called the *Madonna of Humility*. In this iconographical model, the Virgin is seated on the ground as an act of humility (although, admittedly, she is sitting on a very ornate cushion). This iconographical type is never seen in medieval works or in paleo-Christian art. It was invented in Siena, in the circle associated with Simone Martini, in the first half of the fourteenth century. With Simone Martini himself, it passed on to the Anjou court in Naples, where we know of some fairly early examples, and from there it was diffused throughout Europe. We also have Bohemian, French and German examples. Then, the theme of the Madonna of Humility suffered a decline, until it was taken up again in Florence in the latter part of the fourteenth century and the early fifteenth, until about 1410–15. But in Siena, the Madonna of Humility became a characteristic local motif, especially in the archaic style of Sassetta. Later, this theme disappears from painting. You may find the occasional example, specially requested by a patron, but, as a common motif, it disappears altogether.

23. Stefano di Giovanni (known as
Sassetta). *Madonna of Humility.*
Staatliche Museum, West Berlin.

Coming back to our recomposed triptych, there is no doubt at all as to the hypothesis reached through systematic, scholarly research. Everything matches perfectly, both the style and the *punzonature*, those decorative incisions in the metallic background which are made with punches. Every workshop had its own individual punches and its own designs. We still have some of these tools which were characteristic of the great artists of the fourteenth and fifteenth centuries. Very often, nothing of the picture survives except the gold background, but the punched incisions enable us to tell exactly who painted it.

In the triptych, the curvilinear and rectilinear shapes of the upper part also correspond. If we examine all the photographs of the two pictures from Washington on the same scale as the two from Pittsburgh and the panel from Berlin, we will see that there is not a shadow of doubt: everything matches perfectly.

It sometimes happens in art-historical research that one can identify the individual artist, recognise the dismembered and scattered parts which belong to the picture, and still not arrive at an understanding of what the painting means. This happened to me with another work by Sassetta which has now ended up in a museum in Melbourne, Australia. It is an extremely important picture which was 24 part of the first work by Stefano di Giovanni (Sassetta): a polyptych executed between 1423 and 1426 for the *Arte della lana* [Wool Guild] in Siena, and which was catastrophically dispersed during the seventeenth and eighteenth centuries. Some parts have utterly vanished and we have not yet been able to trace them. There is no doubt, though, as to the identification of the author of this panel, nor of its belonging to the *Arte della lana* polyptych, for the latter is mentioned in an eighteenth-century source and described as an event taking place outside the walls of the city, where a priest is celebrating Mass. Everything corresponds, the description is very precise, but nobody could make out what the picture represented until, recently, a scholar put forward a most convincing hypothesis, that is, that the heretic who is being burned at the stake is Jan Hus. This made it possible to solve the iconographical riddle of the *Arte della lana* polyptych. In effect, it was painted in celebration of the Eucharist. The main panel, which must have been broken up into pieces, depicted the consecrated Host being adored by angels, while below, in the middle, the predella showed the scene of the institution of the Eucharist. One compartment of the predella – the panel in the Melbourne Museum – was dedicated to the burning of the Bohemian heretic, Jan Hus. This picture is iconographically unique, and a highly important testimony, for there exist no other examples in Italian painting, nor, I believe, in European painting (with the sole exception of Bohemia) which illustrate the death of Jan Hus. The painting is of outstanding importance because it is linked to the Council of Constance, whose deliberations concerned the value of the Eucharist, and the incarnation in the Eucharist. This picture should really have gone back to Siena, but unfortunately its significance only came to be understood when it was already the property of a foreign museum. Research has to proceed step by step, it is very difficult to jump straight to a conclusion. And, frankly, I would never have been able to identify the subject of this very strange panel.

24. Stefano di Giovanni (known as
Sassetta). The Burning of the Heretic,
Jan Hus. National Gallery of Victoria,
Melbourne.

There were other motives, besides the commercial ones, that led to the dis-
membering of the so-called Primitive paintings. Very often, it happened that the
beneficiaries under a will wanted to divide up the goods between them. Since none
of the heirs would relent and agree to the object in question being given, intact, to
one of their number, it had to be taken to pieces. The same havoc was often
wreaked with complete dinner services of the same pattern, with cutlery and linen,
and even with sets of books in several volumes. This splitting up, which is due to
the hatred of each of the heirs for the others, is downright folly, and they simply do
not understand how vital it is to leave the painting whole, nor do they realise how
much it loses in value when taken apart.

Coming back to Sassetta's little triptych, it should be said that *altaroli*, or
miniature altars of this kind were very common, especially in Florence, where they
were mass-produced. What were they used for? They were objects of domestic
devotion; morning and evening, the family gathered before them to recite the
communal prayers. These 'portable triptychs' were kept in bedrooms or in other
rooms in the house. They were made in vast quantities, because the trade was not
merely local – these little pictures were sent to many parts of Italy and even
exported beyond the Alps.

We have detailed documents about this trade, some concerning a famous
merchant from Prato, Francesco Datini who, while he was abroad, ordered a
painting to be done in such-and-such a style and even mentioned the names of
several painters, including Iacopo di Cione. And we also know from the documents
that these little triptychs were sold at fairs in France. At that period, there were no
shops that sold paintings, but itinerant merchants carried these little *altaroli*,
along with other goods, wherever they went, and this is why paintings of this kind
came to be so widespread abroad.

This trade was carried on mainly in the fourteenth century, as we can see from
evidence in many parts of Europe, in Spain, France and even Bohemia. Often these
pictures bear heraldic emblems, many of them Italian, and some of them have even
been identified. But there are some that bear the coats-of-arms of foreign families,
which goes to show how the use of these domestic altars was adopted throughout
Europe. In spite of the fact that only about 10 per cent of these paintings have
survived (and possibly even fewer), we have dozens of pictures, often whole groups
from the same *bottega*. This points to production on a truly industrial scale,
involving all the workers in the studio: carpenters, gold-beaters, apprentices,
assistants and, finally, painters. So, it must have been a very well-coordinated
activity: the studio would produce a large number of little pictures which were
then sold locally or exported.

Very often, then, we retrieve these pictorial complexes a bit at a time, because
they were dismembered for commercial reasons or as the result of a will. Here now
is one of these random pieces, a fourteenth-century example that presents a
problem. It is a panel with cusps depicting the *Virgin enthroned with Saints*, and it
is painted in the style of the studio of Bernardo Daddi, a famous Florentine painter
who lived in the second quarter of the fourteenth century. Why do I say 'studio of'

25. Bernardo Daddi (studio of).
Virgin Enthroned with Saints.
Formerly in a private collection in London.

and not Bernardo Daddi? Because all the stylistic data point to Daddi, but the execution is not up to his standard; we may legitimately deduce from this that the painter himself, as head of the studio, provided the cartoons and the models, while the actual execution was left to his assistants and apprentices. This was a fairly common practice in prolific *botteghe* such as Daddi's, from whose studio a great many pictures have survived.

The panel reveals certain characteristics and connotations that tell us a good deal. First of all, the picture was almost certainly painted for a Florentine patron because it portrays John the Baptist, the patron saint of Florence. Secondly, the outline of the picture, with its cusp, is typical of the centre of a small triptych, not a diptych. In the Florence of Daddi's time, the two wings of a diptych were always rectangular, without cusps. Now we have to see if we can trace the two wings which were on either side of this composition. Not an easy task, since many of the pictures from Daddi's studio have been dispersed.

Before proceeding to the identification of the wings, it is essential to measure the centre panel very accurately, and to make a careful examination of the embossed decoration on the gold ground, which you see along the upper borders of this little tablet. As it happens, the two wings can be traced with absolute certainty. Not long ago, they reappeared at a London auction; the stylistic data, the ornamentation, the dimensions, everything conspired to reunite them with the picture that had triggered off the research. Note, however, that a different fate has led to their being in a poorer state of preservation than the centre panel. The wings show symptoms of a harsh cleaning which has slightly dimmed them, while the middle panel is in, I will not say perfect, but very good condition. Happily, it did not fall into the hands of a clumsy restorer. 26-27

There is a rather curious detail in one of the wings of the reconstructed triptych. One compartment of the left-hand tablet contains a most unusual portrayal of the Magdalen, dressed in red and embracing the empty cross. This is a very strange, even rare theme, but it is found again, almost identical, in a series of Florentine works by various hands, all dating between 1330 and 1360. This indicates that there must have been a very important prototype by a famous artist (we know nothing about it, so probably it has been destroyed), and during these thirty years it was copied by a number of painters. I believe the prototype, if not from Giotto's own hand, must at least have been by Maso di Banco, a great artist in whose work this theme appears; it was taken up again by Daddi's studio and other painters of the period. When reconstructing an artist's *opus*, it is useful to bear in mind that we can get clues as to the structure of his vanished works, or at least reflections of the composition, from the derivative works by other artists that have survived.

Still pursuing the same theme of art-historical research, I want to show you another example, a picture which came from the Marchese Gigli Campana's collection in Rome. Before ending up in the Petit Palais in Avignon, this painting was sent to the museum in the little city of Le Mans, where it was catalogued under quite impossible names. As you see, it is in a good state of preservation. The only damage it has suffered is a blow with some blunt implement, which has dented one 28

26-27. Bernardo Daddi (studio of). Wings of a Triptych. Formerly in a private collection in London.

part of the painting. As you can also see, it has cusps. Now, even with an approximate knowledge of the stylistic data, you can soon see that it comes from Siena. In fourteenth-century Siena, there were very specific norms concerning the subject matter, as well as the form, of paintings.

There were triptychs, but, more especially, diptychs, and these, unlike the Florentine typology, almost always have cusped wings. The proportions of this tablet – narrow, elongated and cuspidated – indicate that they are the leaves of a diptych. As for the subject matter, if one wing shows the Crucifixion, the other is bound to show the Madonna enthroned, either alone or with saints or angels. This was a structural convention, similar to the ones which, nowadays, dictate that newspapers shall have the main headline on the front page, and that a film shall start with the title, then the names of the director and the principal actors. Or, to take another example, the convention which says that portraits must represent the sitter in such-and-such a manner, and not while engaged in activities or attitudes considered inappropriate to the art of portrait painting. So, taking these conventions as our point of departure, and following through with the research, we are eventually led to the other half of the diptych: the *Madonna enthroned with Child*, 29 which I discovered in the depository of the Pushkin Museum in Moscow. We see that everything works out perfectly: the outline, the measurements, the gold decorations, and the style (Sienese) of a painter very close to the early work of Lippo Vanni. The two pieces are, however, in different states of preservation because, like the Daddi triptych, they have been through different vicissitudes from the moment they were separated.

Sometimes, when one of the pictures is in a deplorable state, it is difficult to see a convincing logic to the reconstruction. For example, if the wings are in good condition, but the centre has been almost completely wrecked, nothing remaining except the embossed gold background. Or, vice versa, if the picture is intact but the gold has been scraped off. Yet there are cases, even important ones, in which paintings in disastrous condition have still been proved to belong to positively reconstructed complexes.

Here is another typical example. These two fragments of a polyptych illustrate 30-31 the Annunciation. Seen side by side, all the data match, in spite of the fact that the cusps have apparently been re-cut in a rather arbitrary and brutal fashion. The panel on the right, with the Virgin, is in the vaults of the Pushkin Museum in Moscow, the one on the left ended up in the private residence of Pierpont Morgan's librarian. Who could have foreseen such odd circumstances! The two pictures are companions and, on examining the style, it is clear that the author must be a Sienese painter straddling the end of the fourteenth and the beginning of the fifteenth centuries. In fact, Andrea di Bartolo, a most prolific painter characterised by a style that scarcely evolved. In a case like this, once you have put the two pieces together again, you still cannot say what complex they belonged to. Here we have one of those instances where research can go so far and no further. Why? Because, first of all, the panels have been taken out of their frames and their outlines altered; secondly, because a great many of this painter's works have been dispersed. So,

28-29. Lippo Vanni (attributed). Wings of a Diptych. Crucifixion, Gigli Campana collection, Musée du Petit Palais, Avignon, and *Madonna enthroned with Child*, Pushkin Museum, Moscow.

30. Andrea di Bartolo. The Angel of the Annunciation. Formerly in a private collection in New York.
31. Andrea di Bartolo. The Annunciated Virgin. Pushkin Museum, Moscow.

32. Ambrogio Lorenzetti. Crucifixion. Fogg
Art Museum, Cambridge, Massachusetts.

33. Pietro Lorenzetti. Madonna Enthroned.
Staatliche Museum, West Berlin.

unless one has very accurate descriptions, or very leading external evidence to work from, one comes to a halt. It is impossible to name the author of every painting, and is similarly impossible to reconstruct all the scattered complexes.

Now we will look at a great masterpiece of fourteenth-century Sienese painting; 32 it hangs in the Fogg Art Museum in Cambridge, Massachusetts, which is annexed to Harvard University. This panel is not in the best of conditions, but, at any rate, it is perfectly legible and one of the most dramatic pictures in fourteenth-century art. Notice, for instance, the powerful way in which the fainting of the Virgin at the foot of the cross is illustrated in the lower left-hand corner. Here again we have one wing of a diptych, as its outline and dimensions indicate, and, basing our deductions on the precise laws governing the subject matter, we can say that, since this is a Cruxifixion, the other wing should be a Madonna enthroned, alone, with Child, or with angels or saints.

The most curious thing about it is that, while the Cambridge painting shows unequivocally the stylistic traits of Ambrogio Lorenzetti, a great fourteenth-century Sienese painter who died in 1348, the pendant, which has been traced to Berlin, is the work of his brother, Pietro. The Crucifixion has come down to us complete with its frame, including the cusp, but the Berlin picture has been cut 33 down to make a small rectangle, that is, its outline was modified to suit the fashion of a later epoch. Now that it is rectangular, how do we know it is the pendant to the Cambridge painting? First of all, as already stated, because of the subject. Then, from the width. And again, along the upper edges, we have vestiges of the embossing which is of the same design as in the Crucifixion, and we even have the beginning of the cusp. In what remains of the upper part, the measurements match perfectly; the same is true of the type of wood, its thickness, and, up to a point, the *craquelure*. Pictures prepared in the same studio and preserved in analogous conditions produce a similar *craquelure* because the wood was identical, cut from the same tree. For those who do not know the word, the *craquelure* is that network of small cracks that appears over the centuries when the gesso and the colour painted on it dry out. This is known as *craquelure* in French, and *cretto* in Italian.

There are some wonderfully preserved pictures which do not show any cracking at all. For example, a fine painting on wood, circa 1420–30, by Francesco di Antonio di Bartolomeo, which hangs in the Accademia in Florence. Incompetent judges might be tempted to say that the picture is a fake, because there has not been time for the *craquelure* to form. There are other pictures which were 'incamottati' or 'incamiciati': a coating or lining of very fine linen was placed between the wood and the gesso, or, a sheet of parchment was glued to the wood, the gesso was then spread over this and, finally, it was painted. There is an *incamottato* picture in the National Museum in Aquila, the *Madonna of Sivignano*, dating from the thirteenth century. As long as they have not been ruined by restorers, burned by candles or desiccated by the sun, these *incamottati* paintings can sometimes survive without any *craquelure*, and this may give rise to sceptical remarks from people who do not know of this technique and are incapable of recognising the typology of the picture.

Coming back to the diptych in Berlin and in Cambridge, Massachusetts, this recomposed work shows that the two brothers did not work in separate studios, as was thought at one time, but shared the same studio and the same work. Both of them died in the great Black Death of 1348, which raged in central Italy and provoked a disaster of such proportions that many Italian cities, and indeed whole regions, never really recovered from it. The Lorenzetti brothers' sharing of the

34-35 same studio is further demonstrated by another diptych, one half of which is in the Pinacoteca in Siena, and the other, a gift from the Kress Foundation, is in the Museum in Tulsa, Oklahoma. Here again we see, on one side, the Madonna with saints, on the other, the Crucifixion. The characteristics of these two wings of the diptych are actually those common to both Pietro and Ambrogio. One cannot say: this wing is in Pietro's style, that one in Ambrogio's. The execution must have been by another hand, certainly an assistant's, or an apprentice's, working from the drawings and cartoons with which the *bottega* was provided.

Sometimes, a picture may appear to be a fragment from a pictorial complex when, in fact, it is not a fragment at all. These two pictures caused me some of the unhappiest moments in my career, because, after I had discovered what they were – and they were two extremely important paintings – I had the unpleasant experience of seeing my material stolen by a scholar who published all my research without mentioning my name. These are two fine paintings, two sublime masterpieces of Italian painting of the quattrocento, which appeared on the London market correctly attributed to Filippino Lippi, a great Florentine painter of the second half of the quattrocento, who died young in 1504. They were thought to be fragments of a great altar-piece. Each one portrays two standing saints, and it was believed that, originally, they had been the side-panels flanking a central Madonna. When I studied them closely, I discovered that the saint on the left was not, as had

36-37 been maintained, an anonymous saint, but St Benedict. They had, therefore, been painted for a Benedictine church. Moreover, I began to suspect that the saint on the right, also incorrectly named, was really San Frediano, the protector of Lucca. Now, the known data told us that Filippino Lippi had painted two pictures in Lucca. But they were not parts of a triptych, they were side-pieces to a niche that contained, in the centre, the statue of St Anthony Abbot. These two pictures are mentioned by Vasari and other sources; the church for which they were painted was of the Benedictine order, and San Frediano is the patron saint of Lucca. There is no doubt, then, that these paintings are parts, not fragments, of a rather rare combination which sometimes occurs in the late Florentine quattrocento: triptychs consisting of a sculpture (in terracotta, marble or wood) in the centre, and paintings at either side. A complete example still exists in Empoli, in the Museo della Collegiata: the side paintings are by Francesco Botticini and the centre-piece, a St Sebastian, is by Rossellino. Complexes of this kind are occasionally found elsewhere.

During the eighteenth century, the church in Lucca was renovated. The two pictures had fallen out of favour, so they were sold privately and, after various moves, they emigrated, first to England and later to Pasadena, California, where

34. Pietro and Ambrogio Lorenzetti.
Madonna with Saints. Kress collection,
Museum of Tulsa, Oklahoma.

35. Pietro and Ambrogio Lorenzetti.
Crucifixion. Pinacoteca, Siena.

36-37. Filippo Lippi. Two Saints (St Benedict and St Frediano). Norton Simon Museum, Pasadena, California.

38. Andrea Sansovino. St Anthony Abbot.
Church of Sant'Andrea, Lucca.

38   they can be seen today in the Norton Simon Museum. The statue of St Anthony, a
masterpiece by Sansovino which has been completely repainted in oil Heaven
knows how many times, and totally disfigured, is in another church in Lucca. This
is a very interesting case, because it concerns what appeared to be a fragment but
was, in reality, a component of an unusual ensemble.

The discovery of these two paintings by Filippino Lippi, which were believed to
have vanished for ever, is yet another proof that important works of art hide
themselves away, move around, remain undetected, but, sooner or later, come to
light. So much has been destroyed, but so much remains. We should never despair
until there is proof positive that the object has been irretrievably lost.

This is true not only of paintings, but also of sculptures, even antique ones. Here
39   now is a marble fragment from a large sarcophagus which, up until about 1939, was
lying abandoned in a farmhouse not far from the present-day airport of Fiumicino,
near Rome; it is now in a private collection.

On the left of the sarcophagus, you see a man who is looking towards the left. He
is wearing the *toga tabulata* and the senatorial ring, and holding a scroll in his
hand. Obviously, he is a senator. Immediately on the right, we see another figure,
an *orante*. Her hands are raised in the Christian gesture of prayer. Undoubtedly,
then, this is the sarcophagus of a Christian senator and, in fact, the mutilated figure
on the right is Eve, holding a large leaf over her belly with both hands.

There are some curious aspects to this fragment. First, the style, almost in-
decipherable in the sense that it is no longer a truly Roman, or classical style, yet
nor is it medieval. But there are certain characteristics that are normally defined as
Romanesque – Eve's hands, for instance. And look at those two strange heads in the
background, whose hair seems to be blowing in the wind. We do not know exactly
what they signify. The heads are both delineated from two different viewpoints:
one frontal and the other in profile, but you would have to examine the original to
perceive this trick of perspective. Notice another very odd thing: the face of the
praying woman is barely rough-hewn. Several sarcophagi exist in which the heads
of the principal figures have been left in this rough state. Presumably this is
because the sarcophagi were made *en masse* and the portraits were only finished off
when the workshop received an order from a particular customer, or perhaps only
at the moment of the purchaser's death. But in this case the hypothesis really will
not hold water, because this is far and away the biggest Christian sarcophagus we
know. If we make a mental picture of it as it was when complete, we have, in the
centre, the figure of the senator in the act of *dextrarum junctio*, that is, he is
lowering his right hand to clasp his wife's hand. Then we have the *orante*, or
praying woman, then Eve. The Tree of Knowledge must have been there and, on the
right, Adam. The senator's wife must have been on the left, together with another
figure to correspond to the praying woman. Then, there would have been another
scene with two or three figures, but we know nothing about these. The mentally
completed sarcophagus measures almost three metres in height and five metres in
width. Truly colossal proportions, and certainly not the sort of object anyone
would put on the market in the hope of finding a customer; this must have been an

39. Fragment of a Roman sarcophagus, early
fifth century AD. Private collection, Rome.

ad hoc commission, made for a specific client. There could, however, be another explanation as to why some of these portraits are unfinished; I do not rule out the possibility that the rough-hewn head of the woman was destined to receive, at the last moment, a plaster funeral mask.

About fifteen years ago, through the Superintendency of Ostia Antica, the Italian government acquired a quantity of marble fragments, mostly architectonic, and sepulchres which had been set into the walls of the Bishop's palace at Porto, once an important city, which is also situated not far from Fiumicino Airport. Amongst these fragments, which have been removed to the Museum in Ostia Antica, there is another piece of the sarcophagus we are discussing. Here, you see the left part with the woman turning to the right in the gesture of *dextrarum junctio*. Casts have been taken and the two fragments found to match. Between the man and the woman, there is a large hole which was made in the Middle Ages when the immense sepulchre, which must have contained valuable treasures, was desecrated and robbed of its contents.

At the end of the fourth and the beginning of the fifth centuries, there existed near Porto a large hospice for pilgrims, a *xenodochium*, built by a Christian senator who was later buried in the church belonging to the hospice. Probably this was *our* senator. This extremely rich man is known to have died on the night of 24 August AD 410, that is, at the very moment when Alaric's Visigoths were forcing their way into the capital of the Empire through a breach in the walls of Rome near Porta Salaria. And we know that, precisely at that moment, Pammachius died in his palace in the heart of the city, near the Tiber. Now, Pammachius was the husband of St Paula, who died during a pilgrimage to Jerusalem, and he was a friend of St Jerome, whom he often entertained. There is every probability, then, that Pammachius and our senator are one and the same person, and that what we have here is his sarcophagus. Everything corresponds: the place where the fragments were found, the fact that he was a Christian senator, the huge dimensions which indicate great wealth and, finally, the style. Because, if the hypothesis is correct, it would also explain the style: this would be an extremely rare surviving remnant from the time of the Emperor Honorius, the son of Theodosius, a period from which very little remains. That is to say, we are straddling the classical tradition of the antique world, which is in decline, and the rise of a new plastic-architectonic concept which will eventually become the Romanesque.

Art-historical research presents a great variety of problems. There is an intriguing cycle of paintings in Anticoli Corrado, a little town in the valley of the Aniene in Latium, which provokes an entirely different set of questions. For a long time, Anticoli Corrado was famous as the town of artists' models. Up until the beginning of the nineteenth century, it was an artists' colony. Many Scandinavians and Germans, and a few French (Corot, for instance) made their way there because it was famed for the beauty of its women and their willingness to pose for painters. Even in recent times, some important artists have worked in this little town, Arturo Martini for one.

Today, Anticoli Corrado is horribly disfigured through the negligence of the

40. Fragment of a Roman sarcophagus, early
fifth century AD. Museum of Ostia Antica.

41. Sts Cosmas and Damian. Church of St
Peter, Anticoli Corrado.

42. Detail of a fresco. Church of St Peter,
Anticoli Corrado.

43. The Doctors of the Church. Church of
St Peter, Anticoli Corrado.

administration, new building is rampant, illegal and unsightly extensions have been added to old houses, there are peeling facades, hideous plastic, PVC and so on. The small church dedicated to St Peter was left in a ruinous state for a long time and, before the restorations, even the roof had gone and there was grass growing in the nave. On the left, near the entrance, there is an ancient family chapel which still has its cycle of frescoes and these, although crude in quality, are very interesting – we shall see why in a moment. The cycle is dedicated to two oriental saints, Cosmas and Damian, whose cult was also widespread in the West. One of the most important ancient churches in Rome is, in fact, the church of Saints Cosmas and Damian on the Via Sacra in the Roman Forum. This church was installed, quite early on, in a building that had most probably served some civic function before it was converted, it may even have been where the *prefectus urbis*, the city prefect, received consignments of goods. At any rate, the cult of Sts Cosmas and Damian, originating in Asia Minor, became very popular during the Renaissance. Amongst other things, the saints became the protectors of the House of Medici, and the high altar in the church of St Mark's, in Florence, is dedicated to them. Fra Angelico's altar-piece represented Cosmas and Damian before the Madonna, and their legends were illustrated on the predella. We also find them in Germany, in France and elsewhere.

In spite of their very crude quality, the frescoes in Anticoli Corrado present some surprising details: the first is that the friezes which frame them are executed in a manner which is by no means inferior; they are monochrome, with classical motifs on an ochre background. The detail on the cornice of the entrance arch has a family coat-of-arms on it which, unfortunately, has not been identified. It seems very odd that these relatively competent classical friezes should contain such coarse and clumsily painted figures. Moreover, there are several indications that the author of these very third-rate frescoes knew something of Piero della Francesca. 42

Let us take a look at the ceiling. The way it is divided into compartments, with these figures of the Doctors of the Church, is very similar to the vaulted ceiling in the Mazzatosca Chapel in the church of Santa Maria della Verità in Viterbo, which is the work of Lorenzo di Viterbo, a painter strongly influenced by Piero della Francesca. It seems more probable, however, that both the painter in Anticoli Corrado and Lorenzo di Viterbo were inspired by some series of Piero's which they had seen in Rome, very likely in Santa Maria Maggiore where, on one of the ceilings, there is the remains of a fresco by Piero, with the figure of St Luke. 43

If we pass on now to the scenes illustrating the legend of Saints Cosmas and Damian, we notice that, in spite of the extremely poor execution, there are again details that remind us of Piero della Francesca. In the backgrounds, the buildings are arranged one above the other in very complex and very intelligent spatial solutions, and these can in no way be the brain-child of such a poor artist as the man who painted the cycle. In fact, if we study it attentively, we can see that this way of resolving spatial problems recalls very closely certain details of Piero's frescoes in Arezzo. Here is one detail, for example, with the banner bearing the Colonna coat-of-arms very prominently displayed (evidently, when these frescoes 44

45-46

44-45-46. Details of frescoes. Above, Piero
della Francesca, Church of St Francis,
Arezzo. Below, Church of St Peter, Anticoli
Corrado.

were painted, Anticoli Corrado was under the feudal dominion of the Colonna family). Once more, we see a variety of very intelligent and shrewdly conceived solutions, which again bring to mind the influence of Piero della Francesca, although they have been very crudely carried out. It is probable, then, that the painter of these frescoes had seen models by Piero in Rome. We know that Piero had worked in the Vatican, in what is now the first of the Raphael Stanzas, the *Stanza della Segnatura*. We do not know much about what the subjects were, but, according to Vasari, when Raphael received orders to efface Piero's frescoes and paint his own compositions over them, he so admired the work he had to destroy that he made copies first. Unfortunately, they have not come down to us, and who knows where they ended up. Raphael painted four huge thematic frescoes in the *Stanza della Segnatura*: on one of the long walls, the *Disputation concerning the Holy Sacrament*, a great ideological subject, and, facing this, the *School of Athens*, a philosophical subject; on the two smaller walls, we have the Parnassus celebrating Poetry, and the scene representing Jurisprudence. The reason the *Stanza della Segnatura* is arranged in this way – and the same themes are echoed in the four *tondi* on the ceiling – is because originally this room (only later known as *della Segnatura*) must have contained Julius II's library. Below the frescoes, where today there is a painted socle, there must have been cupboards containing, on one side, the theological books and, on the wall facing them, the philosophical works; on the other two walls there would have been, respectively, books of poetry and jurisprudence. There was, therefore, a very shrewd logic to this particular distribution that was taken up and diversified in the frescoes. The subjects themselves are so elaborate, so complicated, that it is absolutely impossible to believe that Raphael invented them himself.

In this case, the same argument we have already propounded for Michelangelo and the Sistine Chapel applies to Raphael. However cultured, however gifted Raphael was, he simply could not have been capable of conceiving a series of subjects that are so complex and involved from the theological and philosophical points of view. I am convinced that there was someone who suggested to the Pope the themes Raphael should portray in the *Stanza della Segnatura*. Further, I suspect that it was the same person who, as already mentioned, suggested the themes for the ceiling of the Sistine Chapel. The most probable candidate is the Augustinian, Egidio da Viterbo.

Be that as it may, there is a very interesting fact relating to the fresco representing Jurisprudence. In this scene, Raphael painted the Emperor Justinian in the act 47 of consigning the Pandects, the books of Roman civil law; the Emperor is seated in profile and, in the background, there are some men wearing very strange headgear. One day, I happened to be visiting the Sistine Chapel at the same time as Roberto Longhi, an art historian of genius. He said to me: 'You see, here Raphael wanted to pay homage to Piero.' I asked him, 'Why?' And he replied: 'Because there is an unmistakable reference to Piero della Francesco here, probably a reflection of something of Piero's that Raphael had seen, and who knows if it might not be the very frescoes he had to destroy?'

47. Raphael and Assistants. Justinian
Consigning the Pandects. Stanza della
Segnatura, the Vatican, Rome.

Now, if we move on to the scene in the Anticoli Corrado frescoes depicting Saints Cosmas and Damian in front of the judge, we will see that, in spite of the 48 wretched workmanship, the compositional plan is essentially a repetition of Raphael's fresco. Here, too, the judge is in profile, seated on a classical chair, and, in the background, you see the same men, wearing the same strange headgear, that we saw in the scene with the Emperor Justinian. This means that both Raphael and the humble author of the Anticoli Corrado frescoes (who was working twenty years before Raphael) were influenced by models in some work by Piero which we no longer know. What can we deduce from this? That it is a mistake to look only at masterpieces and ignore works of art of poor quality, as was done at one time. We must consider the work of art in its context and compare it with the whole figurative repertoire of the same period, even to a distance of two or three generations either side. Only in this way can we understand the soil the great work grew from. I am against the idea of amassing collections of nothing but acknowledged masterpieces, which is what some collectors and experts would consider ideal and, indeed, as is the fashion in some museums in the United States. There are certain American museums which, for some time now, have been in the habit of discarding what they consider to be minor works and keeping only the masterpieces. In my opinion, this is an aberrant practice. This over-ambitious chrestomathy, this anthology of supreme works, is absolutely misleading, and especially so in countries like America, thousands of miles from the places where the works were created, countries in which there is, so to speak, no connecting tissue. Of course, we can admire the quality of these collections of masterpieces, we can learn from them to a limited extent, but the real meaning of the work, in its historical context, is completely lost, and, for the uninstructed visitor, who does not have a cultural background, it can have a totally alienating effect.

With regard to the Anticoli Corrado frescoes, there remains the problem of restoring them. As I have said again and again, the less one tampers with paintings the better. The harm done by restorers in this last half-century is infinitely worse than the ravages of time and wars. But I do believe in conservative restoration. People often ask me if I think the *Primavera* by Botticelli has been restored in an adequate fashion. I would say yes. Up until recently the *Primavera*, one of the great masterpieces of the Italian quattrocento, was disfigured by innumerable layers of discoloured varnish and dirt. It was virtually illegible. The restoration, or rather, the cleaning, since it was not a matter of restoration in the full sense, did nothing more than remove these obfuscating layers to expose the original skin of the painting in its true and proper colours. In fact, it has revealed a detail that was invisible before: in the background on the left, you can now see a distant landscape. So, cleaning has given back to the painting its original spatial depth. But, I insist, restoration should be a very cautious process, and limited to cases in which the colours are dimmed or the canvas is torn. Let me repeat, I am in favour of conservative restoration. At the same time, I would like to point out that, in a lot of Italian and other European museums, we see paintings that have been altered in a strange way, typical of the Romantic era, when pictures were covered in what is

48. Sts Cosmas and Damian before the
Judge. Church of St Peter, Anticoli Corrado.

called 'gallery varnish'. Every picture was treated with the same golden or yellow-ish varnish, which dimmed the tones. As an epoch, the nineteenth century neglected colour; the fact that antique statues were once painted and facades of buildings covered in polychrome, was ignored. So they gave everything the same tonality. Paintings were indiscriminately coated with this golden tone which, nowadays, often leads to a distorted reading of the work, since it is hard to judge the original colour range, and even the spatial qualities of the painting.

This 'gallery varnish' not only distorts, but it makes all pictures look alike, from the fourteenth to the seventeenth centuries. There is another factor: this kind of blondish, golden colouring was thought to be inherent to some schools of painting, notably the Venetian. During the nineteenth century, a lot of Venetian paintings were smarmed with these golden varnishes, so that we tend to read them *'alla D'Annunzio'*, as if the whole of Venetian painting were to be read and interpreted through D'Annunzio's *'Il fuoco'*. When you look at certain pictures, you feel you are reading a page about La Foscarina, her loves and her moods.

Up until a few decades ago, it was a common practice for restorers to clean a picture and then coat it with a substance called 'Indian yellow', to give it a golden tone and a uniform patina. This could have serious results because, if the Indian yellow was genuine, it came from India and was the urine of camels, a substance that can be removed, but, if they used an artificial Indian yellow, it darkened after a while, penetrated the paint and blackened the picture irreversibly. The nineteenth century has left us this most unwelcome legacy. Once more I insist: it is not advisable and it is not wise to clean pictures.

It can also happen that otherwise well-preserved paintings, that have escaped the clutches of bad restorers, can still deteriorate beyond repair because of the materials used by the painter. In the fourteenth and fifteenth centuries, the blue in the most prestigious paintings was obtained by grinding oriental lapis-lazuli to a powder. It was, therefore, a very costly material and very few patrons could indulge in such expense. Of course, when Fra Angelico worked for the Medici, the robes of his Madonnas were always done in lapis-lazuli. Other great painters enjoyed the same privilege. But very often cheaper substances were used, which gave more or less the desired shade of blue, but then, with the passing of time, underwent chemical changes and became blackish. As long as the picture retains its patina, these violent imbalances are not visible but, once cleaned, they show up and can ruin one's enjoyment of the picture. In some instances, the whole painting has slowly changed and darkened. Cleaning, even when done with perfect care, can remove not only the patina but the chromatic and formal unity of the picture. When they were considering the possibility of cleaning a great processional banner by Vincenzo Foppa, they had the foresight to make a small test first; it was seen at once that the colours were drastically altered. Cleaning brought the light colours up even lighter and made the dark tones even darker, so it was decided to leave it with its patina intact. Otherwise, the result would have been a picture of startling contrasts, totally alien to the artist's intentions.

There are other cases where cleaning must be avoided because there is old damage underneath the dirt. In London, there are two coffers decorated with mythological subjects by Filippino Lippi. One has had a thorough cleaning recently, the other has not been touched. On the uncleaned coffer, the patina is, perhaps, a little excessive, but at least the painting seems more or less intact. The cleaning of the other coffer revealed serious damage to all the flesh-tones, not recent damage – as the non-expert might imagine – but the result of a restoration done a hundred, or even two hundred years ago, which was so harsh that the outer skin of paint was rubbed off, and the greenish priming uncovered, in all the areas where there were flesh-tones. So now the figures on the cleaned coffer look wretched and sad, and the green parts are really distressing because they do not tone with the rest of the picture. In such a case, I would not have cleaned the coffer. As I have said before, it is a question of taste, and depends on the restorer or whoever is in charge of the work. There must be reassessments from time to time. Only when the picture is in perfect condition and cleaning can bring it back to its former glory am I in favour of going ahead. Raphael's portrait of Baldassare Castiglione, in the Louvre, came out marvellously after cleaning because the picture itself was intact. Another example is the picture by Bronzino with which we began our conversations, *Venus, Love, Folly and Time* in the National Gallery in London. A small test was made, and this proved that the colour pigment was not in the least altered, nor had the skin of the picture suffered any outrage, so it was possible to proceed confidently with the cleaning. When it comes to frescoes, some of Raphael's, for instance, extreme caution is necessary because, while they may be quite well preserved under all the smoke and the dust, they may have lacerations, or wear and tear to the epidermis, and these will not be noticeable as long as they are covered in dirt, but will be exposed by thorough cleaning. On the other hand, there is one picture I would really like to see cleaned, the *Mona Lisa*. There exists a vast literature which speaks of the mystery, the strange, subtly shaded atmosphere of this masterpiece by Leonardo. But, in fact, there is no mystery and no strangeness, they are merely the effects of innumerable coats of varnish and the dirt beneath the surface of the painting. I saw the *Gioconda* when it was shown at the Metropolitan Museum in New York. They had put extremely strong reflectors in front of it and, although it was behind glass and one could only look at it from a distance, it was plain to see that the *Gioconda* is a very light picture; the Mona Lisa's flesh-tones are really very pale, the sky, against which the snow-covered mountains stand out, is of a delicate and tenuous blue. The picture itself – and this is the most important point – is in perfect condition. The only damaged area is the neck, where there are some wide cracks that have been filled with tempera. Cleaning would remove this retouching but, on the whole, the painting is well preserved and I believe it could stand up to cleaning without too many problems. But, if the picture were stripped of its smoky film and restored to its original skin, the mystery of the *Mona Lisa* would vanish. There would be a howl of protest from the public, who are accustomed to seeing Leonardo's painting in a certain way. Indeed, a tradition has been built up concerning this and similar masterpieces, because they have become familiar to us, and entered our culture, in one particular guise and no other, and the common opinion is that they should be left as they are. Recently, Velasquez's *'Las Meninas'*, in the Prado, Madrid, was cleaned, and there was a spate of furious protests, not because the picture had been damaged in any way, but because it looked different. In its new aspect, it no longer corresponded to the cherished image that had long ago entered into the traditions, and the hearts, of the public.

Unless the work of art has been disfigured by the patina, or dirt, or smoke, to the point where it becomes practically illegible (as had happened with Michelangelo's frescoes in the Sistine Chapel), or where crude and arbitrary retouching has distorted the look of the picture, I believe it is necessary to respect this tradition of taste, to respect the feelings of the masses, and to prevent acts of tyranny. Especially when a work of art has been famous, and familiar, for a long time – centuries even – and when the restorations in the past have been carried out by first-rate artists, it seems to me absurd to intervene without taking the public's wishes into account. Surely, this is obvious, and applies particularly to certain monuments of ancient sculpture that have become an essential part of our cultural heritage. I cannot agree with the kind of scholarly purism that insisted, for example, on removing the hands that had been added on to the Apollo Belvedere. When this statue was discovered at the beginning of the cinquecento, it was immediately given hands, and it was in this restored condition that it took its place in European culture. Taking off the hands and leaving the statue with two amputated stumps was an act of arbitrary pruning, because there was no need to intervene – the hands were in no way an outrage to the work. Still more grievous is what happened recently to the archaic Greek sculptures from the pediments of the 'Aphaia' Temple in Egina, which are in the sculpture gallery in Munich. As I told you in the first conversation, these sculptures were restored by Thorvaldsen, who levelled off and smoothed the fragments of the statues before proceeding to the restoration. In order to remove these additions, they were actually sent all the way to the Thorvaldsen Museum in Copenhagen. The result is that what you now see on exhibition in Munich is a collection of cripples, paraplegics and amputees, very interesting to archaeologists and philologists, but disorientating and repellent to the public.

You cannot lay down one blanket rule regarding restoration. Each case must be pondered over and the decision requires a sense of history, scientific knowledge, and, above all, good taste.

Just a postscript now on the substitution of pictures. In earlier periods, it often happened that the originals were sold and replaced by copies. It is important to understand, in this context, that the concept of one unique and unrepeatable original is relatively modern. Up until the middle of the eighteenth century, the copy was considered to be more or less on a par with the original, especially if it was painted by a first-rate artist. In art galleries, you will often see copies in extremely costly frames because, where the copy was concerned, the elements that interested people were the composition and the iconological and iconographical significance, unlike nowadays, when it is the formal data, or the signature, that attract us.

Fourth Conversation

In this penultimate Conversation, I want to discuss a subject that fascinates experts and the general public alike, and that is: fakes.

There have always been fakes, because, from the moment a work of art begins to arouse interest, and to have a market value, it is bound to be exploited. When it becomes famous, a lot of people want to possess it and this is a strong incentive to reproduce it. And so the forgers set to work.

But not all fakes are done for financial gain, sometimes the motivation is the desire to play a practical joke, to make fools of the experts. The young Michelangelo sculptured a sleeping Cupid, in marble, and passed it off as an antique, classical statue. This Cupid, now lost (although some scholars maintain it is in the Archaeological Museum in Turin, under an erroneous attribution) was then sold for a considerable price and passed into various illustrious collections. Michelangelo did not make it for money, but solely to cock a snook at the *cognoscenti*.

Anton Rafael Mengs, a neo-classical painter of the second half of the eighteenth century, played a similar trick: he painted a fresco (now in the Galleria Nazionale in Rome) with Jove kissing Ganymede, and passed it off as an ancient work he had discovered during some excavations in a Roman ruin. The famous archaeologist Winckelmann fell for it, in spite of the fact that it was painted in a technique entirely alien to the classical world. Perhaps, being homosexual, he found the subject titillating. Whatever the reason, Winckelmann accepted it as genuine.

After the discovery of Pompeii and Herculaneum in the eighteenth century (the same period as Mengs's fresco), the faking of antique paintings increased considerably. The vast number of wall paintings brought to light during the excavations excited tremendous interest and so stimulated the production of fakes. In the museum in Cortona, we have the Muse, Polyhymnia, which was long believed to be genuine, but which is certainly an eighteenth-century fake done in Florence. And there were many other finds, or pseudo-finds, sold to Italian or, more often, foreign collectors. But the important thing to bear in mind is that there have been fakes in every period, right from the earliest times of classical antiquity.

Some of the Roman works which have come down to us are imitations of archaic Greek sculptures. Today, at a distance of two thousand years, it is easy to see that they are simply in the archaic style, but, at the time, they must have looked to many people like authentic archaic Greek pieces, and so of great value. For example, the figure of the Boy extracting a thorn from his foot, in the Capitoline Museums. This is most probably a pastiche created in the Roman era by adding an archaic-style head to a genuine first or second century BC body. It was very likely a deliberate fake. We know from literary sources that other imitations were made from it.

The golden age of fakes begins in the second quarter of the nineteenth century and carries right on into our own time. This is also the period in which the great private collections were started; the period, as we have seen, of the hunt for Primitive paintings. It was mostly paintings from the thirteenth, fourteenth and fifteenth centuries that were faked, as well as those from the first half of the sixteenth and the eighteenth centuries. In this last case, the fakes are generally clumsy imitations of the Venetian painters. There are dozens of false Francesco Guardis, little views of Venice which fall far below the technical perfection, the sublime skill of the artist whose signature they carry. The style and the period were too close, too familiar and too well understood to fool contemporaries, and they were soon unmasked.

There are also a great many pitiful imitations of Gianbattista Tiepolo, ridiculous pieces which give themselves away at first glance. What is much more interesting is the practice of faking the earlier centuries of Italian and Flemish art.

How does the faker operate? His object is to immerse himself in a vanished period and re-create a figurative work that truly belongs to that age. Now, this is an impossible task, first of all because what is gone is gone for ever, and secondly because we view the past with our present-day eyes. Benedetto Croce said: 'All history is contemporary history'. We look at the problems of the ancient world, in all its aspects, through the filter of our own sensibility. In each period, the contemporary sensibility is the creative source of the works produced, but it changes constantly, the sensibilities of the past no longer exist and cannot be re-created. And no matter what efforts the faker makes, some trace of his own period will always remain, and it is this that will betray him.

Besides, it is impossible to identify totally with the past; this is amply demonstrated by the fact that many objects from past eras lie right under our noses for long periods without being understood; they can only be absorbed into our own culture, and our own complexity, when something occurs, some shift in our sensibilities, which enables us to pick up echoes from these objects which have hitherto remained 'silent' for us.

The history of mankind can be conceived in different ways. First, as linear history, that Judaeo-Christian tradition of the revealed religions and, also, of Marxism, which is the lay version of them. According to this concept of history, mankind tends towards an end which must and will be reached: on the one hand, the Last Judgement, on the other, Universal Communism. 'Linear' history is divided into three periods. A first period which, in the revealed religions, is that of absolute happiness, of earthly Paradise, and, in Marxism, the communism of primitive societies. A second period in which we have, on the one hand, Original Sin, the root of all evil, and, on the other, private property, which is equally the root of all evil. The third period is characterised by a solution which will resolve all problems: Redemption on the one side, Communism on the other.

Then there is the cyclical concept of history, which is the way the Greco-Roman historiographers saw it. But whatever concept shapes and informs our interpretation, however we view it, it is evident that we are not the same today as we were

1. Anton Raphael Mengs. Jove and
Ganymede. Galleria Nazionale, Rome.

2. The Boy Extracting a Thorn from his
Foot. Capitoline Museums, Rome.

yesterday, because, in the meantime, there has been a mutation, an accretion of experience that has changed and modified us. Just as, from the biological point of view, we change every day.

Coming back to fakes, the attempt to immerse oneself in a past era and totally identify with it is madness. However hard the faker tries, however long and meticulously he trains himself, there will always be some indication, some tell-tale sign that will nail the false picture to the period in which it was painted. And, interestingly enough, it is precisely those errors that eventually lead to the exposure of the fake – in other words, the modern elements – that appeal most to contemporaries and allow the bogus work to enjoy an ephemeral success, however brief. If you read the comments on some of the nineteenth-century fakes, written by critics of the time, you will realise that these experts were enchanted, and ensnared, by just those elements that, nowadays, make us laugh. But you must take care not to fall into the opposite trap: a lot of art historians are ready to shout 'Fake!' every time they are faced with paintings, sculptures, goldsmiths' art, or drawings which they are incapable of understanding. The 'fake' label has sometimes been attached to objects whose only fault was that they belonged to a style, or a culture, which had not yet been studied. And this phenomenon repeats itself with a certain regularity.

One of the most curious, and notorious, cases of a genuine piece being mistaken for a fake is a painting on wood which came on to the market in Rome several years ago. It is the bust of a lady which, at first sight, seems to show an odd discrepancy: the sitter and the costume she is wearing belong to the late fifteenth century, whereas the painting is, obviously, of a later period. A lot of scholars and connoisseurs declared the picture to be false. But, in fact, it is something of an oddity, it is an oil-painting copied from a marble bust. The sculptured bust of this lady, datable to about 1470–80 and attributable to the circle of Desiderio da Settignano, or some other great Florentine sculptor, was made for a family in Florence. About a century later, the same family wanted to have a painted portrait of this ancestress. They called in the artist and had him paint an oil on wood, taking the bust as his model. The image was copied in the round, but it was painted in colours, as if it were a portrait done from the life. So, it was anything but a fake. The painting is in perfect condition and the stylistic characteristics betray, if not the hand, at least the studio of a Florentine painter, Michele Tosini, known as Michele di Ridolfo del Ghirlandaio because he had been a pupil of Ridolfo, the son of Domenico Ghirlandaio. This is an egregious case of a genuine old painting being mistaken for a fake.

Sometimes, it is the unusual technique which arouses suspicions and leads to the picture being condemned as false. One of the strangest cases I know of concerns this great painting which was found, years ago, in a private collection in Switzerland. It portrays a Madonna and Child between two Saints, within an architectural frame. The signature of Gentile Bellini appears on one of the two columns. Even the inexpert eye can see that there is an unacceptable discrepancy between the time of Gentile Bellini (the second half of the quattrocento) and the style of the

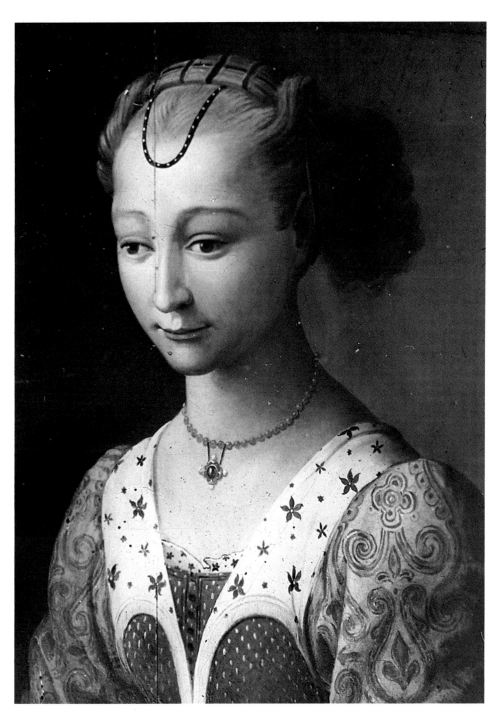

3. Michele di Ridolfo del Ghirlandaio. Bust
of a Lady, copy in oils of a fifteenth-century
marble sculpture. At one time on the
antique market in Rome.

4. Gentile Bellini. Madonna and Child with
two Saints. Private collection, Switzerland.

5. Master of the Misericordia.
Imago pietatis.
Formerly in a private collection, Paris.

group in the centre, which obviously belongs to the cinquecento. In fact, we can go further and say that the central group is based on a celebrated composition in the Doge's Palace in Venice, a fresco painted by Titian in 1523. Still other elements, for instance the figure of the female saint, proclaim a sixteenth-century date of birth. The most extraordinary thing about this picture is that it is not a painting in the true and proper sense, but a collage of coloured and painted silks, applied to canvas. What was this picture? Apparently, a processional banner or the insignia of some fraternity or school, painted by Gentile Bellini. In the course of time, the surface, exposed to sun and rain during processions, must have suffered a great deal and, because of its extreme fragility, it dried out and disintegrated. So the picture must have undergone a series of restorations. The last one, in the sixteenth century, made no attempt to repeat the now lost compositions of Gentile Bellini, but took some more or less contemporary sixteenth-century examples as models. So, what we have today is a kind of stratification, a mosaic, not only of pieces of silk but also of different periods. A work of this kind cannot in any way be defined as a fake. It is simply a picture that, because of the nature of its structure, and the vicissitudes it has been through, is no longer a homogenous whole, but the fruit of various restorations and reworkings.

There are other, completely different reasons why works of art are manipulated and reworked. Here is a very specific and rather rare case. This predella, with a gold background, was found years ago in the antique market in Paris. It depicts the *Imago pietatis*, that is, the dead Christ displaying His wounds, with His body 5 two-thirds of the way out of the tomb, and half-figures of the mourners, the Virgin and St John the Evangelist. This composition was quite common in fourteenth-century Florence and is usually perfectly symmetrical: it has three figures, the Saviour in the middle, upright in the tomb with His arms outstretched, and the two grieving figures at the sides. But in this picture, there is an anomaly. There is a fourth figure, recognisable as St Michael from his sword and wings. Originally the predella of a polyptych, this composition was altered about a hundred years after its birth, but the reasons are unknown. Someone, possibly a private individual or a monk, wanted the figure of St Michael inserted, why we do not know, but probably because of some personal or devotional predilection.

St Michael was painted in by a Florentine painter who tried to imitate the style of the three original figures and the embossing of the halo, that is, the gilded decoration of the background. The original painting belongs to the Florentine school (as the trained eye will see at once) and can be attributed with certainty to an artist whose work is well known, although we do not know his name. As is usual in such cases, he has been given a provisional name, derived from his most important work, the one from which the research began. The name-piece is a vertical painting on wood in the Accademia in Florence, it is known as the *Madonna della Misericordia* and depicts the standing Virgin sheltering the faithful beneath her cloak. Very likely, this painter, the *Maestro della Misericordia*, can be identified with Giovanni Gaddi, brother of the well-known Agnolo Gaddi, and a painter of the first rank in his own right. Many signposts point in this direction, but so far no

6. Giovanni Martorelli. Triptych.
Pinacoteca Nazionale, Bologna.

7. The same triptych after cleaning.

document has come to light with sufficient detail to enable us to link one of the works in the anonymous group to a precise description in the archives. Not only are we lacking, for the moment, a document which could be matched with a picture, but there is not one painting which shows this artist's signature. In the 1950s, I saw this painting in a perfect state of preservation in Paris. A few years ago, it fell into the hands of a collector who considered the figure of St Michael to be an abusive and illicit addition. He had it removed. The painting was scraped, the gold decorations of the halo were ironed out. The gap left after scraping off the figure of St Michael, which had been painted around 1490 by a Florentine artist from the circle of Ghirlandaio, was then filled with new gold. And so, a picture that had come down to us in absolutely perfect condition has been wrecked, reduced to a ruin, out of a stupid and absolutely unforgivable mania for restoring it to the original, a mistaken purism that ignored the historical evolution the picture had gone through.

At other times, it is academic taste that dictates alterations and manipulations
6   to a painting. A typical case is this triptych in the Pinacoteca Nazionale in Bologna. Here, we are seeing it as it was until a few decades ago. Even at first sight, you are immediately aware of the impossible dichotomy between the style of the predella, with the half-figures of the Apostles, and the style of the main panels. While the Apostles are agitated by violent movements and have facial features that, nowadays, we would define as strongly inclined towards Expressionism, the principal figures have something sugary-sweet, cloying and academic about them. They are in a completely different style, and it is hard to believe they are the work of the author of this triptych, Giovanni Martorelli, who was active in Bologna in the fifteenth century. The picture was then cleaned and it was discovered that the principal figures and other parts of the triptych had been distorted, painted over by a restorer precisely because their violent character was not pleasing to the tastes of the time (presumably around 1830–50) when the modifications were carried out.
7   Once the main figures and the other parts were cleaned (and fortunately they had been painted over with tempera and so it was not necessary to scrape or tamper with the surface), the figures that emerged harmonised perfectly with the ones in the predella, as they too were violently agitated and had facial features bordering on the grotesque and caricatural.

In other cases, pictures have been altered, and in large part falsified, for reasons of decency and morality. Because of its Puritanical attitudes, the Counter-Reformation intervened in a heavy-handed way and imposed clothing on a great many of the nude female figures in mythological scenes. And religious paintings suffered, too. The most glaring example is Michelangelo's *Last Judgement*. The moment it was unveiled, the painting aroused violent protests; it was considered indecent because it showed the private parts entirely without benefit of covering. There was even a threat, at one moment, to destroy Michelangelo's masterpiece, and, backed by the Carafa Pope, Paul IV, this threat would have been carried out but for the fierce opposition of many connoisseurs and prelates. But an immediate 'cover-up operation' was begun, veils and draperies were painted over the most

8. Raphael. *Lady with a Unicorn.*
Galleria Borghese, Rome.

offensive parts. At a later stage, they called in the painter Daniele da Volterra (who then became known as Braghettone, a name derived from *braga*, meaning breeches, or knickers), and he proceeded to cover up various sexual organs and buttocks, thus seriously altering the look and the significance of the original painting.

This kind of puritanical distortion is far more common than is generally realised. There are whole galleries, entire collections, in which the nude figures have been dressed. The Galleria Doria Pamphili in Rome, for example, where all the female figures have been covered with heavy clothing, transforming the nude bodies into camouflaged, wrapped-up dummies. The same thing has happened in the Galleria Colonna in Rome. In one of the great masterpieces there, Agnolo Bronzino's *Venus with Eros and a Satyr*, the goddess has been travestied with a heavy drapery. In many cases, these additions were later removed, but unfortunately the wrong kind of tools were often used, such as sharp scalpels, which scraped off not only the extra layer of paint but the skin underneath, and so ruined the original surface. In fact, it is quite a common event to come across – in private collections or on the art market – pictures that are well preserved except for the nude female figures, which are totally defaced from neck to ankle. Only the head, feet and hands remain unscathed. To remove old over-painting by harsh mechanical means is always dangerous and can lead to irreparable damage.

8 The most grievous case of this sort is the *Lady with the Unicorn*, by Raphael, in the Galleria Borghese in Rome. This picture, painted in Raphael's Florentine period, originally depicted the half-figure of a lady holding a unicorn between her hands. Some forty years later, it was completely repainted, with the exception of the face, to transform it into the figure of a martyr-saint. The critic, Roberto Longhi, had the genius to intuit that, beneath the banal repainting of the Florentine cinquecento, there was a work by Raphael. His suggestion was acted upon, but with entirely unsuitable means. By scraping down the over-painted areas, which were almost contemporaneous with Raphael's, the original painting was removed as well, so that today this picture looks like a corpse, or a larva. The whole of the epidermis, the final paint-skin, has been brutally destroyed.

In other cases – alas, rare – the process is carried out by appropriate methods. Eschewing even the use of solvents, the work is done under the microscope, using a very fine platinum point to lift and remove the re-painting. It is a painfully slow process, at the most one square centimetre per day can be cleaned, but the results

9 are always sensational. Mattia Preti's *Susanna and the Elders*, in the Longhi Foundation in Florence, was treated in this way and a splendid restoration emerged. When Roberto Longhi acquired the painting in about 1947–8, the figure of Susanna, although immersed in the bath, was fully dressed! A test was done to remove the over-painting and it was seen that, unless the job was done with extreme care and the utmost delicacy, Mattia Preti's original painting would be lifted off together with the retouching. And so they used the platinum instrument under a microscope to do the job. The cleaning process went on for years, but in the end revealed the nude in such exceptionally fine condition that even the final

varnish, applied by Mattia Preti himself, remained intact. Today, nobody would suspect that, towards the end of the seventeenth century, this picture was disfigured and rendered virtually unrecognisable.

If you are going to take off the layer of paint that has been added, without damage to the underlying surface, it is essential that a considerable time should have elapsed between the original work and the retouching. If the over-painting is done soon after the original, the two layers practically amalgamate, because there has not been time for that coating of dirt and smoke to form which would protect the original painting. In cases like this, if the restorer goes to work with a heavy hand, ruin is inevitable. And we have, alas, all too many examples of ruined pictures in both Italian and foreign museums.

And then there are those restorers who perform miracles to impose what they believe is a subtler and more refined taste on a picture. One of these men was called Vergetas (or Verzetta). He was active in Paris between the end of the nineteenth and the beginning of the twentieth century and worked on countless pictures on behalf of a connoisseur-dealer, Baron Michele Lazzaroni. The expert eye can recognise his efforts at first glance. Bernard Berenson, when he came across one of these works restored by Vergetas, called it a *'lazzaronata'* (a pun on the Baron's name and *lazzaronata*, meaning 'a scoundrelly action'). Very often, Vergetas repainted the pictures with tempera or water-colours, and so did not hurt the original surface, but, on other occasions, he did irremediable damage. I remember seeing, years ago, a great painting by Nicolò Alunno, with the figure of St John the Baptist, which had been so heavily reworked by Vergetas that its authenticity was in doubt. When it was cleaned with a very gentle solvent, the retouching came off easily and, beneath it, the original picture appeared in immaculate condition. Not only had the painter's original varnish been preserved, but even the drops of wax that had fallen on to the canvas from some altar candles. In this case, everything turned out for the best. But elsewhere Vergetas has performed strange and unexpected manipulations that, alas, can no longer be removed. Here, for example, is a large *tondo* of the 10 Madonna and Child with Two Angels belonging to the Metropolitan Museum in New York. Originally, this picture was on wood. Vergetas (or someone working for him) transferred it to canvas and then proceeded to 'sweeten' it. The painting is attributed to the immediate circle of either Domenico Ghirlandaio or his brother-in-law, Sebastiano Mainardi, which dates it to the second half of the quattrocento, but anyone who is familiar with Florentine painting of that period will see at once that there is something sugary, something pathetic in the face of the Child and in the face of the angel on the right. The eyes of these two actually look as if they have been made up with mascara, and neither of them can possibly be accepted as original.

This way of travestying and making-up the figures can be seen again and again in pictures that have passed through Vergetas's hands, it is an instantly recognisable style. Here is another painting on wood showing the same traits. Once again the 11 Child has this sickly-sweet, dreamy look, almost like a Christmas card, in spite of the fact that the picture belongs to a very different school and period from that of

9. Mattia Preti. *Susanna and the Elders.*
Longhi Foundation, Florence.

10. Domenico Ghirlandaio (or Sebastiano
Mainardi)? Madonna and Child with Two
Angels. Metropolitan Museum, New York.

11. Benedetto Bonfigli. Madonna and Child.
Private collection, USA (Formerly Otto
Kahn collection).

the Metropolitan Museum's *tondo*. In the thirties, it belonged to a well-known banker, Otto Kahn, and it is now in a private American collection. It was painted around 1470 by Benedetto Bonfigli, a great painter from Perugia. Vergetas's absurd retouching has transformed, or I should say melted, the two works into one totally unacceptable sugary solution. And yet the Bonfigli is still a very valuable picture, and skilful cleaning could restore it to a pristine state. The present owners have always hesitated, however, because there is a risk of finding a disaster underneath the doll-faces we see now. An alarming number of paintings have been distorted, camouflaged and ruined in this manner. You would scarcely believe me if I told you how many restorers of this type were at work during the end of the nineteenth and the beginning of the twentieth centuries, the period when art-dealing reached its zenith.

In other cases, there have been truly diabolical machinations to produce fakes. Certain private collectors, and even some priests, who owned a famous picture, had a perfect copy made and hung in its place before selling it. And so the original came on to the market first, to end up in some great private collection or museum. Then, at a later stage, the false one, which had been hung in the place of the original, was taken down and sold, and, because of its pedigree and its certain provenance, it was taken to be the real thing.

The result is that now we have several twin copies in circulation, one real, the other a fake. Often forgers succeed in bribing those in charge of holy, or at any rate illustrious, places and so manage to sneak their fake products into art galleries or churches, where they hang them in place of the originals. They then let it be known that the custodians want to get rid of an old picture. Which goes to show that connoisseurs should never believe what they are told, but must always verify it for themselves by examining the picture as meticulously as if it had come out of the blue.

Sometimes, the faker imitates the picture only after it has come on to the market. A typical example is this wing of a thirteenth-century diptych, which 12 came up for sale in Paris in the 1920s, or thereabouts. Whoever owned it at that time had a perfect copy made by a highly skilled craftsman (probably a miniaturist) 13 who copied even the minute details in an irreproachable way, not straying by so much as a hair's breadth, except for certain superficial cracks which are not quite convincing. The cracking, or *craquelure*, can also tell you whether a painting is antique or a modern fake, but sometimes the cracking of the gold can be deceptive. In this case, if you had had only the photographs to examine, without access to the originals, it would have been very hard to distinguish the prototype from the modern copy.

There also exist fakes that have been invented *ex novo*, with a fraudulent end in view, but they rarely achieve these heights of sophistication and expertise. As a rule, the faker only manages to deceive people for a very short time and, even then, only people with little visual training, because each period has its own forms of expression and its own *Zeitgeist*, and these are reflected in, and characterised by, the composition of paintings. You will never find a cuspidated polyptych in the

12. Anonymous Umbrian, fourteenth
century. Crucifixion, wing of a Diptych.
At one time on the antique market in Paris.

13. Copy of the above. At one time on the
antique market in Paris.

fourteenth century, nor in the seventeenth century. At most, you might find that, in the nineteenth-century Gothic revival, certain structures typical of the fourteenth century were taken up again. These fundamental principles, however, are not known to the fakers, who often bring together elements which have been lifted anachronistically from various periods and styles.

One of the most horrible fakes, one of the worst I have ever seen, is a Crucifixion 14 which has, nevertheless, enjoyed such a cyclical history, cropping up again and again, that I have nicknamed it the 'Comet'. Since there is no law which decrees that the fakes, once detected as such, must be destroyed, they are simply hidden away for a while and brought out again perhaps a generation later. Generally, the cycle is made up of the following phases: the appearance of the fake; the fraudulent sale to some unwary collector or art-dealer; the trial, and the eventual conviction for fraud. The faked picture disappears, it is kept 'on ice' for some twenty years or so, then it re-emerges and the whole cycle starts again. But, really, it is just as well there is no law decreeing that fakes must be destroyed, since, given the incompetence of many judges and of many tribunal experts, there is the much graver risk that they would order the destruction of a genuine original painting.

So, this fake, this 'Comet', is a Crucifixion. The Entombment below it is an incredibly clumsy composition and, in my opinion, the whole thing was fabricated in the early twenties, either in France or Spain. I would rule out Italy as the source. There is a glaring contradiction between the style of the picture, which seems to be thirteenth century, and the shape of the backing, a vertical oblong with two curves to round it off at the top. This kind of outline belongs to the quattrocento or, to be exact, the period between 1450 and about 1470, and is typical of a restricted zone in southern Italy, between Amalfi and Gaeta. It does not exist elsewhere. My impression is that this picture was painted on a genuine, antique piece of wood actually from that area. The wood, which is worn, has been scraped down and the faker has painted his new composition, in thirteenth-century style, on top of the old gesso. Often fakers use genuine old boards, sometimes with the antique gold or silver ground still on it, to give an authentic look to their forgeries.

Apart from the abysmal quality, one soon sees, in a fake of this kind, some internal contradictions which betray it as a modern fabrication. We have already noticed the contradiction between the style of the picture and the frame: the style is thirteenth, the frame fifteenth century. Now let us look at the technical data: if you examine the picture in real life, the colour range is highly suspicious, the paints seem to be modern and chemically produced. The actual painting, the application of the successive coats, is very crudely and unskilfully done. Antique pictures were painted in *velature* – thin layers of paint applied in varying degrees of transparency and opacity, glazes and scumbles – rather than *colore a corpo*, full-bodied colours, as is done nowadays. So far, then, we have three counts against this Crucifixion: the contradictions of style, the colours, and the abominable execution. There are more to come. Four: there is a series of decorative arches at the top, apparently Mozarabic, and these do not correspond to the style of the picture. Five: at the bottom, there is a kind of gradine, a predella with the

14. French or Spanish fake. Crucifixion.
Whereabouts unknown.

Deposition, and this is another contradiction, because, in the epoch he is trying to imitate, there were no gradines, no painted predelle. One of the oldest examples, if not *the* oldest, is the predella (now dispersed) which was originally attached to a Florentine polyptych by Pacino da Bonaguida, c. 1325–35. There is also Giotto's polyptych in the Pinacoteca Nazionale in Bologna, where, however, there are not the usual scenes as we know them. Predelle belong to several generations later than the period the faker is trying to imitate. Six: the gestures of the figures are unconvincing. While St John succeeds in expressing a movement of grief which is in harmony with the iconographic and symbolic gestures of the period in question, the posture of the Madonna does not correspond to the unvarying conventions of a painting of the time. And so, as you see, there is a whole series of errors, each clumsier than the last, which immediately give this picture away and reveal it for what it is – an utterly worthless modern fake.

Not all fakes are so crude or of such execrable quality. Some, and they are extremely dangerous, are good enough to deceive even the most highly trained and penetrating eye. Here is a painting that gave more than one expert a hard time, and intrigued a number of art historians, including myself.

The story of this picture began around 1947, when it appeared on the art market 16 in Rome and was purchased by a well-known collector who then approached me, and a first-rate restorer, to confirm the authenticity of the painting. We examined the wood on which it was painted: it was unquestionably antique. The picture was painted on a silver background, and this, too, was found to be datable to the thirteenth century. There was something about the execution, however, that made me suspicious; it was perfect, and yet I was not altogether happy with it. At the bottom, there was something written in rather strange and complicated characters. This, too, was examined by a paleographer who declared it to be perfectly consistent with the period. Then, finally, a most odd thing happened: one day, as I was studying the picture in the restorer's laboratory, I noticed that, if I pressed my thumbnail against the small patterns, composed of three white dots, which decorated the Madonna's robe, my nail penetrated the colour. The paint, therefore, was not perfectly dry, and it is patently impossible that a picture, painted around 1250–70, should not have dried out after seven hundred years. But how on earth had the faker managed to make up this painting which, apart from anything else, showed a completely unknown composition of the figures, for which there was no known prototype? I found the answer by chance. Somebody sent me a present, a large packet of old photographs and, amongst these, there was a large one of a painting absolutely identical to the one in question. It was, however, framed in a kind of box, a very old wooden niche, and there was a superb metal crown, finely wrought with the lilies of the House of Anjou, on the head of the Madonna. So this was a photograph of the original from which the faker had derived his copy. The photograph also proved that there was an original, which must exist, or have existed at one time, in the old Kingdom of Naples, and so that was where the research was carried out. It was quite a vast area to explore, because the Kingdom of Naples included the whole of the Abruzzi, as well as the region south of Gaeta.

15. Abruzzese school, thirteenth century.
Madonna di Sivignano. Museo Nazionale,
L'Aquila.

16. Roman fake, circa 1945. Copy of the
preceding picture. At one time in private
collection, Rome.

Before we started on the research, the restorer who was doing the analyses made some private investigations, and he approached the most prominent fakers of the day. I cannot tell you all the details, as some of them are rather delicate and confidential, but the author of the work was discovered. He turned out to be a highly skilled faker who, at that time, was living in the centre of Rome. This is what had happened: the Madonna whose photograph I now possessed belonged to a very small place called Sivignano, a *frazione* [an outlying hamlet, or country ward] of Capitignano, in the province of Aquila in the Abruzzi. The local priest, in cahoots with another shady character, decided to sell the painting. First, he had it photographed and enlarged (and what I had was one of these enlargements), then he went to Rome to consult the faker. This man managed to acquire a genuine antique board, which still retained its authentic silver background. After destroying the remnants of the old picture, he painted his copy of the Madonna over it, using the enlarged photograph as his guide. The next operation was to have been the substitution of this copy for the original, in such a way that the local inhabitants would not realise anything had changed. But all this took place between 1943 and 1944, and, just at the moment when they were about to make the secret exchange, the battle front drew near, the zone became a theatre of operations and the person who had ordered the fake, and who was supposed to make the switch, died. The original painting therefore remained *in situ*, and the fake was left in the hands of the man who had created it. By this time, the local inhabitants had become suspicious of certain goings-on – secretive dealings between the priest and an outsider, photographs being taken of the Madonna – and so, to save the picture, they took it out of the church and hid it, moving it to a different hiding-place every week so that nobody would know where it was. When we learned the whole story, the restorer and I first confirmed that the painting bought by the collector was the false one, then alerted the *carabinieri*, who went to Sivignano to investigate. After a violent, stone-throwing battle with the people, the *carabinieri* sequestered the picture, which is now in the Museo Nazionale in Aquila. It is the famous *Madonna di Sivignano*, painted on parchment applied to wood. It is in a perfect state of preservation, but unfortunately, during all these endless moves, the precious Anjou crown was lost. Sooner or later, it will appear on the market somewhere, and then it will be sequestered, unless, of course, it has already finished up in some foreign collection.

Let us go back a little: when the man who was the brain behind the intended theft died, the original picture was hidden away by the locals and the faker was left with his false copy. He did not hesitate to sell it, first exploiting the naïveté of three great experts (one of whom is internationally famous and, in my opinion, half blind, because, when we showed him the fake and asked him to confirm what it was, he did not even notice that the Madonna had been stood on her head!). So the fake, armed with three expert opinions praising it and endorsing its value, was sold to the collector. Naturally, when he learned the truth, he denounced the swindle and had restored to him the considerable sum of money he had paid for it. The fake was not destroyed, though, and it recently reappeared on the market. So here we have another typical 'comet' amongst fakes, making one of its cyclical reappearances.

The original picture, which is the work of a painter from the Abruzzi, datable to around 1250, is in exceptionally good condition; it is one of those rare Italian pictures painted, not directly on to the wood, but on a sheet of parchment, first polished with a hard stone, over which the painter spread a very light priming before painting on it in tempera. As the picture has never been corroded by humidity, nor maltreated by a restorer, it is in an almost unique state. It is sad that the crown is missing. The interesting point about this episode is that, if we had not discovered, quite by chance, the photograph of the original from which the fake was copied, it would have remained an almost insoluble mystery.

Sivignano is not a unique case. A lot of pictures have been substituted, and often the people in charge did not even notice. Only recently, for example, the Superintendency of Liguria have been able to prove that the centre panel and the cusps of a large polyptych in the church of San Francesco in Noli have been switched. Yet I saw the cusp on the Rome market as long ago as 1945, or thereabouts. I did not know where it came from because there were no photographs of the polyptych. Photographs are invaluable in identifying these substitutions.

There is a picture in the Ashmolean Museum in Oxford which once hung in the church of San Matteo in Ortignano, near Grosseto, but it was exchanged for a copy. The original is the work of Pietro degli Orioli (known as Giacomo Pacchiarotto). In Tuscany, substituting the original for a copy was a very common practice; there is, for instance, a picture by Domenico Puligo, which is now in the Ringling Museum in Sarasota, and whose substitute hangs in the Chiesa di Badia in Settimo, near Scandicci, not far from Florence. I cannot over-emphasise the importance of photography, because it enables the expert to identify and denounce these fraudulent substitutions. It is, in fact, indispensable, because paintings in churches are rarely checked and verified. There is a stunningly beautiful standing figure of St Lucy, belonging to the Roman school of the thirteenth century, now in the Museum in Grenoble, which is the original of a faked panel that hangs above the high altar in the church of Santa Lucia in Selce in Rome. In this instance, we know that the substitution took place between 1890 and 1900.

Very often, then, the fake that comes on to the market has something grotesque or ridiculous about it, but that does not prevent the *cognoscenti* from taking it for the real thing, nor stop it ending up in an honoured place. One such picture was a large *Madonna and Child enthroned*, which belonged to no less a personage than 17 Sir Joseph Duveen, later Lord Duveen of Millbank, who, in the 1920s and 1930s, was the Prince of Merchants. This large fake was bought by Samuel Kress, a New York collector, who had risen from being a miner to become the owner of a chain of small department stores, the famous *Five and Ten* chain, where only articles costing five to ten cents were sold: needles, safety pins, paper napkins and so on. Kress had assembled a gigantic collection of works of art, containing more than 3,000 objects, some of them of outstanding importance. Unfortunately, the Kress Foundation later distributed these works amongst the National Gallery in

17. Fake Madonna and Child Enthroned.
Study collection, Fogg Art Museum,
Cambridge, Massachusetts.

Washington and a lot of provincial museums in the cities where Kress had made money with his Five and Ten stores. One of the 'gems' of the collection was this fake, which was actually destined for the National Gallery in the US capital; it was authenticated by bundles of testimonials from experts, all of whom declared it to be a supreme masterpiece. It was not until about 1950–2 that the administrators of the gallery, alerted by Mario Modestini (the same Italian restorer who had helped me to identify the *Madonna di Sivignano*), were finally convinced that the picture was a fake. The painting was demoted to a 'study collection', one of those small university collections created for the study of various techniques in painting, fakes and other disciplines. But, even without the restorer's analyses, it is evident that this giant picture, measuring nearly two metres in height, is a colossal 'dud'. There is something about the style that does not ring true – the baby's legs, for example, with those prominent little muscles. You can see that it is not the work of a thirteenth-century artist who is moving towards naturalism and three-dimensional painting, but rather the work of someone who is already very familiar with three-dimensional art and naturalism but is trying to imitate an early abstract style. So here, too, there is an internal contradiction. Unfortunately, these incongruities are not always sufficient to ensure against a fake being mistaken for the genuine article. This fake of Kress's must have been done in Florence. From about 1910 up until 1940, Florence and Siena were the real hotbeds of forgeries. Not only furniture and pictures were reproduced there, as is generally believed, but also miniatures. There are countless false miniatures about, painted during this period, and they were done with immense skill. Often, they are sold off in lots at auctions.

Coming back to our fake Madonna, the more you look at it, the more incongruities you discover. The two angels at the top do not look in the least thirteenth century, they look more like a couple of chorus girls, and the setting they are in would be more suited to a musical comedy. Let me give you a useful tip: when you are suspicious about a picture, take a photograph of it and turn it upside down. In that position, the incongruities, the lack of unity, jump to the eye, especially in the way the folds in the drapery are treated. Another thing in the Kress fake that should have aroused suspicions is that kind of *horror vacui* that pervades it: there is not a millimetre anywhere that is not filled with some decorative detail.

So much for the crude stylistic contradictions in this fake. As far as the technical data are concerned, the eye of the connoisseur will immediately spot the flaws, because it is difficult, if not impossible, to imitate the technique of a thirteenth-century painting. One would need to be a real master-craftsman, like the man who faked the Sivignano picture, though I would say that that was not merely a rare case, but a unique one. The technical data are vital because often they, too, are in contradiction to the style aimed at.

Next, we shall look at a fresco, removed from its setting, which was in a well-known collection in Lombardy up until a few decades ago. It shows the half-figure of the Madonna and Child, in a rectangular frame decorated with mosaic. This fresco was attributed to Bernardo Daddi, an important Florentine artist who died in 1348. In effect, it is in Daddi's style, but the expert will soon

18. Modern imitation of Bernardo Daddi.
Madonna and Child, fresco.
Private collection, Lombardy.

recognise this Madonna and Child as an enlarged copy of a compositional group in one of Daddi's famous triptychs. It is not impossible, of course, that the artist might have repeated himself, but it is rather unlikely. Besides, there is a technical detail that is totally anachronistic. If you look at the outlines of the figures, you will see that they are marked with a series of dots set very closely together. These little dots indicate that the *'Tecnica dello Spolvero'* ['pouncing'] was used, and this was not invented until the fifteenth century, in about 1470 to be exact.

When an artist had to paint a fresco, the composition was first drawn in charcoal on a cartoon. (The finest cartoon in the world, the one Raphael used for the whole of the lower part of his great *School of Athens* in the *Stanza della Segnatura* in the Vatican, is in the Ambrosiana in Milan. The remains of a cartoon for two frescoes in the Pauline Chapel, by Michelangelo, are in the Pinacoteca in Naples.) Once the cartoon was ready, the artist proceeded to perforate the outlines with a pin, making innumerable small holes. Then, the cartoon was nailed to the wall and, with a cloth saturated in charcoal dust, he transferred the outline to the wall by forcing the dust through the holes. Each day, he plastered the area to be painted, between the exact outlines defined by the charcoal dots, and each day he painted *in fresco* on the quicklime plaster. This technique was only invented long after the alleged date of this would-be thirteenth-century fresco. And there are other unconvincing data: the rectangular format, or the 'cosmatic' (named after the Cosmati family, marble-cutters who decorated churches with mosaics in the thirteen century) frame, which would be very unlikely, with these connotations, in the Florence of Daddi's time. Taking all these factors together, one cannot fail to suspect a fake. And yet a number of experts took this bogus effort for the real thing.

There are some fakes, however, which are produced by such diabolical tricks that they are extremely hard to detect. They are not really fakes, in the full sense of the word, but manipulations or alterations. The most outrageous of all was an altar-piece, and this photograph of it is, in its turn, reproduced from a very old 19-2) photograph – almost a daguerreotype, and certainly taken before 1880 – which is in my personal archives. It is a Madonna and Child enthroned, flanked by two saints. On the right is St Sebastian, and on the left, the Archangel Raphael holding the little Tobias by the hand. At the front of the picture, there is a marble step and on its face we see a relief, with a battle scene and a long inscription which includes the name of the donor (seen on the right at the bottom, in less than half-figure). The picture shows the stylistic characteristics of Perugino, but not of the noble master himself. Perugino was a very exacting teacher and all his assistants and pupils, of both the first and second generations, became masters in their own right, some of them of the very first rank. Andrea d'Assisi and Pinturicchio belong to the first generation, Giannicola di Paolo Manni to the second. All very considerable artists. But here, what we have is a feeble and peripheral kind of *Peruginismo*. Apparently, the painter was a rather insignificant master from Umbria, or more likely the Marches, where this fresco would have been in some remote little church, until, very probably, someone took it away at the time of the suppression, or perhaps during the nineteenth century. At some date which it is now impossible to

19. Anonymous artist in the style of
Perugino. Altar-piece, the Madonna and
Child Enthroned, with St Sebastian and the
Archangel Raphael. Whereabouts
unknown.

20. Manipulation of a detail from the
preceding painting. Formerly in the
Institute of Arts, Detroit, Michigan.

establish, the picture was cut, and the lower part, including the figure of the donor, the classical style bas-relief and the last line of the inscription, which read *'Rafaeli erexit, AD 1506 (or 1507)'* were excised. The preceding line ended with the word *'arcangelo'*. It was, therefore, a dedication to the Archangel Raphael. With skilful use of the scraper, *'erexit'* became *'urbinas pinxit'*, therefore *'Raphael erexit'* became *'Raphael urbinas pinxit'*. The dedication to the Archangel Raphael was thus transformed into the statement: 'Painted by Raphael of Urbino'. The picture is antique. Even the 'signature' is antique, it resists solvents. We cannot, in this case, pronounce it a fake, but it is a fiendishly brilliant manipulation, and we must congratulate whoever was the brains behind it, for it was an inspiration of sheer genius. If it were not for the old photograph, which I found purely by chance, there would only be the stylistic evidence to condemn the picture, and I am certain there would still have been experts and connoisseurs ready to swear it was a Raphael, since everything is genuinely antique: the board, the pigment, the remaining letters. Only the 'signature' is slightly damaged, and the date. The picture was, in fact, taken as genuine, and armed with a considerable number of written statements to that effect. It appeared on the New York market and was bought by an important American museum, the Institute of Arts in Detroit. Only in 1948 was it unmasked and returned to the antique dealer who had sold it. But I am told that the dealer gave the Detroit Museum a Flemish triptych in exchange for it, and that this, too, is a fake. Evidently, it was written in the stars that the whole business was to be a swindle from beginning to end!

So far, we have been looking at the problem of fake paintings, but there are also fake sculptures, in marble and in bronze. When it comes to marble, there is a whole range of counterfeiting that goes on, from the re-working of original pieces (whose eroded surfaces are resculptured) to their 'enrichment' as it is called in the technical jargon (meaning that decorative details are added). Often these additions are carried out with great skill, using pieces of marble of similar grain, so that they are not merely restorations but actual falsifications, thought up and executed with the deliberate intention to swindle someone. With bronzes, it is even more perilous, because it takes a lifetime of experience to tell whether the bronze is antique or not. Throughout the entire world today, the number of people capable of distinguishing a new bronze from an antique can be counted on half the fingers of one hand. There have been endless recastings to produce fakes. Many of the bronzes by famous sculptors were already being imitated in ancient times, and sometimes it is difficult to tell the original from the copy, since it is, if not quite contemporaneous, dating from only a few decades later. And finally, during the nineteenth century, there was a great wave of fakes.

When it comes to medals, I believe it is almost impossible to tell whether they are antique or modern, because they are reproduced by the galvanoplasty technique, which reproduces the model exactly. Furthermore, the material used for making these false medals is not a newly made alloy, but an alloy obtained by melting down antique medals of lesser value. For example, the forgers melt down a badly worn piece by an anonymous artist of the quattrocento to create a Pisanello, and so the identification becomes extremely problematic. This system of using bronze of the correct period is very common nowadays. Forgers take thousands of scrap Roman coins, which are very worn, or broken, and melt them down to obtain bronze of the right period for whatever they want to manufacture.

What makes it even harder to point an accusing finger at many of the false bronzes on the market is the fact that they are often sold together with authentic bronzes. Recently, there has been a considerable clandestine exportation of bronze objects from Asia Minor. During the construction of roads and motorways along the coast of Turkey, they discovered some highly important remains of Roman cities, which had been ruthlessly destroyed. Some splendid bronze objects came out of these ruins, and they were then broken up to make as much money as possible out of them – the head was sold to one museum, an arm to another, and so on. There is one statue, currently divided amongst several American museums, that could be completely reconstructed. And, if they did not meet with this fate, a lot of these found objects were cunningly mixed in with fakes as soon as they came on to the international market. You can well understand, then, how difficult it is to distinguish the true from the false.

Perhaps one day, if tastes change and people become more expert at detecting them, these false pieces will be exposed, even without the aid of chemical means, which, in the case of false bronzes, are not particularly helpful, anyway. Some of the marble objects from these excavations are a real acid test for the expert, but sometimes the way the marble has been fragmented is a give-away. If none of the breaks, or gaps, affect the main parts of the work, it is a fair indication that the breakage has not been caused by the ravages of time, or the vandalism of barbarians, but has been cunningly and deliberately done in such a way as to leave the most valuable parts of the work intact.

I will end this digression into marbles and bronzes by reasserting that it is much more difficult to expose the fake in sculpture than it is in painting, because, in the latter, there are more data to go on, more connotations that, suffering the wear and tear of time and the fluctuations of taste, can give clear indications as to date and provenance.

Now I want to return to some more examples of works in the Walters Gallery in Baltimore, where I myself have worked. This collection, although not well known, provides a fund of problems of every sort. This next painting was not part of the Masserenti collection in Rome – which passed, almost in its entirety, into the Walters collection in 1902 – but was bought on the antique market by the owner, Henry Walters. Many of Walters's antiquarian purchases had already entered into the mythology of the art world by the time of his death, and there they remained until the 1950s and 1960s, when the directors began a systematic and scientific examination of all the material, thanks primarily to an excellent laboratory for restorations. Well, this portrait of a man from the Walters collection was attributed to Francesco Bonsignori, the same Veronese painter from the second half of the quattrocento whose curious Madonna, with the Child Jesus sleeping on a marble slab (the Stone of Unction), we saw in the First Conversation. Naturally, this

21. Modern fake formerly attributed to
Bonsignori, then to Brusasorci. Portrait.
Walters Art Gallery, Baltimore, Maryland.

22. The preceding picture under X-rays.

picture, too, arrived on the market with a large wad of authoritative testimonials from scholars and experts. But, once it was decided to investigate the reasons for its baptism, it soon became apparent that Bonsignori had absolutely nothing to do with it. Why, then, was it unanimously attributed to him? Because it is an unwritten law amongst many experts that every school, in every period, shall provide one name to act as a kind of dustbin for all the rejects. When the *cognoscenti* cannot make up their minds who to attribute a painting to, they pull this name out of the hat, We have, thus: Francesco di Gentile da Fabriano for the school of the Marches in the quattrocento; Bonsignori for the Veronese painters; Ercole Grandi for the Ferrarese painters, and, for the Florentine school, the so-called Master of San Miniato; and so on, sometimes with less well-known names, too.

So, thanks to a number of prestigious endorsements, this picture was labelled as the work of Bonsignori, but, when this name turned out to be unconvincing, it was assigned to another Veronese painter, who is also a refuse-bin for oddities: Domenico Brusasorci. Whenever it happens that a Veronese painting, dating from somewhere between the quattrocento and the cinquecento, turns up, and everyone is baffled by it, it is attributed to either Bonsignori or Brusasorci. But even the attribution to Brusasorci – a collective rather than an individually qualifying name – failed to convince. Before cleaning, the picture was submitted to X-rays, which [22] showed unequivocally that, beneath the present painting, there was another, an antique copy of Paolo Veronese's portrait of the Doge Venier. At least two versions of this portrait exist, one in the museum in Budapest, the other in the Museum of Cleveland. This so-called Brusasorci, or Bonsignori, then, was proved to be a modern fake, painted on an old backing from which the original painting (no doubt already in a ruinous condition) had been partly scraped off. It was simply a hybrid botch-up designed to catch the unwary customer. In a case like this, it is not worth removing the fake to expose the underlying copy of Paolo Veronese, which is in poor condition, anyway. It is better to retain the fake, because it is a very interesting document, an indication of the taste of the time, and it can be shown (as it is nowadays in the depository in Baltimore) to those interested in the study and practice of the techniques of forgery.

During the nineteenth century, many galleries collected self-portraits, in imitation of the famous Galleria Granducale in the Uffizi in Florence. So, when you visit what remains of these old galleries, you often find whole series of illustrious self-portraits. The Masserenti collection, bought by Walters, also had its group of self-portraits, including this one attributed to no less a master than Michelangelo. [23] But, the moment you look at it, your suspicions are aroused. It might possibly be, not a self-portrait, but a portrait of Michelangelo painted in the sixteenth century. Yet, when you touch it, there is something dubious about it. The surface feels smooth, like porcelain. Again, X-rays were taken, and they revealed the remains of a sacred picture, with a candlestick on the right, underneath the portrait you see now. So, the backing is certainly what is left of a cinquecento picture (probably an ugly Madonna and Child of wretched quality and in a half-ruined state), and the

23. Nineteenth-century fake. False
self-portrait of Michelangelo. Walters Art
Gallery, Baltimore, Maryland.

portrait of Michelangelo is a nineteenth-century fake painted on top of it. As soon as the cleaning began, the self-portrait started to melt away, because the pigment, not being antique, had no substance at all, and this was further proof of its being a fake. The cleaning process was instantly halted, because, in spite of not being genuine, the picture has great documentary value and it would be wrong to destroy it simply to retrieve an underlying ruin which, sooner or later, would only be thrown out.

Here is another picture from the Walters Gallery, also attributed to Bonsignori. 24 The feeble quality of the painting immediately opened the door to very grave suspicions. For example, that lace hanging on the shoulder is a miserable piece of work. X-rays revealed that there was nothing underneath it. It had been manufac- 25 tured *ex novo*, and a chemical analysis proved that the paints contained aniline compounds, which were not discovered and put on the market until the end of the nineteenth century. Alas, even this fake, attributed to our 'dustbin', Bonsignori, was supported by very authoritative testimonials. Antique dealers are often accused of fraud, but the chief culprits are, on the one hand, gullible collectors, who swallow the bait all too easily, and, on the other, those experts and critics who, for mercenary ends, are willing to indulge in all sorts of dishonest operations. Naturally, the two 'Bonsignoris' we have been looking at cost Henry Walters a great deal of money.

And that is not the end of the story. The Walters Gallery possessed at least three of these self-styled or would-be Bonsignoris: here is the third. Once more, the 26 reading was unconvincing, and again, X-rays were the determining factor. Under the present picture, they revealed another portrait. The faker had kept the bust of 27 this figure, but scraped off and repainted the whole of the face to produce a new work. Of course, an examination of this type is possible only when the museum, or the collector, is willing to discover the truth. But very often owners jib at the idea of seeing their precious masterpiece exposed. Sometimes, they even do so in a violent manner. This occurs particularly with private collectors, and with museums in the New World, because it is very distressing to see works which have cost enormous sums of money – and at least part of which has often come from public subscrip-tions – shown up as worthless and cast on to the rubbish heap. The unmasking of a fake can also be a very serious stumbling-block in the career of a director or curator, especially if he has recommended and carried through the purchase. This is why it frequently happens that the museum resolutely denies that there is any problem, or any doubt, even when the work is patently absurd and unacceptable at the very first glance.

Naturally, forgers do not always use antique backing for their fabrications. Often, as we have seen, they create them *ex novo*, using various devices. But however cleverly they are done – and sometimes they are wonderfully ingenious – a modern backing will always be a flaw and will always expose the swindle sooner or later. This picture appeared, in about 1910, in the collection of Orusov, the 28 Russian Ambassador in Vienna. It has always been attributed to Neroccio di Bartolomeo, a great Sienese painter of the second half of the quattrocento and, as

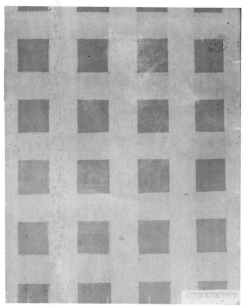

24. Modern fake, formerly attributed to
Bonsignori. Portrait. Walters Art Gallery,
Baltimore, Maryland.
25. The preceding picture under X-rays.
26. Modern fake formerly attributed to
Bonsignori. Portrait. Walters Art Gallery,
Baltimore, Maryland.
27. The preceding picture under X-rays.

such, it has been reproduced in prestigious texts, starting with the *Pitture italiane in America*, by Lionello Venturi. From the Orusov collection, the picture passed into the possession of a great American banker, Philip Lehman, and his son Robert. What is the factor that, in this case, betrays the fake? First of all, from the iconographical point of view, there is a rather bizarre detail: St Sebastian is wearing his hair in two horizontal rows of curls on his forehead, a strange hairstyle that was certainly never seen during the quattrocento. And then there is a technical point, regarding the *craquelure*. As I have already explained, the colour, with the passage of time, forms a network of small cracks because the paint and the wood shrink at different rates. In this case, all the cracks are vertical, and very pronounced. If you take a really good look at it, you will see that the picture is *incamiciato*, that is to say there is a thin lining of linen between the wood and the paint. This practice was fairly common in both the Occident and the Orient, especially in a rather early epoch. The gold, the colour and the gesso of a great many wooden Buddhist sculptures, both Chinese and Japanese, was not applied directly to the wood, but to a cloth which was then glued to the sculpted wood. This technique served to protect the painted part from the damage caused by the movement of the wood.

But in this specific case it can be seen that the *incamiciatura*, which is rather rare for the quattrocento, is false, it has been used solely to create the fake, and the faker proceeded as follows: he took the linen, spread gesso over it, let it dry, then painted over it. When the paint was dry, that is when it no longer stuck to the fingers, he let the linen slip slowly over a flat slab, probably marble, which ended in a right angle. Or, more probably, he pulled the linen downwards, over the edge, to make the paint crack. By repeating this manoeuvre two or three times, he brought the *craquelure* to the desired point. Then he glued the picture to the wooden backing and ironed it, to make it look as though the artificially created cracks were due to the action of time. But, especially if looked at through a magnifying glass, these cracks do not look nautural, you can soon see that they have been cunningly contrived and that what you are looking at is a fake. This technique is often used for fakes which have been totally fabricated, from scratch.

This *craquelure*, essential for the passing-off of a fake Primitive, is sometimes done by crude methods, such as using a pin. If it is, for example, a quattrocento painting on wood, with a gold ground, and there are bald patches right down to the wood, the gesso is applied again and repainted, then, with the aid of a pin, an attempt is made to imitate the antique *craquelure*. But this is rather a poor method and there are much more sophisticated ways of doing it. If the colour has been applied with sodium caseinate, a chemically produced substance, a very odd technique is used. As soon as the picture is painted, it is put into a hot oven, taking care, of course, not to scorch it. It is then taken hot from the oven and put into a very cold atmosphere, usually the deep-freeze. Through repeating this operation hundreds of times, which may take several weeks, the continual abrupt changes of temperature cause a strong traction, so that the wood and the paint surface begin to crack. This can only be done with rather small pictures, since the forger is unlikely to have a freezer available that can take a two-metre-high Madonna – unless, of

28. Fake attributed to Neroccio di
Bartolomeo. Madonna and Child,
Mary Magdalen and St Sebastian.
Philip Lehman collection, New York.

course, he happens to have a butcher's cold-storage room handy. But it is a useful method for the small portraits that are in fashion now. Portraits have always been rare, and those of the quattrocento are extremely rare. And yet you will find an enormous number of false portraits on the market, generally painted with sodium caseinate.

Another point to bear in mind is that the faker, if he is to produce a convincing work, needs an adviser, usually an art historian. But it is hard for the two to agree because, at a certain moment, the faker begins to think he is a genius and so no longer listens to the expert. A lot of fakes give themselves away through iconographical errors that the adviser has tried, in vain, to prevent. The faker is nearly always a coarse and presumptuous man who thinks he knows it all. As for the adviser, it is not always a lust for money that drives him to indulge in this kind of shady activity. He may do it out of a passionate desire to make fools of his colleagues, and to see them covered in ridicule when they fall into the trap.

Here is a striking example of a fake done with great technical skill but full of obvious iconographic mistakes. Years ago, this picture passed through a London auction house and was even reproduced in the catalogue (I do not know whether it was withdrawn later). It was a small panel that appeared to be a fragment from a predella, illustrating a subject that was very widespread in the late fourteenth and throughout the fifteenth century. It is one of the miracles of San Nicola da Myra, a very popular saint who later became known as San Nicola da Bari, when his relics were transferred from Myra, in Asia Minor, to Bari, where they remain today. He is sometimes represented as a bishop and sometimes as an elegant cavalier. The miracle illustrated here concerns three young girls who were so poor that they could not find husbands, so their father decided to set them up in what is commonly called the oldest profession in the world. To save them from this fate worse than death, San Nicola secretly threw three bags of gold, or three balls of solid gold, on to the girls' bed while they were sleeping.

You can see at once that the faker's prime objective has been to imitate the style of Benozzo Gozzoli, a very famous Florentine artist. Gozzoli's work can be seen in the church of San Francesco in Montefalco in Umbria; he also executed a great cycle of frescoes (almost all lost during the Second World War) in the *camposanto* in Pisa. His masterpiece, or at least his most famous work, is the series of frescoes in the Palazzo Medici in Florence. Who is this forger who tried to imitate his style? I do not know, but I consider him to be a real genius because, in this work at any rate, he has shown rare ability from a technical and even a chemical point of view, and I would award him First Class Honours.

Well then, according to the legend – and as you see him in this picture – the saint threw the three bags stuffed with gold, or the three gold balls, through the girls' bedroom window to provide them all with dowries. However, for all his skill, the faker gives himself away by the composition: the reading provokes questions which would not arise with an authentic picture, because when the work is genuine, everything follows, it is logically justified and hangs together.

First, I want to point out some strange features in the architecture. The saint is

29. Fake attributed to Benozzo Gozzoli.
Miracle of San Nicola of Bari. At one time
on the antique market, London.

standing on a ledge that runs all along one side of the building. How odd, though, that the three steps leading up to this ledge are provided with a handrail, whereas there is no support along the rest of the ledge, where the saint is standing and where, obviously, there is a much greater danger of falling off! And how is it that this ledge, quite wide where San Nicola is standing, is too narrow for anybody to walk along on the side facing us? There is no architectonic justification for this.

These are the sort of questions we have to ask ourselves if we are not to be deceived. The forger is very cunning, so cunning, in fact, that he has even inserted a few *pentimenti* into the picture. If you look closely, you will notice that there are some incised lines, later covered over by the painting, as if to witness the fact that the painter, in his careful study of the architectural elements of the composition, made a series of changes. All the more reason to suspect the incongruous features already pointed out.

There are a lot more errors, different in nature, but nonetheless glaring. The room where the miracle is taking place, in the home of poverty-stricken people, is adorned with beautiful marble pilasters, hardly in keeping with the rest of the building. Furthermore – and here we come to some really gross errors – the bedcover on the girls' bed is of a design you are most unlikely to find in a quattrocento painting. Another mistake, perhaps not so obvious but just as important, is in the position of the saint and, particularly, the direction of his gaze. In my opinion, he would not have been able to see into the bedroom from where he is standing. He should have been further to the left. But the most serious mistake of all is still the balustrade, missing just where it is most needed, and made, moreover, of a type of wrought iron that did not exist in the fifteenth century.

All things considered, I am convinced this is a very recent fake, the work of a forger who is probably still active, and who may have to his credit a considerable number of pieces which, to this day, have not been exposed. We have before us, then, a most remarkable personality. In fact, when the picture appeared in London, it was only after lengthy consultations and debates amongst various experts that it was accepted as a modern imitation, and, even then, not because of any stylistic inconsistencies, but on the basis of the compositional features we have discussed, elements which had been carefully picked out from individual clues in the work of Benozzo Gozzoli.

Certain fakes, then, seem to incarnate Benedetto Croce's maxim that all history is contemporary history.

This profile of a woman first appeared on the American market in the 1920s and 1930s; it then came to Italy and is still going on its imperturbable way. It is an attempt to imitate the style of Antonio del Pollaiuolo, and his 'dynamic line', which is the outline that, as it unfolds, reveals the internal bone structure of the figure. (Here, specifically, the prominent clavicle.) There is something about this picture that immediately announces its date of birth as the 1920s, because whoever painted it has certainly seen portraits by Amedeo Modigliani. There is a whiff of Modigliani, especially in the distorted proportions of the neck, and you can at once relate this to the swan neck in Modigliani's portrait of Lunia Czechowska, although here it is so elongated as to seem more like the neck of a goose. If, then, you look at the picture from the bottom up, its absurdity becomes even more apparent, and, if you look carefully at the colours, the blue of the background becomes just as absurd, it is turgid, oddly gelatinous, almost like curdled milk.

Sometimes, fakes are fascinating because the forger introduces into his work reflections of the literature of his own time, creating, as it were, a kind of literary episode which attracts his contemporaries by virtue of its narrative content.

31   Here is a very curious panel which was bought many years ago by the National Gallery in London. It shows three figures in profile: a kind of matron and two children looking out of an open window. The expression on the face of this Herculean female immediately gives you a sense of impending doom. You know that something frightful is about to happen. The woman's gaze, in contrast to the innocent looks of the children, is directed upwards, as if she were invoking divine aid. All three figures are wearing fifteenth-century costume. The window is made of *tondini*, those round pieces of glass, and, from the costumes, one even suspects that there is some heraldic reference here. The woman and the two children evoke the sense of some imminent tragedy, dark and terrible, and one's thoughts instantly fly to the world of Cesare Borgia and the two Malatestas, Sigismondo and Pandolfo, a world of crime, massacres, incest, and violence amongst members of the same family. You feel that these people are locked up in a tower which is their prison, that they are destined for some terrible sacrifice at the hands of a tyrant. The picture combines those dramatic and literary elements which romantic writers – particularly Anglo-Saxon novelists – associate with the Renaissance, and especially the quattrocento: dark passions, ruthless plots, sinister political manoeuvres. This mood is reinforced by every minute detail in the picture. Notice, for example, the landscape, which can be glimpsed through the window: it is a turreted and battlemented castle, which is vaguely reminiscent of the stronghold of the Malatesta in Rimini. And the final touch, as if to emphasise its mysterious origins, is that illegible crest, or seal, high up on the wall. Obviously it is a false one, possibly obtained from an original matrix, but painted in such a way that you cannot decipher it. The whole work is typical of the species of fake that is born under the influence of literature.

Now, once you have waded through the wave of novelettish romanticism brimming over from the painting, and cast aside the gloomy mood that makes you think of families butchering one another and coming to a sticky end, you have to ask yourself what school a picture of this kind could belong to. But there is no answer. The profile, it is true, exists in the fifteenth century, and so does the double profile – the one by Filippo Lippi in the Metropolitan Museum in New York, for instance. There is also a profile of the patroness and her two sons in an altar-piece. But these portraits never show the psychological content, the anxiety and gloom that you read in this picture. The impossibility of placing it in any locality, and this psychological anomaly, prove it to be a forgery, and this is confirmed by a technical examination. This fake has charmed a great many people and, as in other cases, it was precisely those elements that arouse our suspicions that enchanted the

30. Fake attributed to Antonio del
Pollaiuolo. Profile of a Lady.
Whereabouts unknown.

31. Nineteenth-century imitation of
Renaissance-style painter. Three figures in
profile at a window. National Gallery,
London.

purchasers who bought the painting on behalf of the National Gallery. For some time now, the picture has been recognised as an imitation, and nobody, nowadays, would dream of taking it seriously. But fakes of this kind are very interesting because they tell us, in a unique way, how certain cultural movements misread, and misunderstand, cultures of the past.

It would be useful now to examine a sort of composite fake, a small *tondo* [32] painted on wood. It came up at a London auction years ago, and is well known amongst those interested in the Italian quattrocento. This Annunciation is attributed to Nicolò di Liberatore, known as Nicolò Alunno, a painter from Foligno who lived in the second half of the fifteenth century. He was gifted with a most unusual technique which, at times, actually brings to mind nineteenth-century fakes. Alunno is noted for that false, superficial naturalism that dominated some areas of Umbrian painting after the Florentine Benozzo Gozzoli had passed that way, and which has nothing in common with either the Florentine or the Sienese schools. A preliminary examination is enough to start one asking questions, beginning with that incredible throne the Virgin is sitting on, which is of a totally anachronistic shape, not to mention those sharp points that make it positively dangerous; as an architectonic structure, it has nothing whatever to do with the overall style. Obviously, the throne was taken from an older model, and it is not difficult to find: it appears in the background, on the left, in a little panel that, until [33] her death a few years ago, belonged to a great lady, Christabel, Lady Aberconway, who was the companion of Samuel Courtauld, the founder of the Courtauld Institute. Lady Aberconway's picture was reproduced for the first time in the ninth volume of the famous history of Italian art, *The Development of Italian Painting*, by Raimond Van Marle, a great Dutch art historian, which came out in about 1930–1. We have, therefore, a *post quem* date for the execution of the fake, because Lady Aberconway's picture was virtually unknown before then. It was painted by an extraordinary Florentine painter, who precedes Nicolò Alunno by fifty years, and whose historical name unfortunately eludes us, in spite of all the research that has been done. So, according to the convention, he is known as the Master of the Judgement of Paris in the Bargello, because his best-known work is a *desco da parto* (one of those post-natal trays) illustrating this scene, and it is kept in the Palazzo del Bargello, one of the museums in Florence. He is an enchanting painter, very delicate, and with radiant colours. Note how, in the model the faker copied, the throne is in figurative harmony with the rest of the picture, there is no discrepancy. The hand of the anonymous master can be recognised even from the *punzonatura*, the gilded pattern of the haloes, and from the very distinctive outline. These are not the work of a gold-beater, the painter himself certainly applied the decorations. So, we know the prototype from which the throne in the roundel attributed to Nicolò Alunno derives, and we know the date when a reproduction of it was first published.

The main part, with the figures, is lifted wholesale from another picture by Nicolò Alunno, a large and equally well-known painting which is in the Pinacoteca [34] in Bologna and was donated by Pope Pius IX. The faker has suppressed the

32. Fake attributed to Nicolò Alunno.
Annunciation. Formerly in private
collection, London.

33. Master of the Judgement
of Paris in the Bargello.
Madonna Enthroned.
Formerly in the collection
of Lady Aberconway, London.

34. Nicolò Alunno.
Annunciation.
Pinacoteca, Bologna.

background architecture, but he has taken the two figures and seated the Virgin on that weird contraption of a throne which, while justifiable in a fantastic, unrealistic picture in late-Gothic style, like the work by the Master of the Judgement of Paris in the Bargello, is utterly absurd and out of place in the context of the fake composition, where the two main figures are painted with almost caricatural naturalism. And yet this appalling fake, with all the evidence against it – the known sources, the *post quem* date of execution – remains in circulation, armed, naturally, with expert opinions that endorse it as genuine.

Now let us move on to the story of an extremely prolific forger whose works turn up practically every year. Unfortunately, we do not know his name, but he must have been active in Tuscany (Florence and Siena) between 1900 and 1930. This man faked not only paintings, which were always done on fragments of plaster, but also a quantity of absolutely crazy Renaissance-type furniture: credenzas, chairs, coffers and even clothes-stands. All these pieces of furniture have painted inserts in the Renaissance style, either fifteenth-century portraits or allegories with reclining women, which are symbolic figures of the Tuscan school. The fake frescoes are always presented in the form of plaster fragments, to make them look like the remains of important cycles that have been demolished by vandals, or through lack of care. Generally, these fragments have broken, uneven edges and cracks, as if they had been broken and stuck together again. Usually, there are just one or two figures on them but there are some compositions with three or more. The style this faker works in is somewhat anonymous, it contains elements from fifteenth-century central Italy, but nothing specific enough to tell one the exact location. At first sight, these fragments might be Umbrian, but then you discover features from Siena, or even Florence, and these merge into the style of Latium – in other words, a kind of stylistic limbo. Perhaps unwittingly, they reflect certain fashions belonging to the period in which they were painted.

Here is one of these fakes. As you see, the hairstyles are scarcely believable for people of the quattrocento, and whoever painted the object (I will call it an object, rather than a picture or a fresco) had evidently seen films and photographs of certain actresses of the 1920s, the period to which this fake certainly belongs. 35

Sometimes, it is the incident depicted that attracts us and arouses our curiosity. Look at this composition with four heads. On the right, in profile, there is a strange 36 woman holding a scroll with the words *'concordia familiare'* (family harmony) on it. On the other side, we have a trio: him, her and the Other Man. Who is this Other Man, the young one with the dreamy, slightly dazed look? Who is the woman with the scroll? The words seem like a warning, an admonition. Is she a sibyl, then? Or is she one of those *beate*, those virtuous women who were to be found in Tuscany in the fourteenth and fifteenth centuries? She could be Aldobrandesca Ponzia of Siena, or a new Viridiana of Castelfiorentino. It is this literary, romantic character, this story-telling that makes the fake appealing and titillates our curiosity.

Now let us look at what I consider to be one of the most complicated fakes, where the literary, romantic element is entwined with an inextricable tangle of plagiarised data. Here, too, the fake appears to be a fragment saved from a destroyed

35. The 'plaster faker'. Fragment of fresco.
National Gallery, Dublin.

36. The 'plaster faker'. Composition with four figures. National Gallery, Dublin.

37. The 'plaster faker'. Composition with five figures. National Gallery, Dublin.

37   fresco. It shows a group of four people, a man and three women, who are just
passing another man. Obviously, there is a story here: the first woman from the left
seems to be trembling, tormented, one senses that she is agitated because she has
just met the man she is infatuated with, the man on the left with all that hair. Her
woman-friend is in on the secret, she looks at her with some anxiety, and it seems
that the matter must also be known to the man who is escorting them. Observe the
bizarre, literary nature of these people: the guilty woman, the one who is trembling, looks strange, her features are emaciated, as if she were being devoured by
some inner torment, and her body is completely flat, she has no breasts.

Now, to be specific about the sources of this fake: the head of the distressed
woman comes from the masterpiece of a great Sienese painter of the quattrocento,
Matteo di Giovanni, from his Madonna, which is in Percena near Buonconvento.
But the headdress with the twisted ribbon fluttering in the breeze, which adorns
this head of Sienese origin, is derived from a picture by the Florentine, Filippino
Lippi, his *Allegory of Music* in the Berlin Museum. These contrasts, the impossible
combination of Siena and Florence, of Matteo di Giovanni and Filippino Lippi,
would already be enough to demonstrate the inconsistency of the fragment and
condemn it as bogus. But still more serious is the fact that the long-haired man,
the seducer on the left, is taken from Carpaccio. The figures in the background
are rather crude imitations of background figures seen in several paintings by
Carpaccio and Gentile Bellini. So, it is a real patchwork. And this painter has
produced a number of similar patchworks. We have works from his hand that show
wedding processions, tournaments, cavalcades, lessons, and many others.

As I said, there are unfortunately no indications as to his name or the exact place
where he worked. I suspect he may have been active in Florence, but I have no
proof. What is so interesting is to see how his pictures abound with literary
elements, and how obvious, even flagrant, is their derivation from themes that
were fashionable when the fakes were produced. On the one hand, these *femmes
fatales*, destined to sin, to suffer and to arouse grand passions, are reminiscent of
D'Annunzio; and on the other, the physical type in the fragment we have just seen
(which belongs to the National Gallery of Ireland, in Dublin), this thin woman,
devoid of secondary sexual attributes, is like the type of woman who came into
fashion the moment Greta Garbo appeared on the screen. It would be a great
mistake to think that, when identifying a fake, aspects and pointers of this kind can
be ignored. A fake reflects its own period, and the faker working today is inevitably
influenced by comics, illustrated magazines, television and cinema. This is
because every facet of culture becomes involved in a gigantic story, which is one
and only one, an all-embracing whole, and of which the history of art, whether of
real or faked pictures, is no more than a single aspect. In any event, I studied this
faker and published my findings, calling him provisionally the 'plaster faker', from
the material on which his works are painted. Quite possibly, the whole story will
come to light one of these days, and it will certainly be intriguing.

You should never dismiss these links with the cinema and with literature, even
of the lowest and most popular kind, but this is what some art historians do; locked

up in their ivory towers, they refuse to look at comics, or to read novels and detective stories. Everything is grist to the mill, everything is present in the taste and in the style of a particular period. There is nothing that will not help to cast some light on an epoch. And you must never fall into the trap of going into the history of art in search of 'supreme beauty', a term which is utterly meaningless.

Sometimes the faker betrays himself by utilising elements of naturalism that are entirely alien to the period he is trying to imitate. Here is another fragment from the 'plaster faker'. It illustrates a lesson in a university: you can even read the words *'Universitas Studiorum'*. Here too there is a glaring inconsistency of style. There are faces of Umbrian-Sienese type next to a profile that is patently of Ferrarese origin. But the biggest give-away is the gesture of the man who is stroking his lips with a quill pen as he listens to the lecture. Such a gesture is unheard of in a picture from the quattrocento, a century that abounded in symbolic elements and also in data taken from everyday life, but never so naturalistically as to portray a man stroking his lips with a quill. This is obviously derived from the naturalism of the late nineteenth century.

Finally, there is an axiom which expresses the classical mentality, which lasted into the Middle Ages, the Renaissance, and right up till the end of the eighteenth century: every story has a beginning, a middle and an end. There is no such thing as a fragment *per se.* In Greek civilisation, as in the Renaissance, you will never find a statue that does not tell a complete story, or have a complete significance, within itself. A picture like the famous *La derelitta*, the forsaken woman, in the Galleria Pallavicini in Rome, attributed to Botticelli, could not have been given that title in the quattrocento. *La derelitta* is only an episode from the life of Esther: it is, in fact, Mordecai, and not a woman at all, who is weeping outside the door. Titles like 'The Forsaken Woman', and so on, were invented and applied in the Romantic and Post-Romantic eras. In other words, in classical art, there is no generic subject that does not have a precise and particular reference. For example, if a sculpture is labelled 'Statue of a Drunken Woman', it means that what *we* see as the statue of a drunken woman must have been integrated with some other figurative feature that explained the story of the drunken woman, and the whole thing must have referred to some specific episode in the Bible, in mythology or in history.

In the seventeenth century, you can find subjects of this sort, but they are always complete stories: the peasant and his wife weeping beside their dead ass, or the beggar knocking at someone's door and being turned away in a brutal manner. In the nineteenth century and the beginning of the twentieth, people did not understand this compositional principle and so gave works of art totally inappropriate titles, almost as if they had originated as fragments – which is impossible. Remember, also, that up until the end of the eighteenth century, not only was the fragment unknown, but there was no such thing as the intrusion of a naturalistic detail like this one of the man who is stroking his lips with a quill pen.

Finally, let us look at a last example of our 'plaster faker'. This is a strange imitation of a fresco, but it is not even in the Italian style, it is probably German, that is, in the manner of Hans Holbein. Here again, a lecture is in progress, with the

38. The 'plaster faker'. University Lesson. At one time on the antique market in Rome.

39. The 'plaster faker'. Lecture by a Learned Man. At one time on the antique market in Rome.

learned man in the centre. You can see how all the features of the composition show signs of being influenced by sophisticated photography and even the cinema. As before, there is a naturalistic element: the half-open window to let the air in (it seems to be summer time, the atmosphere is suffocating, so it is good to have a little air circulating); and here again we have a man stroking his lips with a quill. These repetitions, in the end, betray the vacuity of the images. The décor of the lecture room is clearly influenced by drawing rooms of the late-Victorian era, cluttered with ornamentation even on the walls. Inevitably, although unconsciously, the faker tends to insert features of his own experience into his work since he is unable to draw on the past, because, let me repeat, the past is dead, and the totality of a piece of music, a picture or a literary work, with all its multitudinous meanings and connotations, is lost to us. At most, we can penetrate the superficial layers of the past, but we can never comprehend in full what the works represented to their contemporaries.

In conclusion, I would like to say a word about the way in which fakes are made to look respectable and authentic. Very often, as we have already seen, a fake is artfully placed amongst the genuine antiquities in a villa, an old *palazzo*, or a church. There is, then, a logistic factor which contributes to the deception of the predestined victim and disarms his critical faculties.

The same technique is often adopted by dishonest dealers, who will insert extraneous objects amongst genuine pieces in an auction. Even great scholars have sometimes fallen into the trap, simply because the fake was cunningly placed in an appropriately noble setting. For example, if an allegedly antique sculpture was shown to them, surrounded by superb paintings and objects of great value, by highly respectable, and perhaps very rich people, whom nobody would suspect of being accomplices in a swindle. Furthermore, there has never been a systematic study of fakes. Only now are we beginning to identify the various groups, to study them and pin them down to particular locations.

When all is said and done, there remain fakers who are very difficult to decipher. There is one, known as the 'pathetic faker', who was working in a very late period (around 1840–60). Pictures from his hand are coming to light now, painted in Flemish, German and Italian styles. This extremely interesting personality produced not only some pseudo-German works which were often taken as genuine and hung in great museums, but also pictures that make one think he must have spent time in Florence and made a long study of the Florentine quattrocento. He is a very sad, very lugubrious painter, his pictures are always funereal. But he is fascinating, because here was a man who even knew the secrets of antique painting on wood, and his technique was excellent. The only things that betray him are the figurative inconsistencies.

Fifth Conversation

In this last Conversation, we are going to examine paintings and sculptures that demonstrate a theme of the utmost importance: the impossibility of applying the same criteria to the reading of works of art from different periods and cultures. Works that have sprung from diverse social and ideological climates, and been executed in different techniques, cannot be read according to a single criterion without leading to serious distortions that invalidate the interpretation and lead us up blind alleys.

1   Let us begin with this view of the Trinità dei Monti in Rome, by the nineteenth-century French painter, Corot. Often in the case of Corot, and with some Impressionist painters, our judgement has to be based on the purely formal attributes, because the very considerable lyrical content is entirely immersed in them. Obviously, this does not apply to all nineteenth-century French painting; countless works of art were produced during the last century which contain elements of a rich cultural background, layers of meaning and even precise symbolism. But it would be no use trying to read this Corot with the same tools that are indispensable for analysing pictures crowded with symbolic, literary or other references, like the works of Gustave Moreau or Odilon Redon. Naturally, with these latter painters, it is also necessary to read the form, but in their case it would be a means of arriving at the less overt contents, the ulterior messages.

Equally, it would be a mistake to apply the purely formal criterion, necessary to the reading of Corot, to earlier works containing elements and messages that, up to the present time, we have been unable to interpret. We must not assume that, because we cannot read them, those messages are not there, or can be ignored. Sometimes, it takes time for the messages to become comprehensible again. Claude-Joseph, the eldest of the three Vernets, is a case in point. This French painter worked first of all on the coast of Provence, especially in Marseilles, and then in Italy, where he painted innumerable canvases, mostly of marine subjects. Thanks to engraved reproductions, his work quickly became popular. Claude-Joseph Vernet was active during the second half of the eighteenth century, but it is only today that we have come to realise there is more to his pictures than a simple description of the landscape, or the seascape. In fact, they contain a series of other elements that cannot possibly be understood without reference to certain Enlightenment theories (propounded, in particular, by Montesquieu). According to these ideas, the climate and the aspect of the sky and the landscape explain the character of the individual nations. There may even be a grain of truth in this theory, but it should be taken with a large pinch of salt, if only because it ignores a vast quantity of historical, religious, political and economic data which must be taken into account when studying the individual characteristics of a nation, given (but not conceded) that these characteristics actually exist. Be that as it may,

Vernet's pictures contain a brilliantly accurate description of the Italian sky and, particularly, the type of clouds seen in Italy, viewed in the light of these theories.

A similar phenomenon can be seen in the work of Valenciennes, a little known and rather rare artist of the same period, who limits himself to painting the roofs of Rome in the lower part of his pictures and the clouds above, captured as he saw them at the various hours of the day and in the various seasons. 2

In Vernet's work, the extremely elaborate description of the coast is often accompanied by precise climatic and meteorological observations. Frequently there are scenes of storms, with the sea beating on the rocky coasts of southern Italy or on the Ligurian Riviera (sometimes, there are glimpses of some architectural monument that place them at a specific point on the Italian coast). But this insistence on tempest, shipwreck and the like cannot be explained without relating it to the claim that they represent aspects of the alleged character of the Italians, who are presumed to be impetuous, passionate and tempestuous. 3

Vernet's pictures, which display very complex formal qualities, were much admired by his contemporaries and, thanks to the skills of excellent engravers, all his major compositions were distributed throughout Europe. For a time, his paintings enjoyed an enormous success, especially in England, where buyers outbid one another at very high prices. But then they suffered the fate that awaits most artistic creations: once the attraction of novelty had worn off, and they had not yet acquired the cultural aura of antique works, they became simply 'old pictures', and therefore negligible. So, Vernet's paintings were taken down from the walls of museums and stacked in the vaults, where they were often left to rot in disastrous conditions, with the result that, when the time came for them to be re-examined and re-evaluated in their proper historical perspective, many of them had, to all practical intents, vanished. Unfortunately, this is the norm rather than an exception.

As I mentioned in an earlier conversation, our own generation has seen and taken part in a similar phenomenon, with the 'Liberty style' under its various denominations – *'floreale'* in Italy, 'art nouveau' in France and England, *'Jugendstil'* in Germany. It was not until the 1960s that art nouveau came to be appreciated again, and by that time many of the most important examples had already been destroyed, all over Europe. The frantic demand for art nouveau objects therefore far exceeded the supply. Yet it was only very recently, in the 1950s, that artefacts from that period came to be systematically destroyed. Some extremely important monuments in Rome, such as the Villino Grassi and the interior of the Villa Ximenes were demolished. And in Paris, during the same years, a whole lot of very beautiful stained glass, some of it influenced by Japanese art, was ruthlessly destroyed. I remember one glorious example in the Rue de Dunai, which reminded me of some of Hokusai's prints. At that time, art nouveau was considered to be a debased style, the lowest of the low.

Today, things have gone to the opposite extreme, to the point where the entrances to the Métro, the Paris underground, which were made of cast iron or varnished wrought iron in extremely intricate patterns, are being fought over by

1. Jean-Baptiste-Camille Corot. View of the
Trinità dei Monti, Rome. Musée d'art et
d'histoire, Geneva.

2. Pierre-Henri de Valenciennes. Study of
the Sky over the Quirinal. The Louvre,
Paris.

3. Claude-Joseph Vernet. The Shipwreck.
Musée d'art et d'histoire, Geneva.

American museums, whereas, at one time, they were despised and were even taken down so as not to outrage the good taste of the Parisians. The same thing has happened with art déco.

What is art déco? It is the style that flourished in Europe and America at the end of the 1920s, following the great *Exposition des Arts Décoratifs* held in Paris in 1925. Personally, I doubt whether art déco is a true and proper style, with autonomous characteristics, it seems to me more like the final phase of art nouveau, modified by the influence of the avant-garde – Cubist painting, the Russian ballet, and an awareness of exotic art, especially Negro art, and Mexican architecture, as well as innumerable influences from other sources. As far as Mexico is concerned, the 'Mexican' novels of D. H. Lawrence contributed to the definition of art déco, as the success of ballets like the famous *Le Train Bleu* did elsewhere. Certain artists and dancers (Vaslav Nijinsky and his sister, Bronislava, for instance) made a decisive contribution by bringing their individual experience of form to the enrichment and modification of the style of art nouveau.

Art déco eventually merged into that curious stylistic phenomenon, the neo-classicism of the 1930s, the full range and substance of which have not yet been sufficiently studied. This is partly because many of its most important monuments were built during the regimes of the dictators, and so we still tend to see them surrounded with the unpleasant connotations that this implies. But if you look at the Città Universitaria in Rome, planned by Marcello Piacentini, the Rockefeller Center in New York, the Théâtre des Champs-Elysées in Paris, and even the Lenin Library in Moscow, you realise that they have the same roots, like many objects in everyday use: some of the Ginori porcelain, for example, made to designs by Giò Ponti, is very similar to the '*farfor*', the Soviet porcelain made in the same years in the great ex-Imperial factories situated near the old St Petersburg, which has twice changed its name meanwhile, first to be 'russified' as Petrograd, then to be 'sovietised' as Leningrad.

In fact, art nouveau, art déco and the neo-classicism of the 1930s are international styles; they spread very rapidly through the Western world, as well as in South America and, more recently and up until at least 1940, the Soviet Union. They are styles which speak a common cultural language, and have a common linguistic structure.

The West has known several others. One of the oldest is the one we call International Gothic (but it is not the first, I believe there are others, even in the heart of the Middle Ages, though, as yet, they are difficult to individuate). The works belonging to this style, which flourished between the end of the fourteenth century and the first half of the fifteenth century, are absolutely interchangeable whether they come from Italy, France, Germany, Spain or sometimes even England.

Towards the end of the sixteenth century, International Mannerism presents an analogous case: its manifestations throughout the whole of Europe are so uniform that it is often very difficult to tell whether a painting was done in Utrecht or Prague, in Florence or Fontainebleau. The same is true of Rococo, which spread through Europe like wildfire at the end of the eighteenth century. Here again, the porcelain and the furniture can easily be confused: there are Rococo objects from Genoa and Bavaria which are almost impossible to tell apart, and some of the Neapolitan products could be mistaken for English or French.

The neo-classical is another international style, which appears in various editions. When looking at a neo-classical architectural drawing, it is very hard indeed to say whether it is Russian or Neapolitan, Spanish or French. Our own century has seen several of these international styles, the latest, still breathing although moribund, being that curious revival of art nouveau which began in the United States around the middle of the 1960s and, thanks to the work of certain designers, spread rapidly, especially from New York. The interior decoration of some restaurants, and the exterior designs on some buses – the work of Peter Max – stimulated some very remarkable works in Italy, South America, Canada and even in certain parts of Asia, such as Hong Kong and Tokyo.

It is not easy to define the historical, cultural and social significance of these movements. But before I develop the argument, I would like to revert to the theme which opened our conversation. I want to show you a painting by Edouard Manet, which is in the National Gallery in London, and a landscape by Claude Monet, which is in the Metropolitan Museum in New York. In the picture by Manet, there are no symbolic connotations and no hidden meanings. The same is true of Monet's picture, where there is a total immersion in nature, which excludes any kind of metaphysical reference.

Reading pictures of this type in the usual way, that is, in purely formal terms, and then applying the same criteria to a medieval enamel or a Byzantine ivory is, let me repeat, a very grave error which deprives the latter works of all their implicit meanings. Critics of the so-called school of 'pure visibility', the formalists, fall into this error and see nothing but the form; they even boast of being utterly uninterested in the iconographical and iconological contents, in other words, the subject matter of the work.

This method of reading a work of art solely on the basis of the style is perfectly in key with the concept of dividing art into hierarchies, into major and minor arts. If you read a critical essay by an art historian, or perhaps a scholar, who bases his judgements purely on the formal attributes, you can be quite sure he has no idea of the artistic value of a piece of furniture (whereas a chair can, in fact, be an exquisite work of art), nor of the value and significance of a coin. He undoubtedly despises the so-called 'applied arts' as inferior.

Failure to appreciate the value of the applied arts cuts you off from the artistic output of entire periods, because, as we have seen, there are cultures which expressed themselves solely through the applied arts.

Here is another extraordinary picture from the National Gallery in London. It is by Edgar Degas and shows the interior of a circus. You can see clearly that this is a picture that must be read purely through its formal qualities. First of all, observe how a painting of this kind could not have been imagined before the advent of photography. Incidentally, when photography was born, most people thought it

4. Edouard Manet. Concert in the Tuileries
Gardens. National Gallery, London.

5. Claude Monet. Landscape. Metropolitan
Museum, New York.

6. Edgar Degas. Interior of a Circus.
National Gallery, London.

would be the death of painting, but, on the contrary, for a large part of the nineteenth century, the rapport between painting and sculpture, on the one hand, and photography on the other, was very intense and fruitful. I believe that, nowadays, the same sort of rapport exists between painting and the cinema. In this picture, you can see how closely the brush is related to the lens of a camera, and the hand that holds the brush to the finger that clicks the shutter after choosing the 'frame'. Think of the close relationship between photography and painting that has been established in our day by Hyper-Realism, a movement that is still flourishing, and how impossible it would be to understand it if you did not study its relationship to films in colour. And the latter, in their turn, are slowly absorbing the influence of Hyper-Realism. The point is, the two phenomena should be studied in parallel.

Obviously, and I must repeat this, there exist works of art that have entirely different connotations and must therefore be read in entirely different ways. As an example, look at this picture from the Musée d'Art et d'Histoire in Geneva, which illustrates a pathetic theme: *The Visit to the Prisoner*. It is by the French-Swiss painter, Alfred van Muyden. Now, a work of this kind cannot be understood unless you place it in the context of the particular political and ideological climate in which it was created. In the picture, you see a woman in the peasant costume of southern Italy, probably from Ciociaria or the Roman Campagna, who is visiting her husband in gaol and holding up their baby son for him to see. At first, it may seem to be nothing but a sentimental, almost caricatural depiction of a touching episode. But, if you relate it to the period and the cultural atmosphere that it belongs to, its significance will appear much less banal.

As everyone knows, the Congress of Vienna, in 1815, re-established the pre-revolutionary frontiers and put the monarchs who had been deposed by the revolutionary armies, and then by Napoleon, back on their thrones. In the early days of the Restoration, there is no clear-cut cultural picture. The reign of Louis XVIII of France, from 1815 to 1824, has no very distinctive character. All we have is a series of pictures that present Louis XVIII's elder brother, Louis XVI, who ended up on the guillotine at the time of the Terror, in a heroic light, or mythologise him as a gentle, charitable man, participating in the sufferings of the people. It is interesting to note that this mythologising of Louis XVI never includes his wife, Marie Antoinette, the Austrian. She was still considered to be responsible for the catastrophe that had befallen the Bourbon family, so there are no pictures of that period in which Marie Antoinette appears in a sweet, noble, mythological light, or in a populist perspective. So much for the first phase of the Restoration.

In the second phase, especially during the reign of Charles X, which ended, as you know, with the Revolution of 1830, we see a double process of mythologisation going on in the vast area that includes France, Belgium, French-Switzerland and sometimes even northern Italy and Tuscany. On the one hand, we have the style nowadays known as Troubadour style, which depicts the Middle Ages in a mythical and heroic light; on the other, an emphasis on the life of the people, but in a totally artificial and distorted way.

Why the Middle Ages? Because the Middle Ages were presented as a profoundly religious, homogenously Catholic era, an era without doubts, which we know to be very far from the reality. If ever there was an epoch tormented by doubts, it was the Medieval. During the reign of Charles X, however, it was portrayed from the viewpoint of the reinstated sovereigns and the old aristocracy whose possessions had been restored; it was shown as an epoch of rigid institutional structure and, above all, a time of social happiness, without revolutions and political disturbances. In these Troubadour-style pictures, the Middle Ages appear not only as a period of intense religious piety, but also as a time of noble feasting, hunting and tournaments, festivities which the people, when they appear in the background, seem content to watch without protest, whereas, we are well aware that the Middle Ages were a time of terrors and social tensions. You have only to think of the terrifying events concerning the Paterines in Milan and the whole of Lombardy (the Paterines were a heretical sect, but the heresies of the Middle Ages always had a social basis) or of the riot of the Ciompi in Florence, in 1378, a riot staged by underpaid weavers, which today we would define as a revolt of the urban proletariat.

The Troubadour style mythologised the Middle Ages through the ideology of the European Restoration, and also presented them as a period of profound religious mysticism, of faith amongst the people. But we know nowadays that the Medieval period was a real hotbed of heresies, of personal interpretations of the Holy Scriptures that were generally totally unacceptable to the ecclesiastical authorities. And we know that often these heretical focal points inflamed whole nations. But all this is ignored in Troubadour art, which presents the Middle Ages as a period of serene mysticism.

Another country that was mythologised, because it had been spared the Revolution, was Spain. And it is interesting to note that it was in precisely those years that western Europe discovered Spanish painting. It may seem impossible to us now, but the great works of Spanish art had remained quite unknown in Italy, France, England and Germany until around the year 1830. Certainly, one or two works were known: the portrait of Innocent X, for example, painted by Velásquez during his second stay in Rome; this splendid portrait, still in the Gallery of Casa Dora Pamphili in Rome, was well known, but it was ignored, partly because it was alien to the local tradition, partly because of the fierce envy the Roman artists felt when faced with a work of such genius.

This ignorance of the art of Velásquez, Murillo and Zurburán was matched by a widespread ignorance of Spanish literature. In Europe, up until 1830, there is no appreciable echo of the great Spanish texts, of Celestina or Lazarillo de Tormes, of Don Quixote or the sonnets of Góngora. All these were unknown until, around 1830, Europe suddenly discovered them, mostly through France. How did it happen?

During the Napoleonic campaign in Spain, and their ephemeral occupation of the Iberian Peninsula, the French had stolen a large number of paintings both from the churches (Saragoza, for instance) and from private collections in Madrid and

7. Alfred van Muyden. The Visit to the
Prisoner. Musée d'art et d'histoire, Geneva.

8. Giovanni Lanfranco. The Arrival of
the Explorers from the Promised Land.
J. Paul Getty Museum, Malibu, California.

other cities. Wherever it was possible to trace them, the Spanish made positively violent demands for their return, even as early as the occupation of Paris in 1814. Nevertheless, a vast number of paintings remained in France and, soon after 1830, were hung in Louis Philippe's so-called Spanish Gallery, and in the very important collection of Maréchal Soult, from which come a great many of the masterpieces of Spanish art now dispersed throughout the world.

The translation of the great Spanish literary works began contemporaneously with this revelation of Spanish art, which was mostly of seventeenth-century painting. Oddly enough, it was in these same years that England sent Protestant missionaries to Spain, who reported back to Great Britain news of the collections and of Spanish art in general; moreover, it was in these same years that the Scotsman, William Stirling, set his hand to what is still, to my mind, the fundamental work on Spanish painting: the three volumes of the *Annals of the Artists of Spain*, published in 1848.

Italy was a different case. In the second phase of the Restoration, Italy was portrayed as the country of good, serene people, religious folk who were happy in their work and went to the holy sanctuaries smiling and singing. It was supposed to be a land without social contrasts, where there was perfect harmony between the clergy and the poor, between the nobles and the labouring classes. And the picture in the Geneva museum adopts these very themes with the intention of touching the heart and arousing feelings of tenderness in the observer. First and foremost, it exploits what we today would call the *kitsch* of childhood: children are always touching, they are innocent little souls, therefore to present them in a dramatic situation is bound to stir the emotions. Much the same applies to the mother: she is presented here, in her national dress, as the good little peasant woman showing the baby to her imprisoned husband. I hope I have made it clear, then, that this picture does not rely on its technical or formal qualities, so much as on its literary content, from which one could draft a short story, or even a novel.

During this period, and especially in France, there were countless pictures of this genre which completely travestied Italy. They depicted our country as the land of happiness, of *joie de vivre*, of dancing peasants, in complete contrast to the reality, which was essentially one of wretched poverty. Apart from a few fortunate landowners, who held absolutely all the wealth, the poverty of the Italian masses was truly horrifying. Do not forget that the average wage in Italy, even in 1914, was no higher than the average wage in India today. We have every right, therefore, to question whether the Italians were in the happy, idyllic situation presented by the painters of the Restoration.

Van Muyden's picture shows how this stereotyped image persisted and was handed down into the second half of the century. The myth of Italy, and of her happy, healthy people, received new vigour after the social upheavals that shook Europe in 1848, and has continued, one might say, almost up the present day through the distorted vision of Italy perpetuated by certain Hollywood films of the second post-war period.

If we go back in time, to before the French Revolution, we see that the meanings, the connotations of the works of art are practically always of a religious nature. The enormous canvas illustrated here belongs to the Getty Museum in Malibu and depicts the return of the explorers from the Promised Land. On the left is the figure of Moses, recognisable from the two horns on his forehead, and on the right are the explorers, who are arriving with an immense bunch of grapes and other gigantic fruit.

8

What can we read from this picture by Giovanni Lanfranco? Apart from the brilliant description of the scene, it is evident that the picture was meant to be viewed from below, looking up; there was, therefore, a play of perspective that explains why the horizon is so low down. But the symbolic significance of the painting lies in one of those concordances between the Old and the New Testaments, and concerns the sacrament of the Eucharist. It is well known that, right from the beginning, Christians have constantly sought for concordance between the Bible of the Hebrews and the evangelical doctrine. The canvas we are examining belonged, with ten others, to a series that related to the institution of the Eucharist. The principal picture (the Last Supper, with Christ instituting the sacrament) is now in the National Gallery of Ireland, in Dublin. The other canvases from the cycle illustrate episodes from the Old Testament (the manna falling from heaven, for example) which all foreshadow and refer to the eventual institution of the Eucharist. Giovanni Lanfranco, who came from Parma, painted this cycle for one of the great basilicas in Rome, St Paul's Outside the Walls. The pictures were hung above the choir (and so at a considerable height) between great stucco frames, in the chapel of the Holy Sacrament. There was, therefore, a direct relationship between the subject matter they illustrated and the place where they were destined to hang. This is the umpteenth case that demonstrates how useless it is to examine a picture solely from the formal point of view; one must always ask oneself why that particular subject was chosen.

Due to time and neglect, rain and humidity penetrated into the chapel. Little by little, the humidity has seriously damaged some of the canvases. This picture is well preserved, but others are in a deplorable state. The only work from the cycle that has remained in Italy now belongs to a private person in Rome, but it is in such a lamentable condition that only about 15 to 20 per cent of the original painting remains, the rest has been reworked.

At a certain moment, this great cycle of the Eucharist was judged to be too badly damaged and was taken off the walls of the chapel of the Holy Sacrament. It was acquired by Napoleon's uncle, Cardinal Fesch, who had put together the gigantic collection, in Rome, that I have already mentioned.

Fesch had collected more than 3,000 pictures in his house, the Palazzo Falconieri in Via Giulia, and in an annexe of Palazzo Ricci, on the same street. When he died, in 1839, the works were put up for auction, and the catalogues are still in existence. The Papal government allowed all the pictures, except the *St Jerome* by Leonardo da Vinci (today in the Vatican Museums), to be taken out of Italy, even though some of them were of outstanding importance. From the Napoleonic era on, successive governments have been in the appalling habit of carrying out commercial transactions of this kind with private individuals, a very dangerous practice which I am totally against: either a collection is of little importance, in which case it can be dismembered and freely exported, or it is important and must be maintained in its integrity.

In this century, there have been two extremely serious examples of this sinister vice in Italy. The first goes back to 1935, when the Gallery that had been in the trusteeship of the Barberini family in Rome was dispersed. An extremely questionable contract was drawn up and as a result some of the most important pictures that had remained in Italy were sold to foreign buyers and exported. For example, Albrecht Dürer's *Christ Among the Doctors*, which he painted in Venice in just five days, ended up in the Thyssen collection in Lugano, which also has Caravaggio's *St Catherine* from the same collection. And there were numerous other extremely significant paintings. The second, more recent example concerns a private collection in Florence. This was a really iniquitous transaction: the State retained, in the form of a donation, certain pictures that would never have been allowed out of the country (and it is doubtful whether, in their day, they were all acquired by entirely legal means), then consented to the export of some outstanding works, including the Zurburán *Still Life* that is now in Pasadena. Admittedly, it may sometimes be necessary to 'grade' pictures and renounce a few of lesser importance, but it is essential to have someone on the committee who really understands the significance of the works involved, and who is not susceptible to certain 'persuasions'.

In any event, these transactions are very dangerous, and better avoided altogether. In the case of these works by Lanfranco (who was born in Emilia but active in Rome and Naples during the seventeenth century), the entire series was exported. The ruined piece that is now in Rome was bought abroad and brought back to Italy. All the pictures from the cycle in the church of St Paul's Outside the Walls have been dispersed, and some have turned up in the most unlikely places. The canvas I showed you was found in the collection of Viscount Massarene on the island of Mull, in Scotland. Other pieces reappeared in Amsterdam, Dublin, Germany and elsewhere. And so a highly important pictorial ensemble belonging to the seventeenth-century Roman school has sadly been scattered.

As I said, this picture was placed in a stucco frame, in a recess in the wall, and the low horizon indicates that it was meant to be looked at from below the lower edge of the frame. This painting had a decisive influence on two artists of the classical school in seventeenth-century Rome: Andrea Sacchi and Carlo Maratta. There is at least one early work by Carlo Maratta, a *Martyrdom of St Andrew*, whose compositional elements were undoubtedly inspired by this prototype. So here is a case where an organic group of pictures, essential to the understanding of the development of a particular school, has been dispersed and can only be reconstituted on paper, and even then it is impossible to comprehend certain aspects which could only be read when the work was in its original setting.

When examining a picture, one should take into account not only the religious connotations, but also other semantic indications, which are often overlooked.

9. Anthony van Dyck. Portrait of Agostino
Pallavicini. J. Paul Getty Museum, Malibu,
California.

9   Heraldic emblems, for example. You see here a great painting, in the Getty
     Museum in Malibu, which was painted in 1623 by Anthony van Dyck during his
     stay in Genoa. It portrays a senator of the Republic of Genoa, and, for a long time, it
     was thought that the sitter belonged to the ducal Durazzo family, whose members
     had held high office in the Republic. Nobody had taken the trouble to note that on
     the curtain in the background, in shadow, there appear the unmistakable heraldic
     emblems of the Pallavicini. Once these were recognised, it was possible to identify
     the man in the portrait as a member of the Pallavicini, another Genoese family
     whose members had served as high functionaries in the Republic of St George. This
     is yet another proof that it is impossible to pass a verdict on a picture without
     having first identified all the available factors, and that it is always dangerous to
     base your judgement on purely formal values. The formal evaluation should be
     made only at the last moment, when all the other elements necessary for a sound
     assessment have been gathered together, and it is only at this point that we are
     enabled to admire the extraordinary virtuosity with which this red drapery has
     been handled; it shows that the artist had made a study of original Titians and had
     also been a pupil of Pieter Paul Rubens. And in fact, van Dyck first studied with
     Rubens in Antwerp, then came to Italy where he set to work actually making
     copies and numerous drawings from the works of Titian. The portrait is a work of
     supreme virtuosity, one of the strongest works van Dyck painted in Genoa.
     Strangely enough, in spite of his splendid portraits of the Genoese aristocracy, van
     Dyck did not succeed in obtaining any large commission for a public building, nor
     even an altar-piece, in the capital of the Republic. He painted small altar-pieces for
     little towns in the province, but not for the city of Genoa, where, evidently, the
     local artists were too jealous of their own prestige.

         So this picture, too, must be read centimetre by centimetre before you can say
     you really know it. It is not possible to comprehend it from a casual glance, which
     is the way most paintings in museums are viewed.

10   Now let us move on to another picture. This panel, from the National Gallery,
     London, is one of the oddest amongst all the works in the style we now call
     Proto-Mannerism. Both the internal characteristics of style, and written evidence
     (it is cited in the old sources) point to a great Florentine painter of the first half of
     the cinquecento: Jacopo Carrucci, known as Pontormo, from the village where he
     was born.

         The work was painted for a series on which various artists collaborated,
     including Andrea del Sarto, Francesco Granacci, Francesco Ubertini, known as Il
     Bacchiacca, and another anonymous artist. The whole series was carried out to
     decorate the bedroom of a Florentine, Pier Francesco Borgherini; some of the pieces
     were inserted in a wooden seat-back, others adorned the bed and the marriage
     chests. The subject matter was the story of Joseph. It would take a long time to
     explain why Borgherini chose this biblical theme for his bedroom. In any case, the
     furnishings of the room were soon dispersed. When it came to be dismantled, only a
     few decades later, the pictures, which had been highly valued right from the
     beginning, were saved, but the furniture itself was lost, including the ornamental

panelling, which must have been very elaborate, and hinged, but which we know very little about. The old sources – and this is confirmed by the measurements of the room which contained the series – inform us, among other things, that the panel we are discussing was situated immediately to the left of the door, on the same wall. It is, in fact, possible to reconstruct the original arrangement on very general lines, but unfortunately the detail eludes us.

In later periods, four of the panels (the two by Andrea del Sarto, which, at the time, were considered to be the most important, and the two by Francesco Granacci) went into what was then the Galleria Granducale and is now the Pitti Gallery, while others were scattered amongst various collections.

Pontormo's picture, one of the most curious products of Italian art in the first half of the cinquecento, illustrates two episodes from the legend of Joseph. The two episodes are not narrated with any continuity, but rather with a startling spatial and temporal break, which is just as unexpected as the settings for the two scenes. At the top on the right, you see the death of Jacob, a drama which is unfolding on top of a bizarre edifice with an open-air staircase, and in a bedroom which is itself virtually open to the sky.

At the bottom on the left, we have the recognition of Joseph. The scene is adorned with weird, indeed incomprehensible columns surmounted by figures, some of which are sculptured, others living. Then there is a whole series of people who have nothing whatever to do with the story: the boy you see in the foreground, sitting on the bottom step, is almost certainly the young Agnolo Bronzino, pupil and later assistant of Pontormo, whose *Venus, Love, Folly and Time* we looked at in the First Conversation.

Apart from the oddity of the composition and settings, the most extraordinary thing in the picture is the background, with those unusual and even improbable buildings of northern aspect, which have been borrowed from engravings by Lucas van Leyden. (You may remember we saw a portrait by this painter in an earlier conversation.)

This picture is one of the most significant in relation to that crisis in the painting of central Italy, and particularly Florence, which today is known as Proto-Mannerism, although it is really the sum total of the crises of individual painters, which manifested itself from around 1505 to 1530–40. In Florence, a simple design no longer satisfied the painters, who found themselves in something of a dead end, and then, partly because of their personal problems, partly because of the general crisis of form in Florentine art, turned to prints and engravings of northern art to find some answers to their questions. Prints by Albrecht Dürer, Lucas van Leyden, Schongauer and other engravers were avidly sought after by the Florentine artists, who re-elaborated them, borrowing details, clues and hints as to general composition.

If I were to comment, centimetre by centimetre, on Pontormo's painting, we would need at least another six or seven conversations. It is a veritable mine of clues, each of which reveals an initial crisis, which the artist resolved by referring to foreign models, which he then reinterpreted in an extremely personal fashion. In

10. Iacopo Carrucci, known as Pontormo.
Legend of Joseph. National Gallery,
London.

11. Stained glass. Philibert II the
Handsome, Duke of Savoy, with his
guardian saint, St Philibert. Abbey of
Bourg-en-Bresse.

this picture, every element is the fruit of an elaborate reworking, and every detail has involved an almost infinite series of preparatory drawings. Some of these studies have survived, and nowadays Pontormo is considered to be one of Italy's major draughtsmen, although what remains of his graphic work – abundant in comparison to other painters' – is only a fraction of what he must have produced, because, as I said, every figure he painted required endless preparation, endless reworking from other sources.

There are some artists – Michelangelo for one – who hate to show their preparatory studies. They like to exhibit only the finished product, and to be known through that alone. This reluctance is not confined to painters and sculptors, there are plenty of poets, writers and novelists who are unwilling to show the complex and wearisome work that went into, say, the final version of a sonnet or a verse. (Just imagine what preliminary efforts a work like the *Divine Comedy* must have cost the author!) So, they themselves destroy their preparatory work. As far as Michelangelo is concerned, we have a corpus of his drawings, published in four volumes by the Istituto Geografico De Agostini in Novara. But these are a minute fraction of the graphic works of Michelangelo. The ceiling of the Sistine Chapel alone, just the nude figures, must have involved thousands of drawings, but we know barely a dozen of them because Michelangelo personally destroyed them, one by one. Those that remain are pages stolen by admirers, or that were lost under a piece of furniture and later retrieved. But we possess practically nothing from the four great allegories in the Medici chapels, although these must have required an immensely long and elaborate period of preparation.

However, it is not only the great works of painting and sculpture that involve long preparation. Stained glass, for instance, which the general public usually thinks of as the work of craftsmen pure and simple, must also go through a preparatory phase, including sketches, drawings, the elaboration of details. Here 11 we see a window in the Abbey of Bourg-en-Bresse in Burgundy, France; it depicts a member of the Savoy family, Philibert II the Handsome, attended by his guardian saint, St Philibert. The first thing you have to ask yourself when you come across a piece of stained glass is, what condition is it in? Glass is among the most fragile and the most frequently restored materials in the history of art. The abbey to which this window belonged was built by Philibert's wife, Margaret of Austria, in about 1530. During the French Revolution, it was requisitioned and turned into a stable. Vandals broke some of the windows with stones, others were wrenched out and destroyed. It was not until the Restoration that they were repaired. Whenever you look at stained glass, therefore, you must establish which pieces are truly original, examine the condition of the lead, and see whether some parts of the glass have been touched up by the restorer to enhance faded colours.

Look at the number of heraldic connotations in this work: the Collar of the Annunciation worn by the principal figure belonged to the royal family of Savoy and was made up of links in the form of knots (a family emblem) with the letters FERT worked into these knots (FERT stands for 'Fortitudo Eius Rhodum Tenuit' meaning 'His strength kept Rhodes', and refers to an episode in the history of the Savoys). Also the predominant colours are red and white, the colours of the Savoy coat-of-arms. So everything is linked, and must be read and interpreted in accordance with the artist's intentions.

In buildings in central Europe, stained-glass windows often served the same function as frescoes or altar-pieces in Italian churches. There are some stained-glass windows, especially in French churches, which are veritable encyclopaedias of sacred and symbolic contents. But they are very difficult to interpret, particularly as regards the symbolism of colour, which is always relevant.

Now I want to show you a picture that contains an entirely different kind of symbolism. It is a tiny panel, just a few centimetres in area, from the Museo Poldi   12
Pezzoli in Milan, and portrays St Francis of Assisi kneeling before Christ. The artist is Carlo Crivelli, who belongs to the Veneto-Marches school. Look at the objects in the background, known as the *arma Christi*, the instruments of the Passion: the spear that pierced His side, the cane with the sponge soaked in vinegar, the scourge. In some paintings, these instruments are introduced as a kind of shorthand for the Passion itself. Sometimes they even include a basin, with Pilate's hands in the act of washing, or the cock that crowed when Peter denied Christ. In about 1475, when Crivelli painted his picture, the use of the *arma Christi* had become rather rare and unfashionable. But it was very common in the first half of the quattrocento, especially in the works of Gothic artists. In many of these, Christ's sepulchre is in the foreground, with Our Saviour rising from it, in half-figure, with his hands held wide apart in the gesture of the *imago pietatis*, and He is surrounded by the *arma Christi*, a synthetic representation of the actual Passion. It is very difficult to establish where and when this system of 'shorthand' symbolism originated. And we are still not clear about the beginnings of the *imago pietatis*, which spread throughout the Orthodox area of eastern Europe but was also common in western Europe. Nobody knows when it was initiated.

So, as you move back, little by little, in time, the sacred connotations become more and more decisive and fundamental, while the profane ones begin to disappear.

Here is another picture, painted by Pisanello for the court of Ferrara, which now   13
belongs to the Louvre. It is undoubtedly a portrait of a Princess of the House of Este. The symbolic connotations here are numerous and can be recognised in the emblem embroidered on the garment (one of the emblems of the House of Este) and in two flowers in the background: a carnation, which, as we have seen, alludes to betrothal and marriage, and the columbine, or 'Venus's Chariot', which could symbolise either the Passion of Christ or amorous passion. In many Milanese paintings of the school of Leonardo in the early cinquecento, the Child Jesus holds a columbine in his hand, the flower which symbolises the Passion, and this is a typical instance of rhetorical prolepsis; that is, an allusion to something that is going to happen later. Look at the sumptuous sleeve on which the emblem is so richly embroidered. This was not unusual, as sleeves were highly valued; they were not considered to be part of the dress, they were separate and could be worn with different dresses. We have a lot of inventories of the possessions of noble-

12. Carlo Crivelli. St Francis before Christ.
Museo Poldi Pezzoli, Milan.

13. Pisanello. Portrait of a Princess of the
House of Este. The Louvre, Paris.

14. Filippo Lippi. Double portrait.
Metropolitan Museum, New York.

15. Alessio Baldovinetti. Portrait of a Lady.
National Gallery, London.

women and princesses in which the embroidered sleeves *'a gozo'*, or *'a gomito'* are
listed separately as precious items. You can see sleeves of this kind in several
antique paintings: for example, in Filippo Lippi's double portrait in the Metropolitan Museum in New York, where there is even a family motto embroidered on
one of the sleeves. A painting in the National Gallery in London also shows an
extremely elaborate sleeve. The picture was attributed to Paolo Uccello and
erroneously identified as a portrait of the Countess Palma di Urbino. It is actually a
Florentine painting, and the artist was certainly Alessio Baldovinetti.

The history of costume, which still remains, in large part, to be elucidated and
written up, is very important to the study of painting. From the design of the
clothes, especially the women's dresses, it is often possible to establish the date, at
least approximately, and, quite often, even the locality and the family. And these
data supply us with collateral confirmation of the stylistic pointers, and so help to
identify the artist (which, of course, could not be done solely from the style of the
clothes).

The history of costume is very interesting, by reason of its continual variety and
the fact that changes in fashion often coincide with ideological changes in society.
These changes are relatively cyclical. For example, there is the constantly recur-
ring question of the female leg, which, from a certain period on, is now displayed,
now covered, as hemlines rise and fall. This happens only after the French
Revolution, before that time it would have been inconceivable for a woman to
show her legs, even in stockings. Masculine costume, too, sometimes reveals
sexual connotations. The use of the cod-piece, for instance, that kind of horn
attached to the crotch of breeches or tights, which often assumes an aggressive and
almost obscene aspect, and against which Ignatius Loyola and Gaetano Thiene
inveighed. It was actually the Counter-Reformation, with its harsh sexual
repression, that banned this accessory to male attire.

Another indication of fashion is the colour scheme. For example, the custom of
wearing black suits, in the sense of 'good' clothes, suitable for men to wear in
society, arose only in the second half of the sixteenth century, and is due to Spanish
influence. It goes back to the time of Philip II, who was said to dress always in
black. As a consequence, black became the standard colour for formal wear in high
society.

Up until the end of the cinquecento, the situation was the reverse: black was a
sign of poverty, it was the colour worn by those who could not afford to buy
colourful clothes, since these were more vulnerable to stains, wear and tear and
fading. The rich, in contrast, tried to outdo one another with their multi-coloured
garments, often wearing different colours on different parts of the body. In central
Italy, you will see frescoes and paintings, dating from the end of the quattrocento
and the beginning of the cinquecento, which show young pages or squires wearing
tights made in the colours of the heraldic livery of the family they served, often
different on each leg. This costume has disappeared in modern times, and now it is
essential to wear the black suit with a neat white collar.

There are some pictures, especially portraits, which give the overall impression

16. Domenico Ghirlandaio. Old Man with
Child. The Louvre, Paris.

of being so simple that you can understand them at first glance. But it is wise to be wary in the reading of even the most apparently simple picture. Here is a typical case: this picture belongs to the Louvre and is the work of an artist who, in my opinion, is very great indeed, although certain modern art historians hold him in contempt, accusing him of being academic and playing to the gallery. I am speaking of Domenico Ghirlandaio.

Here, against a landscape, we see an old man with a warty nose, a nose deformed by Heaven knows what skin disease, who is embracing a little boy who is probably his grandson. Many of the stylistic features betray unmistakably the hand of Ghirlandaio. The picture would be in perfect condition if it were not maimed by some rather peculiar damage. If you look closely, you can see on the old man's forehead a dense network of scratches, all vertical or horizontal except for some slighter, asymmetrical marks. This curious damage is due to the fact that the picture must have been put into a crate that had a nail sticking out of it and, during its journey, probably on a cart or the back of a mule, the nail scratched the surface of the painting. Otherwise, the picture has not been damaged either by time or cleaning. But the most unusual thing about it is that the preparatory drawing, from the hand of Ghirlandaio, still exists, and this is a very rare instance indeed. The only difference is that, in the drawing, which belongs to the National Museum of Stockholm, the old man is portrayed as dead. Evidently, Ghirlandaio was commissioned to do a portrait of this old man after his death, so he drew the features of the corpse and then reinterpreted them, in the painting, as if he were alive. I am convinced that it was the Sassetti, a very important banking family from Florence, who commissioned this picture. They also commissioned other portraits from Ghirlandaio and, more particularly, had the artist paint the interior of their private chapel in the church of the Holy Trinity in Florence, which still exists.

But take a good look at this picture: you will see that there is a discrepancy in the quality. While the figure of the old man is very well integrated and leaves no doubt as to its paternity by Ghirlandaio, the figure of the child is banal, almost anonymous. It seems more like a 'stock figure', a type, rather than an individual. The same is true of the landscape. The probability is that, as with other pictures by Ghirlandaio, assistants from his *bottega* had a hand in the work. Ghirlandaio's studio was very active, very efficient, and a great many of the pictures produced there show the master's hand in the composition and the principal parts, while the rest was evidently left to pupils. A typical example is the Massacre of the Innocents, a scene in the background of the *Nativity* in the Spedale degli Innocenti (the Foundling Hospital) in Florence. The background is clearly not from the hand of Ghirlandaio. It was Bernard Berenson who recognised the artist who painted it, together with some other works from the same hand, and baptised him 'Pupil of Domenico'. Berenson's hypothesis was later confirmed by documentary evidence: the painter was called Bartolomeo di Giovanni, and he was, in fact, a pupil and collaborator of Ghirlandaio.

Several other members of his family worked in Ghirlandaio's studio: David Ghirlandaio, Benedetto Ghirlandaio, and his brother-in-law, Sebastiano Mainardi.

17. Domenico Ghirlandaio. Preparatory
drawing for head of the old man. National
Museum, Stockholm.

18. Bartolomeo di Giovanni. Massacre of
the Innocents. Museum of the Spedale degli
Innocenti (Foundling Hospital), Florence.

19. Bonifacio Bembo. Tarot card.
Accademia Carrara, Bergamo.

But he also employed an enormous number of apprentices, assistants and collaborators; some artists of the first rank learned their trade in his studio. You have only to think of Michelangelo, whose artistic beginnings were in the shadow of Ghirlandaio. The same may be said of Francesco Granacci and many others. Traces of these collaborations can very often be detected in pictures that came out of that extraordinarily productive studio, from which we still have a great many works, in spite of considerable losses. We possess innumerable pictures, yet these represent only 30–35 per cent of Ghirlandaio's output.

As I was saying, the hand of an assistant can be seen in the background, and in the figure of the little boy, in this portrait that hangs in the Louvre. Nevertheless, it is a very respectable bit of painting. Just because an assistant works on it does not mean the picture is to be dismissed; as we have seen, there was no shortage of first-class assistants in this studio. But, from this intense production of portraits created in the studio, I want to turn now to a more general consideration. I want to remind you that, besides these portraits, of which only a small percentage has survived, the Gothic period, especially in its closing years, produced an enormous output of the most disparate objects, all made by artists.

At that time, as I have already mentioned, an artist was considered to be a craftsman, so he was commissioned to do any kind of work within his capacity. The artist made banners and ceremonial shields, he designed armour, masks, clothing, and even furniture. We have documents which tell us that chairs and stools were painted by artists whom we rank as very great indeed.

The artist remained a craftsman up until the cinquecento, when he began his ascent towards what we might call the 'Olympus of the Artists', in the footsteps of Michelangelo and Titian. Michelangelo was the one painter, sculptor and architect who was held in such high esteem by his contemporaries that he could afford to snub a patron like the Pope himself. And, for Titian, the Emperor Charles V actually bent down to pick up a brush. This incident is probably apocryphal, but it is a true enough indication of the new status the artist enjoyed in society during the cinquecento.

At first, the artist made everything, even playing cards. We have packs of Tarot cards from the Lombardy of the quattrocento painted by famous artists. This card, for example, comes from a pack painted by Bonifacio Bembo, from Cremona, and now belongs to the Accademia Carrara in Bergamo. Artists were quite ready to paint the strangest objects and very often, in the documents, the subjects they were to depict on panels or frescoes are specified in minute detail. There is a Lombardian document in which the painter is commissioned to paint a portrait of the patron's dogs, with the added instruction: 'It must be clearly seen that my dogs wear gold collars'. The artist, in short, would turn his hand to anything. It is a modern myth that the artist is above certain functions and vulgar, everyday needs. They even designed desserts, a practice that was carried on into the seventeenth century. As I have already told you, amongst the extraordinary creations of Gian Lorenzo Bernini were some colossal desserts which were first exhibited and then eaten at the grand banquets of the papal aristocracy. They were sculptures in whipped creams, gelatine, biscuits. We also have some Bolognese engravings which show these highly elaborate sweets and, given the facility with which materials like gelatine and whipped cream can be moulded, one can imagine that they were amongst the most florid and prestigious plastic creations of the Baroque era.

Another field in which artists were once very active is goldsmithery, sometimes sacred and sometimes profane. Unfortunately, very few examples of this kind of work have survived, partly because such products, especially if secular, were not revered as works of art at that time, as they would be today. The patron commissioned goldsmith's pieces of incredible intricacy and refinement, yet he would have them melted down without the slightest compunction the moment he was in need of cash.

The Duc de Berry is a typical case in point. We know from documents in the archives that this fifteenth-century aristocrat possessed an extraordinary collection of gold and silver plate; it was not used for the serving of food, but displayed on stands on the occasion of great banquets. We actually have a miniature by the Limbourg brothers which shows the Duc de Berry at table with one of these stands nearby. As soon as the Duc was in need of money, for political reasons or for promoting his family's interests, he had these fabulous pieces melted down, without batting an eyelid. You must remember, moreover, that it was not the kind of artistic tableware that is relatively common today, it was work of the very highest quality, reserved for a tiny élite. One of the reasons why I prefer living nowadays, rather than in the quattrocento, in spite of the great artists of that period, is that the material goods which render life pleasanter and more civilised, and at that time were the privilege of a very few, are now within everybody's reach. Nowadays, it is not only the millionaire who can have a refrigerator, and eat with knives and forks off decent plates. The least of his employees enjoys the same things, although admittedly, he will use stainless steel cutlery and china from a big department store, whereas the rich man will eat with silver forks off fine English, Danish or Ginori porcelain plates. In the thirteenth and fourteenth centuries, there was an immeasurable gulf between the life-style of those who held all the wealth and power and that of the masses.

The rags the poor used to cover themselves with simply cannot be compared to the rich apparel of the ducal courts, any more than a telephone kiosk can be compared to a cathedral. Hundreds of people worked for months and months, for minimal wages, to make the clothing of the Duke of Burgundy, or the Visconti, or the Sforza. These garments were worn once or twice, then they were burned to recover the gold and silver thread. The silks, the velvets, which had been woven for them with enormous effort, were discarded without the slightest regret, except, as I said, for the sleeves of women's garments, which were unstitched and then applied to new dresses.

The same thing happened with tapestries. Again, the most sumptuous ones, woven with gold and silver threads, were burned to recover the precious metals for re-use. This is why we have a mass of documentation about the huge output of tapestries, but a very limited number of actual examples. The cost of these cycles of

20. The Limbourg Brothers. Miniature from
the Book of Hours of the Duc de Berry.
Musée Condé, Chantilly.

21. Jan van Eyck. Portrait of Jan Arnolfini
and his Wife. National Gallery, London.

tapestries which, according to the available documents, decorated the large halls of the palaces and castles of the nobility, is almost unimagineable in terms of our modern economy. Moreover, they cost not only vast sums for the materials, but great labour and study for the artists who prepared the sketches and then the cartoons, as well as years of painstaking work for the weavers. Yet all this was later destroyed without the slightest concern, and, if they were not woven with precious metal threads, the tapestries were cut up to make saddle-cloths and caparisons, or simply burned. And so we have very few of the older, and therefore most important, tapestries left. Today, we have consumerism as a mass phenomenon, but it concerns goods of little value, whereas in the thirteenth and fourteenth centuries, it was the prerogative of the rich and involved extremely costly goods, often of outstanding artistic value.

The next theme I want to discuss is the impossibility of reading northern European, and especially Flemish painting, in the same way that we read Italian. In the latter, we must pass on from the general to the particular, but for a northern European picture we must adopt the opposite procedure: begin by reading the details and go on to the overall impression. This is particularly valid for the paintings of the early-Flemish era.

Flemish painting has very individual characteristics. We might say that it sprang forth fully armed, like Minerva from the head of Jove. It was born with two supreme geniuses, Jan and Hubert van Eyck, who, as we know from old documents, began their activities as miniaturists. Immediately after them came a slight drop in quality and intensity, at first imperceptible, then more and more noticeable. Flemish painting of the second half of the quattrocento, even when you count a colossus like Hugo van der Goes, no longer reached the absolute peak of the van Eyck brothers (distinguishing one from the other is extremely difficult, almost impossible, in fact).

In the first half of the sixteenth century, around 1510, the Flemish artists discovered Italian art and their work and culture were greatly enriched by it; this is the period of the so-called 'Romanists'. Nowadays, a lot of scholars, particularly specialists in Flemish art, consider the Romanists as an abomination, as painters of the fourth rank who betrayed the Flemish cultural tradition. A highly debatable opinion, however, since there are some very respectable artists, and even some great ones, amongst the Romanists.

21   Here, now, is a superb masterpiece from the first phase of Flemish painting: Jan van Eyck's Portrait of Jan Arnolfini and his Wife, in the National Gallery, London. In this masterpiece, van Eyck has already achieved, amongst other things, that play of reflection and of optical perspective that was to reach its highest accomplishment in Velásquez's *Las Meninas*. On the wall at the back of the room where the married couple are standing, you can see a round convex mirror, surrounded by a frame with small round insets in each of which there is a scene from the Passion of Christ (the way these are painted betrays the hand accustomed to painting miniatures), and surmounted by the legend: '*Johannes de Eyck hic fuit*' (Jan van Eyck was here). Now, in the centre of the convex mirror, the artist has portrayed

himself, standing in front of his easel, painting the married couple, whom we see here from the back. There is, in short, a reflection between the observer, the subject of the picture and the moment in which the picture is being painted, no more and no less than in Velásquez's *Las Meninas*. And it is only by starting from this detail of the mirror that we can proceed, centimetre by centimetre, to the reading of the whole painting.

The first thing that strikes you is the enormous importance of the light, which is coming in through the window on the left. It is not that the forms are actually defined by the light, but rather that light, to Flemish artists of the fifteenth century, was what three-dimensional perspective was to the Italians. While Italian painting is based on perspective and the three dimensions, Flemish painting is based on light. It was in Milan that the two schools were grafted together.

The Milanese school, in fact, had a decisive importance as a kind of 'hyphen' between the north and the south, thanks to artists like Donato dei Bardi and Vincenzo Foppa. This grafting of northern light and Italian perspective, which was developed by the Brescian school of Savoldo, favoured the appearance of the founder of modern painting, Michelangelo da Caravaggio. Spanish painting itself, the art of Velásquez and Zurburán, cannot be understood without Caravaggio and his precursors of the Lombardian school.

Coming back to van Eyck's painting, it must be read – and I shall never tire of insisting on this – by the inductive method; only by analysing each minute detail will you be able to arrive at the general, overall idea. This is the exact opposite of the deductive method we must adopt when reading an Italian painting of the same period. The details in van Eyck's pictures, if carefully analysed, are a veritable gold-mine. With incredible skill, he manages to communicate to you the varying surfaces of the different objects, the way in which they absorb or reflect the light. His treatment of stained glass is absolutely prodigious.

Look now at a rather curious detail: the dress Arnolfini's wife is wearing. For a long time, it was believed that the lady was, as they say, in an interesting condition, that she was pregnant. But it is much more likely that it is the style and cut of the dress, with its very high waist, right up under the breasts, and that kind of pouching over the belly that give this impression. You will find the same fashion in Italian pictures, especially Florentine ones, of the same date. This fashion involved not only the shape and cut of the dress, but even a certain way of standing and moving that, oddly enough, recurs more than once in the history of fashion. In France, for example, shortly after Thermidor. We have a lot of pictures and particularly fashion-plates from the years 1794–8, in which the women, the so-called '*merveilleuses*', are wearing dresses of this type and assuming postures intended to accentuate the 'pregnant look'. The psychological implications of a fashion of this kind have yet to be studied and understood.

In van Eyck's picture, there are also chromatic values that still need elucidating. For instance, it is certainly not by chance that the woman is dressed in green; the colour must have some definite symbolic significance, although, in the present state of our knowledge, we cannot say what it is.

22. Jan van Eyck. Portrait with the legend
'Leal Souvenir'. National Gallery, London.

23. Petrus Christus. Portrait of a Man.
National Gallery, London.

Here is another picture by van Eyck which also belongs to the National Gallery
in London. It is a portrait with the legend: '*Leal Souvenir*'. The sitter must have had
this painted as a present for a friend. Notice how important the light is in this
picture, too, and, above all, the exceptionally powerful realism of the figure. The
Italians, however, considered this power as a mark of superficiality.

The truth is, the Italians did not understand these pictures. They admired them
as skilful pieces of work, but not for themselves, as works of art. Michelangelo
detested pictures of this genre, though it is only fair to say that it is unlikely he ever
saw a picture by that supreme genius, Jan van Eyck, since there were none of his
works in Florence or Rome at that time. In any event, he imputed to Flemish
paintings a trivial, sentimental quality which, in his judgement, was successful in
moving simple people, or pious women, to tears (especially if it was a sacred
subject), but lacked real substance. Michelangelo was an extreme exponent of the
Italian mentality, for whom the figure must, above all, be the expression of an
internal structure.

If you examine any Italian painting of the quattro- or cinquecento (and I am not
even saying by Michelangelo, who carried the idea to the absolute limit in the
frescoes in the Sistine Chapel), you will feel that, beneath the surface, there is
always a bony frame, a structure. Even if what is actually shown and described is
only the exterior line, the so-called 'dynamic line', you are aware of the underlying
structure of muscle and bone, which the artist has studied and mastered. In
Pollaiuolo's pictures, for example, you feel the internal structure just through the
course of the external line.

Flemish pictures, on the other hand, do not have this internal structure. Their
paintings live through the light. Light which does not actually define the form, but
animates it – as witness this portrait, the '*Leal Souvenir*'.

Here is another portrait, painted by a Flemish artist of the generation that
immediately followed, and who is considered to be van Eyck's best pupil, Petrus
Christus. This picture, in the National Gallery, London, is in an excellent state of
preservation, but it is not complete. It is certainly one half of a diptych. The other
half, which has not yet been traced and may very well be lost, must have depicted
either the patron saint of this personage or a half-figure of the Madonna and Child.
You can see here a slight, almost imperceptible falling-off in the intensity of the
figure, as compared to the work of van Eyck. It is almost unnoticeable, but it is
undeniably there. Petrus Christus is the Flemish painter who comes closest to
Antonello da Messina. It has even been conjectured that the two may have met
each other in Milan. In the archives of the Duke of Milan, there is an account which
mentions the names of an Antonello, or Antonio Messinese and a Pietro di Bourges
(at that time, it was 'Bourges' and not 'Bruges', just as it was 'Burxelles' and not
'Bruxelles').

It has been pointed out, as an objection, that these two names appear, not in the
section relevant to painters, but in the archers' section. But really, in the frightful
muddle of pre-capitalist household management, this should not be so surprising.
The criteria on which this type of economy was based seem to us quite mad. The

Duke of Milan did not adjust his expenditure to suit his income, but fixed his income on the basis of his expenditure. When he gave a banquet, he did not budget for it within his means, he simply increased taxes to meet the costs. This way of operating, so alien to our own economic principles, led to such chaos in the keeping of accounts that it is hardly to be wondered at if Antonello da Messina and Petrus Christus were entered under the accounts for the archers.

The quality of this picture by Christus is certainly exceptional, but one feels that already something is lacking in comparison to the unmatchable models of Jan van Eyck.

I cannot trace here the whole course of fifteenth-century Flemish art. We have already met the Master of Flémalle in an earlier conversation, and now we must make a brief resumé of the other supreme masters of the Flemish Renaissance: Rogier van der Weyden, Hugo van der Goes, Hans Memling (to name only the major artists), beside whom we must also place the very great Dutch painters. Supreme amongst the latter was an extremely rare painter, Geertgen tot Sint Jans (which means Gerard of St John); in Italy, we have just one minuscule picture of his, in the Pinacoteca Ambrosiana in Milan. This painter must have died very young, and I am convinced he visited Italy and met Fra Angelico and other artists in Florence. 24

We will linger, however, over a portrait that belongs to the period in which Flemish painting was beginning to be influenced by Italian; it is the work of Jan Gossaert, known as Mabuse. First of all, notice the absolute, meticulous surface reality of these portraits, and how once again the light performs its animating role, although in rather less clear and sharp terms than those we have seen in the paintings of Jan van Eyck. There is another very interesting thing to note: the man who painted this picture is not even minimally influenced by classical art, he may have seen antique statues, but they have made no impression on him. Italian art, on the other hand, in all its manifestations, shows the classical precedent, especially the models of Greek sculpture experienced through Roman copies. Flemish painters, even when they come to Italy and allow themselves to be influenced by antique sculpture, remain impervious to classical culture. Around 1530–40, for example, a lot of Flemish artists were very impressed by the Laocöon, but the interpretations they made of it are always in an anti-classical mode. 25

Now I would like to consider another element: the harsh realism with which the sitters' features are rendered. Looking at the portrait of this man, you are immediately aware that he must have had trouble with his teeth and gums. Probably he was afflicted with pyorrhoea. Italian artists hardly ever record defects of this sort, and an Italian portrait always tends to cancel out anything unpleasant in the physiognomy. The Ghirlandaio (picture number 16 in this Conversation) is a rare exception. This is because Italy is a country that lives on rhetoric – in her art, too. I think it would be a good thing to give children courses in anti-rhetoric, to teach them to face up to objective reality.

It must also be said that this ostentatious, almost brutal insistence on reality in Flemish portraiture can strike an Italian eye as a sign of vulgarity. In other words,

24. Geertgen tot Sint Jans. Madonna.
Pinacoteca Ambrosiana, Milan.
25. Jan Gossaert (known as Mabuse).
Double portrait. National Gallery, London.

26. Konrad Witz. *The Miraculous Draught of Fishes.* Musée d'art et d'histoire, Geneva.

the Flemish painter does not hesitate to portray in his sitter defects that, in Italy, would be thought socially degrading. In Italian painting, too, there are people with problems with their teeth, or with ugly or vacuous faces, but they are always members of the lower classes. In fact, the Italians have drawn on antique Flemish painting to enrich their rigorously hierarchical repertoire of facial types.

These two great components of European painting, the northern and the Italian, later came together in countless local combinations, of varying merit and importance. One of the oddest examples is Konrad Witz, a German-Swiss painter, who also worked in Geneva. This is a fragment from an altar-piece, illustrating the *Miraculous Draught of Fishes*; it hangs in the museum in Geneva. This scene from the Gospels is taking place, as you see, in a real landscape. This is an actual view of Lake Geneva, with Mont Blanc in the background and the city on the right, as it must have looked between 1430 and 1450. In the picture, you can see a series of Italianate elements, generally undervalued or misinterpreted. Due to the fact that both Italian and Flemish painting were immediately diffused over a wide area, there exists an infinite number of combinations of this kind between the two great schools, especially in French, German and Iberian painting, and sometimes with rather odd results.

We have already said that Italian pictures were sold at fairs in northern Europe. Then there are the Italian pictures painted for Spanish churches, such as those by Barnaba da Modena. A lot of painters, many of them Florentine, went to Spain: Antonio Veneziano, for instance, went to Toledo. And, as for the Flemish, it must be remembered that Jan van Eyck, like a lot of other artists of the quattrocento, also acted as ambassador to the potentates of the place. It seems he travelled as far as Lisbon. Therefore, Flemish and Italian painting did not stay on their home ground, but spread like wildfire throughout Europe (not, however, eastern Europe, where western art only became known later, thanks to engravings).

Some of these combinations, or graftings, especially in Germany and Spain, anticipate in an astonishing way certain themes and formal problems that were to reappear in European painting centuries later.

Having examined some Flemish works of art, and the 'paranordic' picture by Konrad Witz, I want you to look now at this Italian picture from the quattrocento: a Madonna and Child under a baldaquin held up by angels. This small picture once belonged to the Cook collection in Richmond, Surrey, and it is now in the National Gallery, London. It has been attributed to Fra Angelico, but it is not his work. It is by a painter close to him. The only other work I know from this hand is an illuminated manuscript in the British Library, an annexe of the British Museum. You see how the whole picture can be taken in at one glance. Everything here is based on perspective. Notice how scientifically the third dimension is rendered, as far as the baldaquin is concerned, although the painter has had difficulty inserting his figures, especially the angels, into this perspective. In the case of a small work like this, the technical quality, which must always be investigated before one can express an historical and artistic judgement, is demonstrated by the fact that the picture stands up well to the enormous enlargement of a colour transparency. The blue of the Virgin's mantle, for example, is still almost perfect, because it was done with Persian or Indian lapis-lazuli. Observe, also, the extreme care with which the incisions in the gold have been worked in all the gilded parts.

Here, now, is one of the three panels from the *Rout of San Romano*, by Paolo Uccello, now divided amongst the National Gallery, London, the Uffizi and the Louvre. The flight of the lancers, the fallen warriors in the foreground, the various human figures and the horses are arranged in such a way as to give an impression of depth. Uccello has not quite managed to resolve this problem successfully, however, since he is, all things considered, not a Renaissance painter, as he is generally held to be, but a pseudo-Renaissance painter. His innermost spirit, his mental formation are those of a late-Gothic artist. What is going on in the foreground really has no precise spatial definition, while the background still looks like a painted backdrop. Those three-dimensional indications in the foreground, those rather futile attempts at perspective, are not enough to make him into a Renaissance painter.

Here, on the other hand, in this picture by Sandro Botticelli, which belongs to 29 the Morelli collection in the Accademia Carrara in Bergamo, we see something entirely different. This painting must have been inserted, originally, into a 'spalliera' wainscoting (rather than in a cupboard, as is generally believed). There is a companion picture, in Boston, illustrating the Death of Lucrezia, while the one in Bergamo depicts the Death of Virginia. The subject matter shows that it must have been a pendant, and there must have been a series of panels dedicated to the Roman heroines, inserted into the wall decoration between frames which formed a kind of seat-back or panelling. You see how, here, everything depends on the third dimension, and how the three-dimensional perspective enables you to grasp the overall significance of the picture immediately.

This brings us back to the great theme, which has still not been anything like exhaustively studied: the grafting of the Flemish and the Italian schools. It is not at all clear, for instance, how Vincenzo Foppa, the painter from Brescia, learned about the handling of light in Flemish art. Admittedly, there had already been a great painter, Donato dei Bardi, who had brought together north and south, but we still know very little about a certain Zanetto Bugatto, whom the Duke of Milan sent to Flanders with the express purpose of perfecting his art in the school of Rogier van der Weyden.

But let us look now at a painting from a series which must originally have 30 consisted of seven canvases dedicated to the seven liberal arts (the lower three of the Trivium, and the higher four of the Quadrivium). Only four of these have come to light, two are in the National Gallery, London, two were in the Kaiser Friedrich Museum in Berlin, but were lost in the fire which, a few days after the city had capitulated, destroyed the great pictures from the museum, although they were stored in the *Flak-Turm*, a tower specifically built for defence against air attack.

The seven pictures (the four known ones and the three which are either lost or have not yet been rediscovered) were the wall decorations of a room belonging to Duke Federico da Montefeltro, but not the famous small study in Urbino, which

<small>28</small>

27. Anonymous Florentine, circa 1450.
Madonna and Child. National Gallery,
London.

28. Paolo Uccello. *Rout of San Romano.*
National Gallery, London.

29. Sandro Botticelli. Death of Virginia.
Morelli collection, Accademia Carrara,
Bergamo.

contained the series of the Philosophers (now divided between Urbino and the Louvre). I think it was, rather, his study in the Ducal Palace of Gubbio, the lower part of which emigrated in 1937 and is today in the Metropolitan Museum, New York. In each of the seven pictures, one of the six important personages of the ducal court (the Duke himself making the seventh) is seen kneeling before an enthroned figure who respresents the relevant art, and receiving from him or her a gift, or instructions, or a fundamental text. Above, there is a legend – you can see a fragment of it here – exalting the Duke's various titles.

The Dukedom of Urbino, as I reminded you earlier, was not altogether independent, being under the patronage of the Church of Rome. When the Dukedom died out for lack of an heir in 1631, it was re-absorbed or 'devolved' (as they said then) into the Papal States, and continued to form part of these until 1860.

I want you to notice how these pictures were worked out in accordance with the position they were to occupy. Inlaid cupboards stood against the lower part of the wall. The pictures occupied the higher part. Now, the perspective of these paintings is calculated exactly according to the height at which each individual picture was to be hung, that is, at about two and a half metres from the floor. This explains the curious perspective from the bottom to the top. Even the light in each picture is distributed in such a way as to correspond to the real light coming from the window, which was an irregular shape. Everything was worked out exactly.

The author of these pictures is a Spanish painter, Pedro Berruguete, who is a typical, although at the same time limited, case of a foreign artist educated in Italian volumetric terms, modified by a knowledge of Flemish light. The series was painted as a testimony to the enlightened greatness of Federico da Montefeltro, who succeeded in creating around himself a circle of the very highest cultural level, a circle which gave birth not only to Baldassare Castiglione, the author of *Cortegiano*, but two of the supreme geniuses of Italian art: Raphael and the architect, Donato Bramante. It is to Bramante, who went first to Milan, to the court of Ludovico il Moro, and then to Rome, where he was in the service of Pope Julius II, that we owe, amongst other things, the destruction of the ancient basilica of St Peter's.

Duke Frederick, however, was not that meek and saintly man they would have us believe. He was cruel, even ruthless, and when it was a question of collecting money for his ambitious cultural projects, entirely without scruples. But it is only fair to add that his schemes were not only ambitious, they were consummated to perfection.

31   If, after looking at these works, we now pass on to a picture by Paul Cézanne, we realise at once that, if we are to interpret his works correctly, we must radically alter the parameters of our reading. It is impossible to approach Cézanne with the same methods that we used for a Flemish work of the quattrocento, or one from the Italian Renaissance.

In Cézanne, we see the definitive abandonment of that long tradition in painting which began in the first twenty years of the fifteenth century in Florence, with the discovery of the third dimension and the scientific application of perspective, and which endured up until the Naturalism and Realism of the late nineteenth century. With Cézanne, there is a clean break, a refusal, a polemic confrontation with the Europe figurative tradition.

This does not mean that the tradition died with Cézanne – far from it, it has continued right up until the present moment and shows no signs of quitting the field. And in any case, as I said before, the chapters of art history are purely hypothetical, no more than working tools, and do not correspond to the factual reality of painting, which is never schematic and univocal in the way it is described in books.

To come back to our argument, it would be iniquitous to judge Cézanne with the same visual yardstick that is, quite correctly and appropriately, applied to a Vincenzo Foppa. The same applies to other artists who came after Cézanne: Picasso, for example.

Picasso, who is generally considered to be anti-classical, is in reality a sort of compendium of everything that has been produced in the Mediterranean area over the millennia, except that, instead of looking only at Greco-Roman painting and sculpture, or at the classicism of the Renaissance, he also looked – and in this he was unique – at the Medieval Romanesque, especially the Spanish version, and even at the art of the prehistoric caves. Picasso is a kind of force of nature in perpetual mutation, and he presents an inexhaustible mine of hints and clues. Perhaps one day, in future periods, some of these hints will be reworked by other artists, recycled to create new stylistic developments.

Not all Picasso's work is of the same high quality. There is a large part of his output, especially after 1945, that seems to me personally of much less value. And even in other phases Picasso went through moments of pure academicism, of pure entertainment, even. From his inexhaustible forge of images, however, precious sparks fly out, illuminating, in their turn, works from the past and enabling us to read them in a new way, which we would otherwise have overlooked.

Picasso often carries academicism to excess, just as, at other times, he carries anti-academicism to excess, but there is always that vital charge of the born artist in him, the true genius of painting. More than once I have heard art historians write Picasso off as a mere caricaturist. For me, his greatest achievements are the portraits he painted in the 1930s, yet I have heard someone say, when looking at   32 them: 'These are simply caricatures!' No. There is something more. There is a veritable visual eruption, and the quality is always that of an authentic genius.

In any case, Picasso's art is an actual, vivid demonstration of the fact that, in order to read the figurative arts, you must have a visual education and make a careful study of the historical moment in which a particular work of painting, sculpture or architecture was produced. It is also a refutation of the idea that works of art speak to everyone, and at first glance.

In this connection, I would like to point out that the concept of *kitsch*, so prevalent today, is usually misinterpreted. To define something as kitsch is a totally subjective reaction. It is a way of reading poems, music and figurative works that can render even the most sublime works silly and invalid. Even Dante

30. Pedro Berruguete. Music.
National Gallery, London.

31. Paul Cézanne. Bathers.
National Gallery, London.

Alighieri can be made to seem kitsch. And the reason is, as I said above, that works of art do not necessarily speak to you at the first encounter.

Returning to the art of Picasso, there is one adjective that certainly does not suit him: popular. In spite of some of his political attitudes, it is nonsense to say that Picasso's art was destined for the masses. On the contrary, his art requires a particularly refined visual education. The same is true of certain works from other periods and civilisations. Here, for example, is a Persian miniature of the sixteenth or seventeenth century. This is the product of a world entirely different from our own, a mental world in which three-dimensional perspective does not exist, and which betrays the influence, albeit indirect and 'filtered', of the greatest Asiatic visual culture, the Chinese.

Chinese art, which had moments of great splendour, succeeded in penetrating as far as the territory of present-day Iran and influencing their figurative concepts. The value of a miniature of this kind resides not only in the actual picture, but in the frame and even the writing, which also have aesthetic qualities. It would take too long to explain how Islamic writing is a true and proper creation of the mind, disciplined by very complex procedures. As can be seen from monuments, and also in some tiles and majolica, this writing is the result of mathematical research. I will not go into detail about the calculations that govern the creation of these letters, like certain ornamental motifs that are worked into carpets and on some majolica. Suffice it to say that there are some mathematical series which are, in their turn, related to the Cartesian co-ordinates. It is an extremely elaborate procedure, involving both mystical and symbolic meanings.

It is not only the reading of paintings that requires a special education, sculpture, in fact, presents even more difficult problems. It is a field that has been less explored, and often we find ourselves faced with works that baffle even the most experienced eye. On the other hand, it is much easier to fake the style of an antique sculpture than an antique painting, since the techniques of sculpture are more or less always the same, and the material is always marble, bronze or terracotta.

In order to arrive at an adequate understanding of a sculpture, you need to have a wide culture, a rigorous visual education and, above all, a profound technical knowledge. It is rare to find anyone with this sort of knowledge nowadays, and few people study sculpture. There are very few monographs. There are various reasons why this particular study is generally neglected. And yet it is precisely in this field that there has been an enormous output of fakes ever since the Renaissance.

Where sculpture is concerned, the art historian sometimes comes across astonishing cases. This has happened to me. On one occasion, I was in the store-rooms of a villa near Rome when I found four statues, covered in soil and cobwebs, just lying on the ground at my feet. I asked what they were and was told they were works from the time of King Umberto, and of no value whatsoever. As I was not satisfied with this answer, I asked for the incrustations of dirt to be washed off with a strong jet of water. Four statues emerged which manifestly could not belong to the era of Umberto, since there was irrefutable proof, on the back of one of them, that the marble had been recovered from one of the buildings of ancient Rome. In the time of Umberto, nobody would have dreamed of going to plunder the Forum, or a Roman Temple, to sculpture a statue; they would simply have bought a block of Carrara marble.

The statues represented the Four Seasons. Their style was unusual, the quality exceptional. Looking at them very carefully, I began to suspect that they were early seventeenth century, and decidedly Roman.

If you look at the first of these four statues, representing Spring with the zodiacal 34
signs of Taurus at her feet, you will notice the prodigious technical skill with which the flowers have been sculptured. It occurred to me, although the hypothesis would have to be verified, that it was not impossible the hand of Pietro Bernini, father of Gian Lorenzo, had been at work here. But let us proceed step by step.

The second sculpture, Summer, with the crown of ears of corn and the zodiacal 35
symbols of Leo, is worked with sickle-shaped rhythms and a very definite outline that reminds one of some of the forms of a Lombardian painter, Morazzone, as well as some Roman painters of the period, like Giuseppe Cesari, known as the Cavalier d'Arpino. And whoever made these statues was very familiar with classical sculpture. One of the indications of this is the way the figure of Spring is standing with her legs crossed. This stance appears in a famous statue of classical antiquity, the work of a great Greek artist, Skopas, which portrays Pothos, that is: desire, nostalgia. The original is lost, but the statue must have been very popular and a lot of Roman copies are known. One of these was certainly well known at the end of the cinquecento, because it was in a private collection in Rome. So the motif of the crossed legs, which had assumed a symbolic meaning in the Middle Ages, was taken up again in the Renaissance and reappears here in the work of a man who was very conversant with antique sculpture. Taking into account the technical and stylistic attributes, I was able to get a rough date for the four statues: between 1605 and 1620. Little by little, I was able to whittle it down and be more specific.

Look now at the figure of Autumn. This is a real *tour de force* of the art of the 36
chisel. Like Spring, it is sculptured from a single block of marble and, as you can see, the results are truly stunning. Autumn is characterised by the zodiacal symbol of Scorpio, and it is particularly interesting to note that the composition of the figure reminds one distantly, but distinctly, of a marble by Michelangelo – one of the so-called Prisoners which are now in the Accademia in Florence, but which, between the end of the cinquecento and the beginning of the seicento, were in the walls of the famous grotto in the Boboli Gardens, next to Palazzo Pitti. Therefore, whoever made these statues had seen the work of Cavalier d'Arpino and Morazzone, and also the sculpture of Michelangelo, and had, moreover, a considerable knowledge of classical art, which he interpreted as a breaking away from the limits imposed by the outline of the statue and an insertion, or a 'releasing' of the marble into the surrounding atmosphere.

In effect, there is a certain contrast here between the conception of the figures and the conception of the fruit and flowers. In the flowers of the Spring and in the fruit of the Autumn figures, you feel that the marble vibrates in contact with the surrounding atmosphere, a motif that has distant roots in its Hellenistic source,

32. Pablo Picasso. Portrait of
Marie-Thérèse. Picasso Museum, Paris.

33. Persian Miniature, sixteenth or
seventeenth century. Musée d'art et
d'histoire, Geneva.

34-35-36-37. Pietro and Gian Lorenzo
Bernini. The Four Seasons. Villa
Aldobrandini, Frascati.

but is also already a prelude to the constant interchange between atmosphere and marble that can be seen in Gian Lorenzo Bernini's *Daphne and Apollo*.

This profound awareness of the interpenetration between marble and atmosphere is not really surprising in either Bernini *père* or Bernini *fils*, when you consider that they were both well-known restorers of antique marbles for collectors, and therefore very much at home with the secrets of antique sculpture, especially Hellenistic and Roman, which at that time was the nearest to hand. It is true to say that the virtuosity of these marbles almost achieves the effects of eighteenth-century porcelain. There are no joins, everything is carved out of a single block, and this is done by the extremely skilful use of tools, especially the drill, which was to be very dear to Gian Lorenzo Bernini even in his mature phase, whereas many other sculptors detested it. If you see a sculpture with signs of drilling, you can be quite sure Michelangelo had nothing to do with it; he considered the drill an unworthy tool for a sculptor, and, at the most, good enough for the poor stone-dressers or some miserable dilettante. Michelangelo used only the gradine and the chisel, he would not admit the use of the bow drill, and yet Bernini put this tool to marvellous use.

Now, if you want to date this set of figures accurately, the internal evidence – that is, the stylistic clues – suggests the years 1615–16, a date which coincides perfectly with the stylistic development of both Gian Lorenzo and his father, Pietro. In both cases, it matches exactly. And this dating also helps to explain the odd contrast between the concept of the figures, which is undoubtedly due to Pietro (as is a large part of the execution, since much of it still bears the stamp of the cinquecento, it is still linked to Mannerism and the pictorial data of the period), and the symbolic-decorative accessories of fruit and flowers, which break up the spatial compactness of Mannerism and open it up to the limitless space of the Baroque. The vital significance of the Baroque is, precisely, in this concept of open, infinite space. At this point, we can say definitely that these statues are the work of Bernini *père*, assisted by Bernini *fils*.

The fourth statue, from every point of view the strangest, again shows how 37 iniquitously art historians have judged Pietro Bernini. He was terribly unlucky: he was a great sculptor, but father to a son who was even greater than he was. And so, as often happens, the glory of the son has eclipsed the merits of the father, who is generally considered to be mediocre and second rate. Yet, actually, Pietro was one of the finest sculptors of the international Mannerist school, perhaps the finest of all, as his contemporaries certainly believed. In any case, the statue of Winter (the only damaged one, some vandal has broken off his fingers) is characterised by the zodiacal symbol of Aquarius, and you can see the individual genius of Pietro in this figure of a shepherd who is warming himself at a fire. He is wearing the oriental costume of the barbarian prisoners on the arch of Septimus Severus in Rome, and on other classical monuments. In Pietro's sculpture, there is a constant reference to Roman art, and it is always associated with something piquant, curious and characteristic. For example, the extraordinary, comical expression on the face of Winter. What you are seeing here is a flourishing cultural context that was by no means alien to Pieter Brueghel the Elder, who was known in Rome through his works in the Palazzo Farnese.

So, we have here a very rich and complex cultural soil, from which the genius of Gian Lorenzo Bernini blossoms forth. And this strange figure, half barbarian prisoner and half shepherd from Ciociaria, wrapped in a sheepskin, and with an odd, humorous expression on his face, is one of the finest achievements in sculpture of the late-Mannerist school.

When did Gian Lorenzo spread his wings and fly? Not many years after he worked on the Four Seasons, when his prodigious technical ability was enriched by contact with the works of a non-Italian painter who had worked in Rome, Peter Paul Rubens. Bernini becomes truly himself after studying the pictures Rubens left behind in Rome, and especially the paintings on slate in the Chiesa Nuova, which still exist, and the St Helena, as well as two episodes from the Passion of Christ which were then in the Church of the Holy Cross in Jerusalem, and are now in the Hospital in Grasse, in France. The physical type of the women in Bernini's earliest works is Rubensian. And it was Rubens who taught Bernini the secret of infinite space. In short, Bernini found in Rubens what he had already learned by intuition from his study of Hellenistic-Roman sculpture.

The stylistic assessment I made of the Four Seasons was later confirmed by documentary proofs. The four statues had been found in a villa belonging to a well-known Roman family. When I asked where they had come from, nobody knew. But then I found an old servant who asserted – and he was proved correct – that when the family sold another villa to the Italian state, in 1929, the only objects he was instructed to take away were these four statues. Evidently, in 1929, there was still somebody alive who remembered how important they were. Armed with this information, I did some research in a library and there eventually came to light a document from the early nineteenth century, when the villa was assessed for tax purposes. From this, it came out that the Four Seasons were at that time attributed with absolute certainty to Gian Lorenzo Bernini. The name of the *very* great son had swallowed up the name of the great father.

Index